SIMEON EBEN BALDWIN

Simeon E. Baldwin

SIMEON EBEN BALDWIN

Lawyer, Social Scientist, Statesman

By

FREDERICK H. JACKSON

Foreword by Charles E. Clark

KING'S CROWN PRESS

COLUMBIA UNIVERSITY, NEW YORK, 1955

KING'S CROWN PRESS

is an imprint established by Columbia University Press for the purpose of making certain scholarly material available at minimum cost. Toward that end, the publishers have used standardized formats incorporating every reasonable economy that does not interfere with legibility. The author has assumed responsibility for editorial style and for proofreading.

PUBLISHED IN GREAT BRITAIN, CANADA, INDIA, AND PAKISTAN
BY GEOFFREY CUMBERLEGE, OXFORD UNIVERSITY PRESS
LONDON, TORONTO, BOMBAY AND KARACHI
MANUFACTURED IN THE UNITED STATES OF AMERICA

Library of Congress Catalog Card Number: 54-12724

To My Wife

FOREWORD

When I was a student in the Yale Law School in 1911–12, we had the honor of having the Governor of the State as our Professor of Constitutional Law. He was then a nearly mythical figure, having just retired, laden with honors, as Chief Justice of the State, to conduct with vigor a successful campaign for the governorship. Obviously one could approach him only with awe and respect. I cannot honestly claim that we felt close to him even after a full course and a final examination, which without doubt he personally prepared and meticulously read. But there was, as we saw, on his side the most conscientious discharge of his obligations to their last jot and tittle. On ours I hope we had some appreciation of the time and energy he freely gave, though of course we lacked real knowledge of the sacrifice represented by his consistently regular attendance on classes several times a week.

Baldwin's course involved reading and preparation in important constitutional decisions of the Supreme Court, regular papers, classroom recitations, and a comprehensive final examination. Since my name was near the head of the class list in alphabetical sequence, I had the prominence of a front row seat, right under the teacher's desk. This was a post of some advantage, for the lecturer kept his gaze pretty closely upon his notes, and hearing in the back of the room was difficult. One incident, trivial in itself, suggests that closer intimacy might well have been possible if attempted. I had been called upon to recite and had answered sufficiently so that the Governor stopped me to pass on to another. But then, not getting the answer he sought, he asked if anyone was prepared to answer; whereupon I brashly stuck up my hand almost literally under his nose. This brought forth quite a chuckle and a gleam in his eye when he said: "No, no, I've heard you—is there anyone *else* who knows?"

Of course such is the type of remembrance a student retains, while he forgets the times when he was caught unprepared! I do recall vividly another incident, however, for it illustrates the precision and perhaps, too, the imaginative limits of his type of mind. The reminder comes by way of a lecture note from his course, long preserved and later checked for accuracy, containing his pronouncement "that this [the United States] is a Christian nation," supported and proved true only by the inevitable citation from the law reports. Sure enough, the case cited so holds! *Church of the Holy Trinity v. United States* (143 U.S. 457, at 471).

Over the years of my practice in Connecticut and teaching at Yale, I came to realize the marvelous scope of his interests and his accomplishments. But the sheer bulk of them cannot be appreciated by any mere feat of recollection; they must be recounted in detail for the total impact to be felt. I must confess that, familiar as I thought the picture to be, I did not sense their full force until I read Professor Jackson's scholarly biography now to be published. Baldwin's life deserved at least a good presentation; here it has an excellent one. I think our author has served the good judge well. One could hardly consider Simeon Baldwin a romantic figure; nor is it possible to conceive of a life of him written in the current heroic style, half novel, half fact, with an eye on the movies, which appears to have become fashionable as a form of biography. And the task before a biographer presented some unusual difficulties from the sheer bulk of the material, particularly the perhaps two hundred items written by the subject himself. The result, it seems to me, is a representation essentially true to life as a picture of a sturdy Puritan, terse and blunt and uncompromising, but devoted and unyielding in pursuit of his ideals and with substantial impact on his generation.

This last facet of his career, his permanent impress on his times, is naturally the most important part of the work, the one most needed to be explored. And it seems to me that here it is done with excellent appraisal of Baldwin's truly wonderful industry and his strength in many fields—railroad lawyer, appellate judge, international legal scholar, bar association leader, political scientist, historian, governor, and, throughout his life for nearly sixty years, a teacher of law. Not only this, but in practically all these fields he was a recognized leader. The number of learned societies in different fields of which he was at one time president is some showing of this. I think Professor Jackson well demonstrates this catholicity of scholarly activity in all fields except one; this he notes, but without stressing that here, too, was a display of rare qualities of leadership. I am referring to Baldwin's work for improved court procedure in the State exemplified by the Connecticut Code of Civil Practice of 1880, which, at the time and, indeed, until the renewed widespread activity of the last two decades, was probably the most advanced of all American codes. It followed the Field reform of 1848 in New York, and the procedural reforms in England of 1873 and 1875, but was most notable in accepting and adapting for use here the English improvements on the original New York model. This of course was at a time when knowledge or imitation of English methods was unusual; but the success of the Connecticut system was such (as I have noted in my *Code Pleading* 19, 20, 97, 113, 114, 239, 2d Ed. 1947) as to be later followed in substantial details in the modern widely imitated Federal Rules of Civil Procedure.

One other matter, ably developed by Professor Jackson, I should like to note because it, too, shows Baldwin far in advance of his time. In 1876 he was instrumental in shaping the first American graduate course in law, stressing a broader education than one purely professional, encompassing history, the political and social sciences, and other disciplines which should be allied to law. But not content with this expanded curriculum Baldwin himself carried on his own personal system of integration and cooperation, so much so in fact that he became a distinguished protagonist of these other disciplines and served as president, in turn, of their learned societies. No other lawyer or law teacher has been so widely active or so widely honored in other fields of scholastic learning. More than this, some fifty years after Baldwin's beginning the law schools started to discover the social sciences. A major development in the last three decades has been the increasing concern of the law schools for the kind of integration of studies which still seems best exemplified in Baldwin's own career.

In some of the most interesting passages in the book Professor Jackson speculates as to why Baldwin's fame has not been more widespread and more lasting. Certain fortuitous circumstances undoubtedly prevented any accretions to snowball his name into modern prominence; he failed to attain a national platform such as is naturally accorded a justice of the Supreme Court of the United States; his writing was spare and lean like his personality, so that it did not entice admirers or imitators; and his political views, generally conservative for his day, were too far ahead of the present retreat to conservatism to accord him place as a major prophet of a new era. What fame he acquired was therefore the product of his own hard and devoted labors, entirely self-created and self-engendered. Looked at from this point of view I think the world has not been too unkind to his memory. Now, some four decades after his withdrawal from active public service, his memory is green in at least three places. In the annals of the nationally organized bar of the country he has been given due mead of praise, particularly during the recent seventy-fifth year birthday celebration, as its founder and original guiding spirit. In the field of procedural reform, his is still an original force, as above noted. And in the Law School, which he saved from disaster and cherished and maintained so long, where his name is continued in an honored professorship, I think that few will not know—however much the details may be lost in the mist of the past—that here more than any other person was the School's savior and patron. Not a few, recalling how his allegiance never wavered even when the School, toward the close of his life, adopted teaching methods he had always abhorred, will find true greatness in a loyalty that surpassed any thought of self.

The thought just uttered finds eloquent expression in a striking tribute from the *Yale Law Journal* at the time of his his death (36 *Yale L.J.* 680, 682; unsigned, but very probably from the pen of Professor Corbin). There it is said: "He was confident, definite and inflexible; and yet his modesty and sense of proportion are strongly witnessed by his unswerving loyalty to this law school, a loyalty expressed even in his last will and testament, in spite of its departure from at least one of his long supported policies. Such a man is the man to live with. He is the man whose memory will be kept green; partly, indeed, because of his ideas and his unusual achievements, but even more largely because of his life and character. The Yale Law School will be proud to continue to build upon the broad and massive foundations laid by this man throughout his long and noble life."

A man who deserves and receives a tribute such as this has not lived in vain. I am glad that he has now found a biographer worthy of the task.

CHARLES E. CLARK
U.S. CIRCUIT JUDGE
UNITED STATES COURT OF APPEALS

New Haven, Conn.
August 2, 1954

PREFACE

THIS STUDY of the life of Simeon Eben Baldwin developed from a doctoral dissertation accepted by the University of Pennsylvania in 1950. It was written under the supervision of Professor Roy F. Nichols to whom I am deeply indebted for his kindly criticism and encouragement. Professors Robert E. Spiller and E. Sculley Bradley of the University of Pennsylvania read the manuscript and raised issues which stimulated me to think further about certain matters. I also wish to acknowledge with thanks the helpful suggestions of Professor Elliott Cheatham of Columbia University who read the manuscript in its entirety.

The research for the volume was undertaken in the Sterling Library at Yale University. The staff was unfailingly courteous and helpful and none more so than Mrs. Zara Jones Powers, Curator of the Historical Manuscripts Collection. The Library graciously granted me permission to use the Baldwin Collection and to publish the results of my study.

The Baldwin family has cordially cooperated from the very beginning of the project. Mrs. Warren R. Gilman, daughter of Simeon E. Baldwin, and Mr. Bradley B. Gilman, his grandson, have answered numerous requests for information and have clarified many matters relating to Baldwin's family life.

Many of Simeon E. Baldwin's contemporaries, associates, and former students have passed on to me their recollections and answered specific queries. Their help was especially valuable in crystallizing my conception of the character and personality of Baldwin.

Miss Joan McQuary and Mr. David Howell Jones of Columbia University Press have assisted and advised me regarding various problems of editing and publishing.

I wish to thank the *American Historical Review* for permission to use portions of an article I wrote entitled "Simeon E. Baldwin and the Clerical Control of Yale," which appeared in that journal in July, 1952.

My wife, Eleanor W. Jackson, like the wives of many writers in academic life, has aided at every point, from helping support the family while the investigation was being carried on to editing and typing the fruits of the research.

FREDERICK H. JACKSON

Urbana, Illinois
March, 1954

CONTENTS

SIMEON EBEN BALDWIN

THE SETTING

The New Haven where Simeon Eben Baldwin was born on February 5, 1840, was Connecticut's first city. The little coastal port, nestled snugly on the level terrain between its two protecting hills, East Rock and West Rock, contained 12,960 persons and was growing rapidly, nearly doubling its population before 1850.[1] The center of the city was then as now the green. The three substantial churches which grace the center of these two blocks of elm-shaded grass had then stood more than twenty years. Impressive still today in their dignity and beauty, these buildings were among the foremost architectural adornments of New Haven during much of the nineteenth century. They indicate the prominent role religion played in the lives of New Haveners a century ago. The denominations inhabiting these buildings—two were Congregationalist and one Episcopalian—reflected a change which had come over Connecticut as the eighteenth century blended into the nineteenth. The nearly universal Congregationalism of the seventeenth and early eighteenth centuries gave way to a variety of sects—Episcopalians, Baptists, and Methodists notably—as the colonial era drew to a close. So strong had these dissenters become that in 1818 they forced the disestablishment of Congregationalism, and under the new constitution of that year the preferential status of the religion of Thomas Hooker and John Davenport was removed.[2]

The importance of religion to New Haveners did not preclude their taking great interest in more practical concerns such as commerce and manufacturing. The decade of the forties saw the transition from water transportation on the Connecticut River, the New Haven-Northampton (Massachusetts) Canal, and Long Island Sound to the rapidly expanding railroads. By the early fifties the state was honeycombed with a rail network.[3]

Manufacturing in Connecticut dated back to colonial times and mushroomed in the nineteenth century. The area around

New Haven contained numerous factories. Eli Whitney's arms plant at Whitneyville in the town of Hamden was perhaps the most famous.[4] Established in 1798, it was noted as one of the first factories to make use of the principle of the interchangeability of parts. Whitney's fame perhaps ultimately will rest more upon this novel feature—the very core of the system of mass-produced goods—than upon the invention of the cotton gin.

Another notable early enterprise was the woolen mill of Colonel David Humphreys at Humphreysville, now Seymour. President Jefferson ordered cloth for a suit there in 1808. "The best fine cloth in the United States," he wrote to a New Haven Democrat, "is, I am told, at the manufacture of Colo. Humphreys in your neighborhood." [5]

A survey of manufactures made in 1845 at the instance of the Connecticut General Assembly revealed that in that year there were thirty-seven shops in New Haven, employing 2,137 people.[6] The principal products manufactured were paper, clocks, saddles and harnesses, carriages, wagons, chairs and cabinets, tin and sheet iron, tobacco and "segars," locofoco matches, India rubber suspenders, leather goods, sash and blinds, varnish, and augers.[7]

More than most eastern states Connecticut had retained in 1840 its homogeneity of colonial times. The inhospitable soil had long since ceased to support the natural increase of the population. The natives, moreover, were unfriendly to foreigners, and special permission from the legislature was necessary for aliens to hold land. They were admitted to suffrage with extreme reluctance.[8] In spite of discouragements small groups of foreigners came. In the forties a Jewish congregation was found in New Haven.[9] The Irish also were arriving in ever larger numbers and injecting another strain into the body politic. From every point of view, however, the old Protestant English stock was dominant. It controlled government, economic life, religion, schools and colleges, and everything else considered worth the effort.

Into this environment on February 5, 1840, Simeon Eben

Baldwin, the ninth and last child of Roger Sherman Baldwin and Emily Pitkin Perkins Baldwin, was born.[10] Baldwin's parents possessed everything desirable—distinguished ancestry, a well-established and esteemed position in the community, culture and intelligence, and an ample income though not great wealth.

Mrs. Baldwin, born January 1, 1796, at Hartford, was the daughter of Enoch Perkins, a lawyer of sound judgment and extensive reading who was universally respected for his integrity and strength of character. Her mother, Anna Pitkin, was the daughter of the Reverend Timothy Pitkin of Farmington. Mrs. Baldwin's parents were descended from long lines of Puritan ancestors, including five colonial governors [11] and a president of Yale College, the Reverend Thomas Clap.[12]

Mrs. Baldwin was an extremely energetic woman and besides raising her large family found time to serve on the board of the New Haven Orphan Asylum and the Hospital Society of Connecticut. A devout Congregationalist, she saw the hand of the Lord constantly working in the affairs of the day. She was a woman of intelligence and of strong opinions and took a keen interest in political affairs. A gracious hostess, she was ideally suited to be the wife of one of Connecticut's chief political figures and lawyers.

Roger Sherman Baldwin, born January 4, 1793, at New Haven, was the grandson of one of Connecticut's most distinguished revolutionary patriots, Roger Sherman. Baldwin's father was Simeon Baldwin, the youngest son of a farmer-blacksmith at Norwich, Connecticut. In 1777 Simeon Baldwin came to New Haven to attend Yale and spent his life there in the practice of the law and on the bench. He married a daughter of Roger Sherman and upon her death wed her sister. A staunch Federalist, he served a term in Congress (1803–05) and sat for nearly ten years (1808–18) on the Supreme Court of his state. He was one of the founders and secretary of an anti-slavery society called in the curious terminology of that day "The Connecticut Society for the promotion of freedom, and for the relief of persons unlawfully held in bondage." [13]

Following in his father's footsteps Roger Sherman Baldwin attended Yale, graduating in 1811. He then entered the Litchfield Law School, the most distinguished in America at that time, and in 1814 was admitted to the bar. Starting in his father's office, he soon opened one for himself and slowly and persistently built up a practice. His father's anti-slavery activities were not lost on the son, for in one of his early law suits he secured the release of a Negro seized as a fugitive slave.[14] Years later his most celebrated legal action also pertained to the freeing of slaves unlawfully detained. This was the famed Amistad case in which Roger Sherman Baldwin was associated with the aged former President John Quincy Adams in the defense of the unfortunate blacks whom he described as "contending for freedom and for life with two powerful governments arrayed against them." [15]

A Federalist in his early years, Roger Sherman Baldwin supported Andrew Jackson for a short time. When the Whig party was founded in the 1830s, however, he joined it and remained faithful until it disintegrated in the fifties. Baldwin then helped organize the Republican party in Connecticut.

In politics he took an active part, serving in the Connecticut Senate in 1837 and 1838 and in its House of Representatives in 1841 and 1842. In 1843 he ran for governor but was not elected. On his defeat Mrs. Baldwin, who devoutly believed that all things happened for good and sufficient reasons, even the election of Democrats, wrote to her son, Edward:

> My only comfort under it is, that God reigns—, his power is stronger than the strongest, there must be therefore, wise & good reasons why this present evil is permitted—and in this belief I can rest— [16]

In 1844 and 1845 Mr. Baldwin won the gubernatorial elections and served two annual terms with distinction. The death of one of Connecticut's United States Senators in 1847 brought him an appointment to the Senate, which was confirmed by the next session of the General Assembly. A senator during the momentous days of the Mexican War and the debates over slavery which resulted in the Compromise of 1850, Mr. Baldwin stalwartly resisted all measures which would extend or protect slavery. He opposed the Mexican War as an unjust aggression by a powerful nation on a weak neighbor, and because he thought its purpose was clearly to spread slavery.

Senator Baldwin remained in Washington until his term expired in 1851. With him it was a matter of principle never to move his hand to secure a political office for himself and never to pledge himself in advance to any specific course of action in order to win support. This conception of duty cost him reelection to the Senate. He resumed the practice of law in the fifties and in his last years received $10,000 a year from his legal practice. He is believed to be the first Connecticut lawyer to have earned such a large income.[17] In his last year of life a prominent fellow citizen described him as "the greatest lawyer in the State & one by talents & character commanding universal respect."[18]

Roger Sherman Baldwin's religious beliefs were the source of much concern to his wife. In the early fifties Mrs. Baldwin wrote of her husband:

> Oh! how I long to have him as years go on become more decided in his religious character—. But the habits become so fixed that even an inward change works slowly outwards.[19]

Mr. Baldwin's life was a model of that of a Christian. Yet, although he attended church, he had never made any overt declaration of faith. A friend writing shortly after the Governor's death summed up his religious position thus:

> Neither he [Mr. Ingersoll], his brother, Gov. Baldwin nor Gen. Kimberly were what is called "professors of religion" though the wives of those who were married were so, and still are. Perhaps I mentioned to you that Dr. Dutton [Rev. Samuel W. S. Dutton] in his discourse [at the funeral of Governor Baldwin] stated that he once sought an interview with Gov. Baldwin at his office (probably at the instigation of Mrs. B) to confer with him on the subject—he was received with much courtesy & the Gove after listening to him said, that he did not feel that he had the power to speak of such matters—meaning probably as most sensible persons think, that questions of this nature must be judged by every individual for himself and are too sacred for dis-

cussion with others—personal religion being a matter exclusively between each person and his Creator & that no clergyman knows more or can obtain greater light than is attainable by every reflecting & intelligent man or woman—Dr. Dutton added that she who knew him best believed him to be a Christian though he never made any avowal beyond the facts growing out of a most exemplary life.[20]

Mr. Baldwin's final public service was as a delegate to the Peace Convention in Washington in February, 1861. Assembled at the call of Virginia as a last attempt to avert civil war, the governors of the states appointed delegates, and Governor Buckingham chose Mr. Baldwin as one of Connecticut's representatives.[21] His lifelong abhorrence of slavery led Mr. Baldwin into the camp of the extremists which opposed compromise. The majority overruled and recommended amendments to the Constitution for the protection of slavery. Similar to the already-discarded Crittenden plan, the Peace Convention's proposals were rejected by a Senate committee and not even considered in the House of Representatives.[22]

Less than two years later, February, 1863, Mr. Baldwin died after a brief illness. His widow lived on another decade, passing away in August, 1874.

Of Simeon E. Baldwin's eight brothers and sisters three had died before he was born in 1840. Of the boys remaining Edward was at that time seventeen and a student at Yale; Roger was thirteen; and George, seven. The two girls, Elizabeth and Henrietta, were fifteen and nine, respectively.

Edward graduated from Yale in 1842, studied law there, and served as his father's secretary while the legislature met in 1844 and 1845, when the elder Baldwin was governor. In the fall of 1844 he entered a law office in New York and two years later hung out his own shingle there. Just as he was establishing himself, an attack of bleeding of the lungs seized him in November of 1846, and it soon became apparent that he had tuberculosis. Edward sailed for the Mediterranean and spent the winter and spring in Italy. This journey and a summer at a water-cure establishment in Northampton, Massachusetts, seemed to improve his health. When Governor Baldwin was appointed to the Senate late in 1847, Edward took over his New Haven affairs. These new responsibilities proved too great a strain on his frail constitution and may have precipitated another severe attack of bleeding. His decline from this point was steady, and he died on July 6, 1848, at Northampton.[23]

The Baldwins had scarcely become reconciled to their loss when the effects of an event which took place 3,000 miles away cast another shadow over the family. At Sutter's fort in California gold was discovered. Waves of Californians made for the hills, as the news of the strike went by steamer to Panama and up the Atlantic ship lanes to the cities of the East. It was late in 1848 when the California fever hit New Haven's young men. Among those smitten was Roger Sherman Baldwin, Jr. Twenty-two years of age, a graduate of Yale in 1847, he had attended the law lectures at his Alma Mater in the fall of that year. His mother worried about his habits: he kept late hours and drank and smoked too much, she thought. When he was invited to go into his Uncle Thomas' law office in Hartford, Mrs. Baldwin hoped the change would improve him.[24] He returned home in May, however, saying that the young ladies of Hartford did not mix with studying law and that he would try to enter a New York law office in the fall. Meanwhile he attended the sessions of the General Assembly in New Haven and was with his brother in his last weeks of life at Northampton.

In the fall he arranged to enter the New York law office of a relative, William M. Evarts.[25] Roger did not stay long enough to find out whether he liked his New York association, for he was overcome in December by the urge to go to California. A group of his classmates corresponded and decided to embark together. On Christmas afternoon Roger told his mother he was determined to go with or without family consent. His father's approval, however, was secured and $500—later more—was given him for expenses.[26]

Next came weeks of indecision and hasty preparations as the boys tried to decide upon the most advantageous route, to collect supplies, and to arrange for passage. Largely because of the disease rampant on the Isthmus of Panama, they determined to try a new venture, the Nicaragua route. They signed with a man who agreed to take them from New York to San Juan on the Nicaragua east coast, thence up the San Juan River, across Lakes Nicaragua and Managua, and finally overland the short distance to the Pacific. An agent was sent ahead to Panama to charter a ship which was to pick up the group on the west coast of Nicaragua and take them to California. On February 20, 1849, the group saw New York disappear behind them and in good time reached San Juan.

Life in Nicaragua was a sojourn in another world for Roger, who was forced to spend several months there because the Pacific connections miscarried. This episode is delightfully related in a series of Roger's letters which were later published in the *Century Magazine*.[27]

In the fall of 1849 the party finally reached its destination. The young men from New Haven were among the many who failed to gain wealth, but experience aplenty came their way. Roger spent a hitch with his pick at the "diggins," tired of this, and worked for a time in the San Francisco Customs House, practicing law simultaneously. He later was a Wells Fargo agent, receiving gold from the miners and arranging for its transportation to San Francisco.

Year after year passed, and the Baldwins continually urged Roger to come home, if only for a visit. To their earnest entreaties he would not yield, apparently wanting to make his fortune before returning to New Haven. The delay was fatal, however, for in 1856 he fell from his horse, receiving injuries from which he never recovered. His death came on November 12, 1856.

Life was kinder to the Baldwin daughters, although their early lives were dogged by ill health and disappointments. Both Elizabeth and Henrietta studied at the various young ladies' schools in New Haven. Elizabeth, who lived with her parents until she was over thirty, also attended language classes conducted by members of the Yale faculty. Both girls were inveterate visitors at the homes of relatives and friends from Boston to Washington. Such excursions were on a reciprocal basis, and the Baldwin household frequently had cousins or friends as guests, some staying as long as a whole winter.

The visits of the girls were sometimes not without events of moment. Elizabeth, for example, on one of her visits to Boston was tendered the hand of a wealthy merchant, who was considerably older than she. Mrs. Baldwin wrote to her husband that she had informed Elizabeth that Mr. Howe is a "very respectable man and she must give a respectful reply." [28]

A more serious romance involved Henrietta with a student at Yale. Dwight Foster of Worcester, Massachusetts, had been seeing much of her, and early in 1848 Mrs. Baldwin wrote to her husband that she was not surprised at Dwight's avowal of his love for Henrietta. Mrs. Baldwin had anticipated this situation and mother-like, learned all she could about Dwight's background:

I had taken occasion when speaking of our friends, the Washburns of Worcester, to Mrs. Davis, to mention *his* name, and was gratified with the manner in which she spoke of the family and of the young man himself in whom their hopes and solicitudes were centered. She said that his father was a gentleman of wealth, and that he had in a manner withdrawn from his profession, and interested himself much in the promotion of objects connected with the general schemes of philanthropy and benevolence in which the religious community was engaged. Feeling satisfied that there can be no other objection than that which arises from his youth, I leave the matter entirely in your hands to adopt such course in regard to it as shall best commend itself to your judgment.[29]

The young people decided to keep the engagement secret for a time, and not until the following July did Hettie tell her brother, Roger, how matters stood.

Before I finish I want to tell you what I have been afraid to for some time and which you have probably guessed or known for longer—that I am *engaged* to Dwight Foster—I was afraid you would laugh at me—or would not like it—or him—was the reason I did not tell you long ago—I was engaged to him last winter—only mother and father forbid it—However—it was my own affair and I *was* engaged and they could not help it—and now they have had to yield—as they *cannot* make any real objection—except that we are young—and that is a fault we are improving in every day—I wish you would write and tell me what you think—I want you to like it—and him—and me—will you? [30]

Because Henrietta had been sickly as a child, the Baldwins were greatly alarmed when she developed a cough during the period Edward was in his fatal illness. Soon after Edward's death, therefore, Mrs. Baldwin took Hettie and Simeon off for a carriage trip through Litchfield County, Connecticut, hoping the country air would cure her cough. When this failed to produce the desired improvement, her parents decided to send her to a warmer climate for the winter of 1848–49, and she was entrusted to the care of a minister in North Carolina. Although she continued to be troubled with a cough for several years, Hettie slowly improved after this winter. The following year she was invited to accompany Mr. and Mrs. Foster and Dwight's two sisters on a grand tour throughout the South.[31] The party went down the Atlantic coast visiting the principal cities, across the Gulf states to New Orleans, and finally up the Mississippi and Ohio Rivers and back to New England.

Hettie was married in August, 1850. Her husband had by this time established himself as a lawyer in Worcester.

Meanwhile Elizabeth, five years older than Hettie, remained at home. She visited her friends and relatives all over the East, assisted her mother in the management of the household, and took charge of it whenever Mrs. Baldwin was away from home. In Mrs. Baldwin's absence she acted as a second mother to Simeon.

In the early fifties Elizabeth suffered a great bereavement. She had become acquainted with Clinton Camp, a promising young student with the usual dim material prospects of a scholar a century ago. Much against her parents' wishes Elizabeth became engaged. Shortly thereafter her fiancé sailed for Europe to study for his Ph.D. and while there died of tuberculosis in 1853.[32]

Out of the ashes of this experience came a new life for Elizabeth. One of Clinton Camp's fellow students in Germany was William D. Whitney. On his return to America he was appointed to the faculty at Yale as professor of Sanskrit. He supplemented his meager salary by giving German lessons to Elizabeth and other New Haven young ladies.[33] The friendship between William and Elizabeth ripened into love, and they were married on August 28, 1856.

George, nearest to Simeon in age, followed his older brothers through Yale, graduating in 1853, and into the law. In the fall of 1854 he went to the bustling city of Chicago where he was at first head clerk in a legal firm [34] and later practiced law. In 1858 he entered a partnership with his brother-in-law, Dwight Foster, in Worcester.[35] George volunteered for service during the Civil War and saw action as an officer with the 15th Massachusetts Volunteers. After the cessation of hostilities George went back to his law partnership in Worcester and later Boston. As a lawyer he prospered. He remained a bachelor, and for many years spent large parts of the year travelling about the world.

Completing the family scene during Simeon's boyhood were the elderly parents of Mr. Baldwin, Simeon and Elizabeth (Sherman) Baldwin, who lived nearby with their spinster daughter, Rebecca. Both were in their seventies when Simeon was born. Their late years had been saddened by the insanity of their youngest son, Charles, who remained at the Hartford Retreat for the Insane over thirty years. Roger Sherman Baldwin customarily spent Sunday evening with his parents and frequently would be accompanied by little Simeon. Mrs. Baldwin died in 1850, and her husband followed a year later.

EARLIEST IMPRESSIONS

SIMEON E. BALDWIN'S CHILDHOOD was that of a normal, happy boy in a prosperous, well-ordered household. Although five brothers and sisters lived at home in his infancy, one by one they departed until by the time Simeon was ten only Elizabeth and George remained.

In his early years most of Simeon's activities centered around the Baldwin homestead, a substantial, square, brownstone structure built in 1840, the year in which he was born. Surrounded by a low, ornamental, iron fence and with an unostentatious porch in front, the house was one of solid dignity and in perfect harmony with its inhabitants.[1]

The record of Simeon's early years must be pieced together from scattered references to extraordinary happenings. His precocity was recognized early by the family and commented upon frequently. On Valentine's Day of 1845, for example, Mrs. Baldwin wrote to her eldest son, Edward, that Simeon, then just five,

> actually printed out entirely himself one [a Valentine] to Lucy Bacon and carried it over to her—He has learned to make letters and put them together on a slate—. *Without any partiality* he is a wonder of a child.[2]

His unexpected retorts were a source of much amusement to the family. Elizabeth regaled her brother with a pair of these, which were uttered when Sim was five.

> Sim's last—no letter would be complete without at least one gem from his conversation. Aunt Rebecca invited father to dine with them on the 4th and he said, "Oh I'm busy, I can't come." Sim thought it rather an ungracious reply and by way of softening it a little—said—"Father is always very undoubtful about invitations—he always dines at home, home is his *sweet reposing*." The other evening he was apparently asleep in his trundle bed—Henrietta spoke to mother in a whisper, so as not to awake him. "Henrietta"—said he—"you need not address your remarks in such a *pensive* whisper." [3]

In the fall of 1845 Simeon entered school for the first time. A year later he had learned to write well enough to pen his first letter.

Dear Edward

We are all well and we want to know whether you are coming up here at Thanksgiving. Do come.

I go to Miss Whittlesy's school and get good marks every day. This is the first letter I ever printed. The next I hope I shall be able to write. Give my love to Sim [his cousin].

Your brother,
Simeon.[4]

Soon thereafter, when Sim was not yet seven, Mrs. Baldwin told Edward that he was studying French under Henrietta "so very correctly, and all himself that even you must acknowledge he is rather a remarkable child—." [5]

George and Simeon seemed to get along well together, but Roger and his smaller brother were often at odds. In the spring of Sim's eighth year they were on the best of terms, however, and Roger made Simeon a little fishing pole.[6] A year later, when the little boy wrote to Roger, then in his uncle's Hartford law office, asking for fishing equipment, the following sophomoric reply came back:

Mr. Simeon Baldwin, alias Aldiboronitphoscophoriobligonchronon-hotonthatogas

Sir—

My old fishing rod is a relic—a fond memorial of past joys. It has travelled with me more than five thousand miles—has caught me more than a thousand pounds of fish—it has been my only companion for long days & weeks—has rejoiced with me when fortune smiled & stuck by me when she frowned her darkest— All the money you have would not buy it and all the love I bear you would not make me give it to you—ergo you cannot have it—My reel you asked for—when I am rich enough to buy another—for its all I have—from my own earnings—which will probably be long after you have descended to the "silent tomb" you may have it—Finally your humble request embraced my sinkers—Take them they are yours—If you can find them—All lines hooks gut & other articles of tackle not herein before mentioned and not shut up in my drawers which it will be worth your life to open are your own

Your loving friend,
RSB [7]

Mr. Baldwin was appointed to the Senate in the fall of 1847. Sim wrote to him occasionally and according to his mother "literally 'leaped for joy' " [8] when his father replied.

Because of his father's position in Washington Simeon, though only eight years of age, became concerned with the affairs of the nation. The treaty ending the Mexican War was being debated in the Senate, and Simeon's deep interest in the matter is described in a letter written by Elizabeth to her father.

Little Sim looks healthy enough and we think grows brighter every day. He reads the newspapers and takes a deep interest in politics, especially *your* proceedings, as we discovered the other night. There has been a report in the papers, unauthorized I suppose, that you would vote against the treaty [with Mexico at the end of the Mexican War], and a good deal has been said about it—which he must have read, for Saturday night when going to bed Mother overheard him saying his prayers—and he commenced, "I thank thee, oh God, that it has not yet been proved, that father voted against that treaty." I should not be surprised if Simeon should have a vote in the Senate himself some day.[9]

Soon thereafter Senator Baldwin sent Sim a speech recently delivered in Congress. Simeon was very pleased and said he would read it. He began to but soon grew tired and laid it down. A few evenings later his mother heard him

talking as I thought in a very loud voice in the kitchen and occasionally such shouts of laughter—that after some time I sent for him to go to bed—He came in with a pamphlet in his hand—and said he had only been reading to the servant girls and an Irishman who had come in to see them Mr. Bell's speech. . . . But said I what was all the laughing I heard—. Oh said he, "that was only when I threw in something of my own such as—The audience will please be very attentive to this." [10]

As he grew older his mother took him with her when she made trips out of town. In the spring of his ninth year they visited his grandmother and aunts in Hartford and on the return trip stopped over at Meriden to call on his uncle's family. The events which transpired there were the subject of a letter from Simeon to his father:

Dear Father

When I recieved your letter today I found it had been waiting for me some time as I was then at Hartford I had a very pleasant time there and started for Meriden on Wednesday to stay there two or three hours and start to go home in the afternoon train. We went to the new church and parsonage the church was very tasteful with a clock with four faces. We spent a long time in admiring it after that we went to the parsonage which was a square house with folding doors between the kitchen and parlor and upstair there were Uncle Georges study and workshop We also spent a long while looking till at last we heard the [railroad] cars close by we all then begun to run but were a minute to late so we were left Mother looked very sober and asked when the next train would go they told her at ten oclock she said that would be too late After that we went to select some paper for the new house but did not find but one kind to suit us. In the evening Mother decided to go home so we went to an Inquiry Meetting in the new lecture room after it closed we went to cars got in and went along so fast that I fell asleep and woke up just as we had come to New Haven we imediately got into a carriage and drove off and soon got home

We thought we had got in in good season as it was only half past eleven but when we got here we found them sound asleep we rung and rung an half hour till at last the girls came and we got to bed.[11]

Sim was constantly surprising the family with his achievements. One Sunday evening in April, 1848, he composed a hymn. For an eight-year-old the result was considerably better than might be expected. The most admiring reader is forced to admit, however, that the metrical structure breaks down quite dismally in the last stanza.

How quickly time doth pass away
While we in pleasures spend the day
How fast the tide of time rolls on
From early morn till set of sun.

Some people spend their time in sin
Others in gaming houses win
While those who love the Lord their God
Obey each item of his word.

And a reward to them will be given
When they reach the judgment seat in heaven
The Lord hath prepared a palace for them
As also he's given to Moses and Shem.[12]

The summer of 1848 was a sad one for the Baldwin family. On July 6 Edward died. The shadow of the disease which ended his life hung over Henrietta, and Mrs. Baldwin decided to take her family by horse and carriage through the Litchfield Hills of Connecticut in hopes that the country air would help Hettie. Simeon enjoyed the leisurely trip, especially bathing in the streams they passed.[13]

The Baldwin family was scattered in the winter of 1848–9, and the homestead was very quiet. Senator Baldwin was in Washington all winter. Elizabeth was on a long visit to friends and relatives in New York, Philadelphia, Wilmington (Delaware) and Washington. Henrietta was spending the winter in North Carolina. Roger was in New York until he decided in December to join the exodus to California. Several weeks of feverish preparations ensued, and after a number of false alarms he sailed on February 20. A deep calm settled over the family after this flurry of activity. Only George, a freshman at Yale, and Simeon were at home with their mother.

When the weather prevented their playing out-of-doors, Sim and his friends used their ingenuity to amuse themselves within. One of their short-lived projects, undoubtedly inspired by Senator Baldwin's position in the Senate, was described by Sim in a letter to his father:

We that is Charles Blackman Charles Tomlinson Henry M. Dutton and myself have formed a little Senate among ourselves Charly Blackman being the Speaker. I wish you would propose in your next letter some bills to be discussed upon before the "Senate." The place for meeting is a recess just above Mr. Blackmans stairs and is furnished with a small table with a writing desk, three chairs and stools for the

Senators and a large Black sofa for the spectators besides a spittoon which together with the table writing desk and a chair formed the the the Speakers furniture.[14]

Another enterprise the boys started was a little store in a large closet in the Baldwin home where they bought and sold with members of the family. Of this and other matters Sim wrote to Henrietta in January.

My Dear Sister

I hope you will excuse me for writing Sunday but for about three days I have been laid up with the earache and the consequence is I have been obliged to stay at home to-day. In reply to your inquiries if my "forlorn little cat" still persists in returning to me I will answer that to my great grief she does not, and that I seen nothing of her since you have been gone. You also asked in your letter if my firm of Baldwin & Blackman, C. Tomlinson, Travelling agent, still prosper. they do though if you should enclose a hundred dollar bill in your next letter it would not be amiss. . . .[15]

"The Firm" was doing a brisk business later in the winter, as one of Simeon's letters to his father attested, although the Senate had permanently adjourned.

I must inform you that our "Senate" is entirely broken up. Mr. and Mrs. Blackman bought 6 cents worth of tobacco water of "firm of Baldwin-Blackman & Co", and Mrs. Blackman lately employed us to manufacture some eye water for her. Our capital is now up to fifty eight cts and is daily increasing. We are going to invent a new kind of pills, and as you are in Washington now we expect that you will procure a paten right for them, their name is the Dry Ginger pills. We would like to have you secure a patent right for us soon that we can begin selling them.[16]

The affairs of the company were materially aided in April when Hettie sent not the $100 her brother hinted at, but a dollar bill.[17]

Baldwin and Blackman was by no means a fly-by-night concern, young as its proprietors were. Nearly a year later the records reveal that George Baldwin borrowed seventy-five cents from the firm, promising to pay seventy-six cents in return.[18] The following August, however, after nearly two years of trade,

Baldwin and Blackman closed its doors for the last time. Mrs. Baldwin told the sad tale and its tragic denouement to her husband:

Simmy is in trouble this morning. We have induced him to break up his shop as we wanted the large closet—and thought it made him—or would make him mercenary—To soften it to him—we bought in the family many little things—and as the Firm has a capital of some amount—, he and Charley Blackman divided finally $1.50 cts apiece—And this was highly gratifying—. It seems that he carried it with him yesterday in his pocket when he went bathing—and late last evening it was missing from his little pocket in his blouse—. It was too dark then to make a search—. But he has gone to the "Cedars" this morning with "Ole" [his dog] and the tears in his eyes.—Feeling like a merchant whose cargo has been wrecked, uninsured—.[19]

Simeon was extremely diligent in his school work and in the spring of 1850 his father, while commending his fine record, urged him to play as well as study.[20] Perhaps the admonition was not needed, for Simeon ended an essay dated April 30, 1850, with the exclamation "I have left school for the summer! Hurrah!" [21] After the spring holidays in May Mrs. Baldwin decided that Sim's eyes needed more rest and therefore kept him out of school for the summer term.[22]

The concern Sim had been showing for politics persisted. He not only read the newspapers and followed the events transpiring at Washington, but also took a lively interest in the affairs of Connecticut. In June of 1850 he informed his father that he was attending the sessions of the state House of Representatives, then sitting in New Haven.[23]

In January, 1851, a new era opened for Simeon. He entered the Hopkins Grammar School. This was the big boys' school, and according to his mother Sim dreaded breaking in exceedingly. He feared being the smallest and being knocked about by the older boys. Mrs. Baldwin, however, had no doubt that he would stand up for himself well enough.[24] He entered with heart and soul into his school work, came home every day in a state of great excitement, and took sides strongly on everything that occurred.[25] At the end of the first week Mrs. Baldwin wrote to her husband:

. . . I found him last evening with his Latin reader in bed, with him—so as he said "that he could look over his lesson the first thing in the morning." No danger but what he will make a scholar if his health and life are spared.[26]

In the spring of 1851 Senator Baldwin's term in the Senate expired. Because he refused to take any steps to secure his renomination, although he would have accepted had it come unsolicited, the legislature became deadlocked, and no senator was chosen.[27] When the next General Assembly convened a year later, it was controlled by the Democrats, and a member of that party was selected.[28]

Shortly after his father returned from Washington, Simeon left for a visit with his sister, Hettie, in Worcester, Massachusetts. The eleven-year-old boy enjoyed this adventure into a new world. Writing to his other sister, he said a bit sourly that he had met the Burnsides, his brother-in-law's relatives, and had received their opinion of him, that he was a "prepossessing gentlemanly young man." [29]

Sim had scarcely begun school in the fall of 1851 when he received a blow on the eye from a football which caused him temporarily to lose his sight.[30] He suffered all through life from weak eyes, and although this incident was not the first reference to his eye trouble, it marked the beginning of a period of several years during which his education had to be interrupted or curtailed. He was obliged to leave school at once, and although his sight returned rapidly, he could not read for months. In December his eyes were improving but were not yet strong enough for school. He spent many weary hours during the winter playing chess when Mrs. Baldwin could not read to him.[31] He eagerly awaited the spring, for his forced inactivity would then be broken by work on a nearby farm.[32] His eyes recovered sufficiently to allow him to return to school for the summer term. They soon became painful, however, and it was necessary for him to leave again in July.[33]

In August his father took him on an excursion on the newly

completed railroad between New Haven and New London. From there they went upstate to Norwich and Stafford Springs, one of the minor watering places of the nineteenth century, where Mrs. Baldwin, Elizabeth, George, Hettie, Dwight and their newborn baby had already arrived.[34]

Late in 1852, before Sim was thirteen, he began assuming responsibility for the New Haven real estate of his Uncle Simeon, who lived in New York. He collected the rents and forwarded the money to his uncle, saw to the renewing of leases, and arranged for minor repairs. These duties continued through his college days in New Haven.

Sim's firsthand acquaintance with the practical affairs of adult life was remarkable for a boy of twelve. His experience as his uncle's agent taught him something about the problems of real estate management. From his father very likely he learned a smattering of legal information, such as the meaning of a patent and something of the law-making process and parliamentary procedure. His attendance at the sessions of the Connecticut Legislature is an instance of his precocious interest in public affairs. Simeon's opportunities for enlarging his world were great, and he did not waste them.

In May of 1853 Sim went to the farm of his mother's cousins at Becket in Berkshire County, Massachusetts, to work for the summer. His eyes still prevented his reading to any extent, and the family was anxious that he have some work to occupy him during the warm weather. The remarks of the thirteen-year-old boy on farm life and the farmers with whom he lived illustrated his sharp powers of observation and must have brought more than one laugh to the family at home.

Referring to the father and son with whom he was staying Sim said:

> The old man is the kindest and whenever I work with him, he gives me resting spells, but Charles wants to drive everything through so that he waits for nobody—so much so, indeed that every morning he will begin reading and prayers, while half of the family are eating breakfast.[35]

Mrs. Baldwin replied that work would never hurt him and that it was better to be with driving than with shiftless people.

Your own habits you know my dear Son, were rather of the "putting off" character—and you must consider yourself as taking a course of lessons in promptness and dispatch.[36]

Simeon's opinion of his farm relatives did not improve with time. To his mother he confided:

I have now entered upon the fourth week of my sojourn here and so feel duly qualified to form a good opinion of your two cousins—and that opinion is—that the old man is kind to nobody, except himself—the young man to nobody—not even himself.[37]

The manner in which farmers lived in the 1850s was quite a revelation to the city-bred boy. He wrote his mother that he had to brush his teeth out in the lamb shed where there was running water and that he was the only one on the farm who brushed them at all.[38]

Simeon's chief complaints while on the farm were the quality of the food and the lack of leisure.

This week I have plenty of hard work and pork and potatoes—when I came here you told me farmers had plenty of milk—but precious little is the milk that anybody gets here except Charles and he lives principally upon it—they make what he leaves into butter and cheese—He also told me in his letter that my sports would be trouting—but I presume I never shall have any more leisure than I have at present—i.e. none at all.[39]

Meanwhile life in New Haven moved on apace. Elizabeth was very distraught during the summer because of the death of her fiancé. George had completed college, graduated in July, and was trying to make up his mind as to the future. Of the professions the ministry, medicine and teaching held no attraction for him, and law into which over half of his class was going seemed greatly overcrowded.[40] George was an average student, distrusted his own powers, and needed encouragement from others, his father wrote to his son, Roger.[41] Of his youngest son, Mr. Baldwin said:

Simeon, if his eyes and health do not fail, gives promise of making a first rate scholar. He exhibits a maturity of mind far beyond his years. He has not been particularly fond of work at home, but I judge from his letters that he is in a fair way to learn at Becket how it suits him.[42]

As Sim was about to leave Becket Charles Perkins wrote a letter to Mrs. Baldwin which indicated that Sim's good qualities were well appreciated. He said:

It has never been my lot to become acquainted with any youth of his age, of so universally correct deportment, industry and perseverance as we have found in him; and an amount of knowledge & general information rarely if ever to be met with in one of his age. We have found him all the while he has been with us a very interesting acquisition to our family. He has all those manly qualities, which make up a gentleman of the first order. In conduct and intelligence he has reached the man in advance of age.[43]

The hard work of the summer was counterbalanced by a good deal of play in the fall of 1853. At that time Sim became deeply engaged in the activities of the Clio Society. This group of early teenagers had formed a club, apparently patterned after the Yale secret societies, which was complete with skeleton, handshakes, passwords, and ritual. According to a brief manuscript account,[44] the society was founded in 1849, and Sim was a charter member. One of its earlier meeting places was Mr. White's hen-house, but in September, 1853, it removed to a room in the third story of the Baldwin house. The members would take turns giving mock orations and passing a jug of cider around to enliven the occasion.

The society had its own songs, and the words of "Cana Clionis" to the tune of "Camptown Races" are still extant.

Cana Clionis

I

Impossible 'tis this noise to repress—du dah, du dah
Mr. President I move we have a recess—du dah, du dah day
Put up the minutes, gag the secretary—du dah, du dah
Let's have a song and be quite merry—du dah, du dah day.

Chorus:

Then loudly let us sing
And let us one and all
Be bound to make the rafters ring
Of jolly CLIO HALL.

2

We Clionians sing this song—du dah, du dah
Clio's bound to go it strong—du dah, du dah day
Although we may seem but few—du dah, du dah
Yet we are a jolly crew—du dah, du dah day.

Chorus

3

From school and study we are free—du dah, du dah
We fear no ruthless Dominie—du dah, du dah day
No more at desks are we tied down—du dah, du dah
But roll our barrell chairs around—du dah, du dah day.

Chorus

4

Then never let our spirits flag—du dah, du dah
While of Clio we can brag—du dah, du dah day
May Pegasus ne'er want a rider—du dah, du dah
To sing the glories of oysters and cider—du dah, du dah day.

Chorus [45]

The Clio Society occasionally extended the privileges of membership to prominent citizens, and undoubtedly the most distinguished to be enrolled was Senator William H. Seward. From his letter of acceptance it is evident that the Senator believed that the society was interested in spreading Whig principles:

Jan 29, 1854

Dear Sir

I pray you to make known to the Alpha Chapter of the Clio Society my most respectful and grateful acceptance of the compliment they have offered me by tendering me the privileges of their association, and to assure them of my sincere wishes that they may be useful and successful in diffusing knowledge of the sentiments, principles and policy of the Whig Party identical as they are I think with the cause of our country and of civil liberty throughout the world. I remain, dear sir with great respect,

Your humble servant,
William H. Seward.[46]

Senator Seward spoke at the Yale commencement in the summer of 1854 and stayed at the Baldwins' while in New Haven. Ed Blake, a fellow Clionian, wrote to Simeon, who was not at home, about the occasion in the following words:

On the whole, he acted just as you would imagine him to do, when he reads his oration over by himself before delivering it. He made no gestures, or at least, but very few. He commenced his speech with one hand in his pantaloon's pocket, and ended it while scratching a mosquito bite on the back of his hand! However he is a great man or he wouldn't be in the Clio Society, and we must not be too severe upon him. Friday noon, not knowing that he had gone I was going to carry him a summons (in an envelope with the Clio Seal) but learning to my sorrow that he was not in town I did not carry it. Wouldn't it have been a joke to have had him at our meeting? I do not know whether or not, your pater took him up to the "hallowed precincts" and as I have no means of ascertaining without exciting suspicion you must sound Freddie and write to me.[47]

In March of 1854 Simeon was recording secretary of Clio, and his minutes of a meeting reveal something more of the nature and activities of the society.

Meeting was called to order at half past seven o'clock by Timothy Bishop . . . and almost immediately Mr. West Steever stiff from the effects of his initiation and attesting to the excellence of the Society's goat made his appearance and was called upon for a speech. The confusion which prevailed during his remarks was such that we can not attempt to give this gentleman's address. It was characterized throughout by eloquence and historic lore. The report of the committee on procuring the second skeleton was then read by Mr. H. M. Dutton, the substance was that one could be procured at the expense of $5.00, perfect, with the exception of the left thigh bone. This defect was noted immaterial and the committee were ordered to purchase it immediately. The question of ways and means was then discussed and the Treasurer reported a balance of $1.83 in the treasury. After some debate a tax of 66 cts was levied on each member. The order of the evening was then taken up, i.e. the election of a poet for the 1st of May. The contest for this office between Messrs Blake, Dutton, Bristol and Steever was kept up with great vigor until at last Mr. Bristol and Steever dropped off, and all the members . . . were divided between Messrs. Blake & Dutton. At this junction the excitement became intense. Mr. Dutton was called to order three times and Mr. Tyler's dagger was several times employed in menacing the unruly. In the midst of the balloting a skuffling of feet was heard outside, a violent knock at the door was given and somebody rushed downstairs falling over the warming pan in his ascent [*sic*]. The commotion caused by this having subsided after three more ballots Mr. Blake was elected Poet, and a short speech thanking the society for the distinguished honor, etc. The society then fell to eating nuts at which agreeable pastime they . . . [exhibited] much dexterity until about nine it was carried to adjourn.[48]

Simeon E. Baldwin
Recording Secretary

Simeon was unable to attend school during the fall, winter, or spring of 1853–4 because of his eyes, and time frequently hung heavily on his hands. He employed it in part to write in a little diary, which illuminates the everyday life of a boy in New Haven in the fifties. It also contains comments on his reading and on men and events which it is difficult to realize came from a boy of fourteen. The following is a representative sampling of his observations.

January 11, 1854. Wrote an article about Skull & Bones [a Yale senior secret society] & put it in the paper. Everyone thought it must be official. Very strange they said. Ha Ha Ha said Ed Blake & I.

January 14. Bought Johnson's Work (calf) for $1.50.

January 16. Am looking into Miss Edgeworth novels. Find them pretty good.

January 18. Mother has decided on a new plan for my torment. I am to go to Brinsmade's & learn how to carpenter. She says it will keep me from the temptation of reading. Awful time today.

January 24. Had a miserable time at Mr. Brinsmade's as usual. Very cold. . . . Sup. Court commenced its session here today. Mr. Blackman very crafty in cross witnessing. Wrote Seward's letter [inviting him to be an honorary member of the Clio Society].

January 29. . . . Mother left for Worcester. Discovered a secret drawer in my bookcase & my great uncle's diploma signed by Pres Clap, my great great uncle [Rev. Thomas Clap, President of Yale College from 1739 to 1766].

January 30. . . . Father spoke today. When he begins a speech his pitch is painful but as he proceeds it becomes well modulated & effective.

February 4. Brinsmade not at the shop. City meeting to appoint an agent to sign city water bonds. Awful row. About 1100 voters present. Hardly any gentlemen. Effected little or nothing. Mayor Skinner was in despair & when the motion to adjourn was carried he was transported.

February 5. Birthday. Formed a number of good resolutions which I hope I may have strength to keep. Snowed quite deep.

February 8. Snow & rain. Paths very hard to make. Sealed some Valentines. Jennings has a sort of dogged look. Found guilty of murder in the first degree. Did not appear to be much moved by it.

February 14. Went over Boardman's Building in State St. just erected. Very fine block. Finished Clio Oration. Had fine fun carrying Valentines. Bought Francis Bacon, Humphrey Clinker for 53 cts. . . .

February 15. Wednesday. Whig State Convention. Rather meagre attendance at first but soon filled up. Henry Dutton for governor got 129 votes. Total number cast 159. . . .

February 16. Clio received a capital answer from its humble servant "Bill Seward F.C.S." [Fellow of Clio Society]. It was read amid great aplause and he was appointed . . . our corresponding secretary at Washington. All the seven were there. Had splendid time speechifying. Got a valentine.

February 17. O. W. Holmes lectures . . . before the Institute . . . Holmes made a pretty good lecture—funny at first, afterwards rather sentimental than otherwise. Spoke as if he was paid for being funny.

February 18. A month yesterday to St. Patrick's day. Rumour whispers that the Padres will turn out, with Gen. Washington painted, kneeling and kissing the popes toe. . . .

March 3. . . . Have been skimming along Don Juan. I don't think it anything very splendid and it certainly is very immoral.

March 5. Read part of Prof. Edwards treatise on the authenticity of the Pentateuch. Exceedingly interesting. Len. Bacon preached this afternoon, rather affected but still good.

March 7. . . . Played running games for the first time this year. . . .

March 11. Went flat fishing and had Fisherman's luck. Bought a moulding plane for 25 cts at auction second hand. . . .

March 14. . . . Put up my birdhouse. . . .

March 15. . . . Painted the birdhouse. Filed a saw and sharpened a bit. Went out to Judges Cave with Ed. The inscription is effaced, a great rascal he who did it.

March 16. . . . I found worms *today*, & am a great mind to go trouting tomorrow. . . .

March 19. Read a book of Paradise Lost. . . .[49]

As Sim indicated with disgust, his going to Mr. Brinsmade's carpenter shop was an idea of his mother's to keep him occupied during the time in which he could not attend school. From Worcester Mrs. Baldwin wrote her husband on this project:

How is Simeon getting on with Mr. Brinsmade—. I have written that I think he had better go to the shop—after dinner as well as before—and I hope you will enforce it if you think it best for him—. And if you see Mr. Brinsmade—ask him if he cannot find or make work for him for a compensation—. I dread so his forming idle habits—from having hours on his hands to trifle away—. When I think of this I long to be at home.[50]

When Elizabeth's fiancé, Clinton Camp, died in 1853, Elizabeth went to visit his family in Trumansburg, a tiny village on Lake Cayuga in upper New York. In April of 1854 Simeon went to Trumansburg to work on the Camp farm. In a letter to his friend, Edward Blake, Sim exercised his acute powers of observation and described his host and his daily routine:

Hon. Herman Camp is a Connecticut born man, and a regular Yankee man. He began life without any advantages of education, as a clerk in this village, and went on step by step, until he is now, Pres of a Bank, and last year of the State Temperance Society, has been in the Legislature &. He is a man of sound sense and a firstrate "gentleman farmer." Once or twice he has been out in the field and showed that he is a good worker. My life with him now is, wake up at about six and come down, the first one, all the others are too lazy, save Mr. Camp, take breakfast, and then go to prayers which cover the best part of an hour, and include several pages of Scotts Notes, in which he explains all the hard words as, for instance "Practical". . . .[51]

In turn, Ed kept Sim well posted on the happenings in the boys' world at home. Affairs at the Hopkins Grammar School were apparently at a rather low ebb.

We have great times at the Grammar School nowadays. It is worse than the worst under "Salmon". . . . Little lets the boys do just as they please and whenever anyone of them cuts up a caper he laughs as much as any of the boys and sometimes more. The boys generally collect together in the cabinet get up a subscription, send down to the pie-bakery for pies cakes beer and ginger pop draw them up into the window by a string and then the Programme is "Eat drink and be merry." Horace Smith keeps a bottle of brandy sugar a tumbler and a toddy stick in his desk and takes a glass of brandy and water every now and then. Tom Wells keeps a bottle of wine in his and occasionally swigs at it with an infinite relish.[52]

In view of the conditions described it is not altogether surprising that Mr. Baldwin wrote to Sim later in the month that the family has

not fully decided what school you will attend. It is not yet certainly known who will have charge of the Grammar School, and I understand that it has lost some reputation of late, owing to some ungovernable boys among the pupils.[53]

Returning from Trumansburg in September of 1854, Simeon was still unable to study full time. He attended classes four half days a week and studied Latin at home an hour a day.[54] In the early spring he acted as escort to his sister, Elizabeth, on a hurried trip to Trumansburg, where her friend, Henrietta Camp, had just died. Simeon left his sister there and returned to New Haven in order not to miss any more school.[55]

One of the high spots of the summer of 1855 was a camping trip to Lake Saltonstall on the outskirts of New Haven.[56] Simeon's friends, Edward Blake and the White brothers, Tom and Roger, joined him on this annual event. The boys went out on a Monday and cooked their meals and slept in their tents for a week. Swimming and boating were the principal attractions, and the campers had the kind of a good time that only a group of boys can enjoy.

By this time Sim's eyes were almost completely well, and he was about to begin the last two years of uninterrupted study at the Hopkins Grammar School. Writing to Roger in August, 1855, Mr. Baldwin said:

Simeon, whose studies have been much interrupted for the the last two years by the state of his eyes we think will now be able to resume them with advantage. He was able to attend during the greater part of the last term at the Grammar School, and though many & perhaps most of the boys are older than himself, he received in the report read at the examinations by the Rector, the *highest* commendation for scholarship.[57]

Sim began to be invited to social gatherings in his last years at Hopkins, but avoided such affairs as much as possible. His mother had worried about the same attitude on the part of his older brothers but decided not to distress herself about it with Simeon.[58] His interests in these years turned ever more strongly to books. He frequented book auctions and spent every cent he had or could beguile from his mother to increase his library. Among his acquisitions at this time was Grote's twelve-volume *History of Greece*, which his mother read aloud to him.[59]

In the spring of 1856 Sim made his first long journey. His Aunt Charlotte, Mrs. Baldwin's maiden sister, wanted to visit her brother in Chicago, and Simeon went along as her escort.[60] Late in April they left from Hartford and stopped to visit relatives in Utica and Rochester.[61] They made a side trip to Niagara Falls, stopped overnight in Detroit, and eventually completed the last leg of the journey to Chicago. There they stayed at the home of Sim's Uncle George, who was pastor of the First Congregational Church.[62] Late in May they traveled across Illinois to Rock Island to see the Mississippi and took a boat trip on the mighty river to Galena and back to Rock Island.

In June Simeon began the return trip alone and stopped off

for a couple of weeks to visit the Camps at Trumansburg.[63] From there he went to New York City and after a few days with his cousins returned to New Haven about the end of June.

Before the summer of 1856 was over Simeon had another excursion. Early in August he and his mother indulged their love of mountains with a trip to New Hampshire. There they eschewed carriages and horses and wandered about the White Mountains on foot. The sixty-year-old woman climbed Mt. Washington with Simeon, spending a night at the Tip Top House. Mrs. Baldwin's accounts of the mountain scenery were very vivid as she unsuccessfully urged her husband to join them.[64]

While he was away Sim received a lengthy letter from Jim Blake, recounting the latest school scandal.

I would advise you to make the most of your respite from study, for Whiton this term has added a cubit to the stature of his ferocity and has turned out Cutter, and threatened Ives . . . and myself with a like punishment. The circumstances of the "Cutter row" were these. Cutter asked Whiton one day in school when the subject of excuses was being discussed, whether it was necessary to specify the *disease* which was the cause of abscence. Whiton asked him what his motive was in asking the question and C. said it was for the sake of obtaining a reply. W. said that a person who would make such a answer as that was either a fool or a knave and asked which he (W.) was to consider him? Cutter replied that he was "not particular which." Whereupon Whiton told him to leave the room. The next day when C. came to school again Whiton told him to rise and make these three statements: 1st that he was sorry for being impudent, 2nd that he did not intend to be impudent, and 3d that he was aware that he *was* impudent;— and told him that if he did not immediately and without a moments reflection make these statements unconditionally, he must be expelled. Cutter said that he wanted time for thought and requested leave to see W. after school about it. W. would not consent to this and reiterated his demands. C. then declared that he had no intention of being impudent, and that *if* he was he was sorry; but that he did not think he had been so, as the nature of Ws questions did not admit of any other answers than the ones he had given him,—and that for him to say the 3d would be to tell an untruth, which he could not consent to do.

Thereupon he was expelled. Recently however Whiton moderated his demands greatly so that Cutter did not consider it inconsistent with his honor to comply with them and is now back again in the school—though by a very precarious tenure, as Whiton takes every opportunity of insulting and annoying him.[65]

Simeon's friend also presented an interesting description of the activities of the Polymnia Society, one of the organizations at Hopkins Grammar School in which Simeon participated during his last years there. The principal function of this group appears to have been debating. The society had been formed in 1849, had died and been revived several times during the fifties, and in 1856 and 1857 was flourishing.[66] Polymnia had never been better attended or more firmly established, Jim Blake wrote. Recently they had the first impromptu debate of the society in which all the members present participated.

The question was "Quid faciemus τῶν βαρβάρων" [*sic*] which being interpreted signifies; "What shall we do with the paddies?" [Irishmen]—and the debate became so interesting that for the first time in the history of the society no recess was asked for or granted. I think this fact will do away with many of the foolish objections which have been made to debating in the society and that hereafter debates will become quite frequent. At the same meeting in which we fully established the success of regular and systematic debating some rules were past forbidding the personal sharpshooting that Wilson you and I have carried on so much; and the miserable quibbling about the minutes that has been so fashionable, and restricting the incessant appeals from the decision of the chair which have been such a bore,—the latter unanimously, and the rest by a vote of 4 to one. So you see that radical changes have been made since you went away and you must expect to find Polymnia quite a different person than she was before.[67]

During his last years at the Grammar School Sim found time for general reading in addition to his school work. In 1855 he acquired Prescott's *Philip the Second* and was awaiting Elizabeth's return home so that she, Mrs. Baldwin, and Simeon could read it aloud together.[68] Early in 1857 he mentions reading Dr. E. K. Kane's stories of his arctic navigations and Lord Mahon (probably his *The History of England from the Peace of*

Utrecht to the Peace of Versailles, 1713–1783 [7 vols. 1836–1853]) and also tackling Madame de Stael's *Delphine* in French.[69]

Simeon generally ranked very well in school, although sometimes he slipped apparently because he did not try. The following tabulation based on his Hopkins Grammar School report cards shows how he stood over the period from October, 1855, to July, 1857. The teacher's comments whenever they appeared are also included. His class varied between 27 and 36 during the period.

Date	*Rank in Scholarship*	*Rank in Conduct*
Oct. 1, 1855 general scholarship very good—inclined to be too neighborly in school hours	3	26
Dec. 1, 1855 general scholarship very good—deportment good	2	8
Feb. 1, 1856	1	1
Mar. 1, 1856 deportment not satisfactory	6	20
Oct. 16, 1856	2	15
Dec. 16, 1856	1	1
Mar. 16, 1857	1	14
Apr. 22, 1857	7	29
July 1, 1857	11	28
July 25, 1857 able to rank first—he should not be content with mediocrity	11	1

The school was one of the oldest in America, having been founded in 1660, and like most secondary schools in the nineteenth century steeped its scholars strongly in the classics. In December, 1855, Sim was studying Virgil, Greek grammar, Latin prosody, modern history, English composition, written translation and declamation. In the latter part of his senior year his studies included Virgil, the *Odyssey*, Greek grammar, Latin prose composition, Latin grammar, Caesar's *Civil Wars*, algebra, and English grammar.

On June 1st of his senior year Simeon won a prize for the best essay on the question "Has the annexation of territory since 1840 been advantageous to the United States?" In July he graduated as valedictorian of his class and delivered two orations, one in Latin and one in English.

Thus Sim ended his school days surrounded by success. On July 27, 1857, came an official notice of what had, of course, been a foregone conclusion—that he was admitted to the freshman class at Yale.[70]

COLLEGE YEARS

YALE IN THE 1850s was a religiously oriented liberal arts college to which small and struggling professional schools had been added. Its total student population in 1857 was 565, and its faculty numbered about 40. The President of Yale was the Reverend Theodore D. Woolsey, a Congregational minister, and during his quarter-century of leadership (1846–1871) the institution advanced more rapidly than in any previous period of similar length. During his incumbency, the college made improvements in the methods of instruction, increased and strengthened the faculty, enriched the curriculum, made the degree requirements more exacting, found the money for new buildings, and raised the endowment. As a final move at the end of his period of tenure, the Connecticut General Assembly passed an act to allow alumni representation in the corporation.[1]

The college chiefly consisted of the large Academical Department,[2] the undergraduate liberal arts school, containing in 1857 447 of the 565 registered students. The remainder of the students was divided among the Department of Philosophy and the Arts (36),[3] the Medical Department (29), the Law Department (31), and the Theological Department (22). These specialized departments were partially for graduate professional study but by no means exclusively so. Only slightly more than one-third of the students in these departments had bachelors' degrees in 1857.

The college was firmly in clerical hands, where it remained until late in the nineteenth century. Its corporation consisted of the President, always a Congregational minister, the Connecticut governor, lieutenant governor, the six senior state senators, all ex officio, and ten Congregational ministers all of whom were traditionally residents of Connecticut. The latter were self-perpetuating.

If the corporation was provincial, the student body was by comparison quite cosmopolitan. The geographical distribution of Simeon E. Baldwin's class, 1861, for example, was as follows:

New York	25
Connecticut	23
Massachusetts	11
Pennsylvania	9
Ohio	6
Maryland	4
New Jersey and New Hampshire	3 each
Kentucky, Mississippi and Delaware	2 each
Wisconsin, Michigan, Indiana, Texas, Missouri, Vermont, Maine, Illinois, and Washington, D.C.	1 each
Total	99

The course of instruction in the Academical Department was built around the languages and civilizations of ancient Greece and Rome. During all six terms of the first two years Greek, Latin, mathematics, and rhetoric were the basic studies. The only other subject was a one-term course in ancient history. All freshman and sophomore subjects were compulsory.

In the junior year Greek, Latin, and rhetoric were still required for two out of three terms, natural philosophy, chemistry, astronomy, and logic were added, and a few electives allowed—namely, advanced mathematics, ancient and modern languages, and mineralogy.

The senior year consisted largely in lecture courses on astronomy, history, mental philosophy, rhetoric, chemistry, moral philosophy, political philosophy, the Constitution of the United States, theology, meteorology, anatomy, and geology. Much more opportunity for individual preference was allowed in this year than in the previous three.

The cost of a college education at that time was not high. Tuition was $45 a year, and the total expense of a student averaged from $234 to $324 a year, according to the college catalogue's estimate. For a New Haven boy who lived with his family considerably under $100 would have carried him through the year.

The college year was divided into three terms, the first running from mid-September to mid-December followed by a two-week Christmas holiday; the second from January to early April followed by a three-week spring vacation; and the third from May to late in July, when Commencement was held. The summer recess was about seven weeks long.

Such was Yale College when Simeon E. Baldwin entered in September of 1857. One of the earliest mementos of his college years is the draft of a speech accepting membership in Brothers in Unity, a student literary society founded in 1768.[4] It and its rival, the Linonian Society, possessed at that time large and fine collections of general literature—about 12,000 volumes each.[5] Nearly everyone in the college joined one or the other of the literary societies, and each could use the library facilities of the other.[6] The two groups also engaged periodically in debates.

Sim's brother, George, wrote to him in the fall of his freshman year, warning him against the dangers of campus politics and throwing light on the extracurricular activities of Yale undergraduates in the fifties:

> Let me claim an elder brothers right . . . and give you a little advice. Don't be a violent "party" man. College politics have assumed a controlling influence of late entirely uncommensurate with their real importance and have created more cliques and occasioned more enmities among classmates than any other cause whatever. What matter is it whether A or B is elected Reader or vice secretary of Linonian Society, or whether K does, or not, bear off the larger share of college honors. Dont let these trifles create any heartburnings between you and your fellows or alienate you from a single friend. and above all dont prejudge your classmates now. The class leaders of Freshman year are generally men of showy and superficial parts who find their level before graduation and are superceded by men of more substantial and more modest merits.[7]

Early in the fall of his first year Simeon was admitted to Delta Kappa, one of the three freshman societies. Election to this was somewhat more selective than to the literary societies, about 40 of the 99 members of the class being chosen. Later he was treasurer of the organization.[8]

During the spring vacation of his freshman year Simeon accompanied his father on a brief trip to Washington. The elder Baldwin's position as a former senator enabled Simeon to see something of official social life in the Capital. Mr. Baldwin described the visit to his son, George:

I availed myself of the opportunity afforded by a short vacation at the adjournment of the U. S. Circuit Court, to visit Washington with Simeon for a few days. He was of course delighted with everything—and it was a great pleasure to me to meet with so many of my old friends in the Senate. We dined with Gov. Seward, and with Mr. Bell, attended a levee at the White House, and a very large party at Mr. Douglas' given on the occasion of the assembling of the Medical Convention, consisting of nearly 600 physicians from every part of the U. S. at Washington.[9]

The freshman year was soon over and to commemorate the class of 1861's becoming sophomores a song was composed, possibly by Simeon:

A Wondrous thing has come to pass—
Old Yale has lost her Freshman Class—
All on this pleasant Summer's day
It seemed to vanish right away.

Yes! Freshman year has taken flight,
And sophomores we stand to night.
One stage of College life is done:
Too soon the others will be run.

Short is the space till Junior year
Shall teach us to electioneer,
And how most easily to break
Whatever pledge one has to make.

Then a few months will hurry by,
And leave us just below the sky,
In that high space, where Seniors dwell,
In greatness unapproachable—

But often as we change our name,
The Class forever stands the same;
And till our latest hours be run,
We all are joined in '61.[10]

In July of 1858 Simeon made a vigorous defense of the Brothers in Unity, which reflected the rivalry between Linonia and Brothers. They can speak of the antiquity of Linonia, he said, and they can say that the Brothers is only an offshoot; and we can tell them that it is not the first time that from some old stump rotting away in the darkness of the forests has sprung up a shoot, which has gained new life in the decay of the parent stock, and finally overtopped and overshadowed it.[11] Sim also defended both of the literary societies against their detractors, who were sure they had outlived their usefulness. Most of their critics, he pointed out, were the ones who attended only one meeting. Many are the men, said Sim, who have been faithful members for as little as a year and yet can testify to the present benefits of the societies. The first speech a man makes there is usually hesitating and ill-assured. A few months later the same man can speak offhand on a question about which he has not thought before the debate began with all the self-reliance, self-assurance and fluency which once gained never deserts him through life.[12]

In his second year Sim was elected to Alpha Sigma Phi, one of the two sophomore societies, along with thirty-two other members of his class.[13] Apparently this society was something of a disappointment to the young man, and in his usual forthright manner, he pointed out the group's shortcomings. The stated object of the organization was the promotion of drama, but no one appeared to take any interest in it. In view of the frequent parliamentary squabbles it was disgraceful, he maintained, that the society did not own a copy of Cushing's manual, a minute's reference to which would often have saved an hour's arguing. The society had almost every man it wanted and a good hall. The only thing needed to make it worth-while was for the members to take a little more interest in it.[14] At different times Simeon was corresponding secretary, vice-president, and president of Alpha Sigma Phi.[15]

During this year Sim was also a member of the Sophomore Wicket Club. Having been driven off the public green by the city authorities, the group petitioned the college for another playing field.[16] Simeon was also active in the college chess club. He took part in intercollegiate matches and was president of the club in his senior year.[17]

In January, 1859, the annual prize debates of the literary societies were held, and in the Brothers' contest Simeon won first prize in the sophomore competition.[18]

In writing to a friend Sim described one of the traditions of the sophomore year which took place after the end of the first term—the burial of Euclid.

The time honored rite of the Burial of Euclid was duly performed with the appropriate ceremonies by the Sophomore Class, a few weeks since. Now that the requisitions of study have been so much increased, Euclid has become one of the easiest of the text-books, but custom has decreed that Euclid must be buried, & in College, custom is stronger than anything else. The great end of the occasion has now become to run upon the Freshmen.

This unhappy Class, their name being printed in the programme of performances in *green* ink are sarcastically informed in one of the Songs that although

"*. . . no monstrous* problems now shall flunk
The Class of '61
Yet know ye wretched Freshmen
That Euclid is not dead;
He is not dead but sleepeth
Upon Lethean bed.
If he be dead to Sophomores
He is not dead to you
Long shall he live, long shall he live
To fizzle '62."

The Faculty used to forbid the Burial & proceed against its authors with great severity, but for the last few years, they have let it pass without any notice.[19]

During the spring vacation Sim and his friends went on a

walking and fishing trip to Litchfield County, one of the most beautiful regions of Connecticut.[20] Soon thereafter his mother wrote that:

Sim is swallowed up in College affairs— He has just come in saying that in a meeting of the "Brothers" Society George Perkins [his cousin] had been nominated for vice librarian—and he himself for junior orator—"which honor he had declined"—His eyes have been bad this summer and a great draw back to him—which he feels keenly —and he complaining during the rainy weather—that the noise of the children in the house playing or crying is a great nuisance.

He has been so much alone and had his own quiet ways, that it is well for him to have some disturbing forces. We must all meet them.[21]

A skillful organizer and indefatigable worker, Sim drew up a petition in May of 1859 for the establishment of a vocal society at Yale. His interest in music also led him to compose the words to no less than three songs commemorating the end of sophomore year. The two best are as follows:

Air: Vi Volla Rolla Rolla Ra

We've passed the greatest bore in College,
Vi volla rolla rolla ra
As every Soph'more will acknowledge;
Vi volla rolla rolla ra
Hurrah Hurrah for '61,
For Junior year is now begun.
Vi volla rolla rolla ra
Vi volla rolla rolla ra
Vi volla rolla rolla ra

Then louder shout the jolly chorus,
Vi volla rolla rolla ra
Biennial no more hangs o'er us;
Vi volla rolla rolla ra
To that we bid a long adieu
And take today a start anew.
Vi volla rolla rolla ra
Vi volla rolla rolla ra
Vi volla rolla rolla ra

As fond remembrance counts her treasures,
Vi volla rolla rolla ra
When flown are College cares & pleasures;
Vi volla rolla rolla ra
Whatever else her hand may blot,
This day shall never be forgot.
Vi volla rolla rolla ra
Vi volla rolla rolla ra
Vi volla rolla rolla ra [22]

The second is to the tune of "It's a Way We Have at Old Yale, Sir."

Oh! on this day millenial
Of memory perennial
We've finished our Biennial
And entered Junior year.

Our college cares are over;
Hence forth we live in clover
Our "ordo saclum nova"
Today commences here.

We're ready to acknowledge,
That we all came to College
To acquire useful knowledge,
From all parts of the land.

But then too much of a good thing
The wisest join in condemning,
And Junior year never does bring
Much wish to study for stand.

Then louder shout the chorus;
There's nothing more to bore us,
And two glad years before us
To spend in College yet.

When fond remembrance measures
In after years her treasures—
Our college cares and pleasures
This day we'll n'er forget.[23]

Sim won a number of scholastic honors during his sophomore year. Besides the Brothers' Debating prize he was given the Berkeley Premiums for excellence in Latin Composition and the first award in English Composition.[24]

One of the essays which helped Simeon win the latter prize perhaps provides a clue to his philosophy of life and a key to the explanation of his future conduct. It was entitled "The Second Life of Man." From this one might judge that it was concerned with the conception of the afterlife of the mid-nineteenth-century Congregationalism in which Simeon was raised. On the contrary, Simeon was referring to the reputation which a man acquires while living and which survives his death. Perhaps the real explanation of his strivings for success and leadership in a wide variety of activities was the desire for fame, for "the second life of man" referred to in this early essay.

It should not be supposed from this, however, that Simeon did not believe in the future life of the orthodox Christian. Another essay clarifies his position on this subject. This deals with Daniel Webster, and in it Simeon deplores the fact that Webster died without any hopes beyond the grave.

> It is painful indeed, to see so great a mind as W's living a long life, in full view of the principles of Christianity, paying them all deference, not disputing their truth, and yet never once embracing them, & making them his own.[25]

The summer vacation of this year soon arrived, and Simeon spent part of it in Worcester. He went there late in July to witness the annual boat races between Yale and Harvard,[26] and early in August escorted his mother, sister, and her children to New Hampshire.[27] While Simeon reveled in fishing, Mrs. Baldwin enjoyed the mountain views. She was pleased that Simeon was happy in her company and remarked to her husband that he seemed to talk easily with those about him.[28]

In the fall of 1859 Simeon joined Psi Upsilon, one of the three junior societies at Yale. Twenty-one members of his class were elected to this group, while the other two societies, Delta Kappa Epsilon and Alpha Delta Phi, chose twenty-six each.[29]

These societies met every Tuesday night where rumor reported (for the societies were secret) "literary exercises" took place and a lunch was afterwards eaten. Once in each term a more elaborate program was prepared, including short plays and speeches, enlivened by jokes concerning a variety of college affairs. On these occasions an unusually good supper accompanied the evening's festivities.[30]

As his junior year advanced Simeon showed signs of increasing intellectual maturity. This tendency may be illustrated by an essay written at this time in which he argued for freedom of the press. He granted that freedom of the press helped to spread infidelity, the doctrines of which would otherwise be little known. With a free press truth and falsehood could vie, and errors could thus be contradicted. If the press was restricted, on the other hand, error might go uncorrected provided that it coincided with the prejudices or aims of a government or a church or an age. Simeon astutely pointed out that the accepted principles of one age were often the proscribed theories of the last.[31] The young man could be and frequently was decided in his views. Yet this early recognition of the relativity of some kinds of truth served to temper his partisanship and made it easier for him to change his opinion when he felt that his past judgments were fallacious.

Another evidence of Simeon's intellectual growth was his ardent interest in politics. This, as the previous chapter has indicated, was originally aroused a decade previously when his father was a senator. By the spring of 1860 he was assuming an active role in the new political party which was that year to nominate and elect Abraham Lincoln. Along with other young Republicans of New Haven he helped build a great barn called National Hall, where party speakers held forth. This enterprise was constructed largely from dollar subscriptions and the volunteer labor of its supporters.[32] Simeon was also one of the organizers and an officer of the Yale Republican Club in 1860.[33]

At this time he was also actively engaged in a new literary venture called the *University Quarterly*.[34] This was a periodical by and for the undergraduates of the colleges of America.

Founded by Yale students, edited and printed in New Haven, the *Quarterly* had boards of editors on other campuses who solicited articles on literary, historical, and educational subjects, contributed news from their institutions, and handled subscriptions. Simeon was one of the three editors from his class at Yale who took an active part in the work of the magazine. Eight creditable issues of the *Quarterly* appeared between January, 1860, and October, 1861. The advent of the Civil War made publication extremely difficult, however, and with the October, 1861, number publication was suspended.

In the fall of 1860 Simeon entered his senior year as an outstanding man of his class. He was one of the Yale board of editors of the *University Quarterly*, president of the Yale Chess Club, one of the best scholars, writers, and speakers in his class, and a member of Phi Beta Kappa. In addition, he had belonged to the highest-ranking social fraternities throughout his college years and climaxed his career by being one of the fifteen elected to Skull and Bones,[35] the most coveted senior society. The history and significance of this organization are described in an informal account of Yale written in the 1880s.

This association was organized in 1832 by fifteen members of the Class of 1833, one of whom is now Ex-Attorney General Taft. Fifteen members are elected from every senior class, the elections being given out a short time previous to Commencement in junior year. Early evening is the time chosen for notifying of their election the men that have been chosen, and several hundred students, and ladies with their escorts, always gather on the campus, between North College and Durfee, to witness the ceremony. The members proceed from the hall one at a time, search among the students for the ones elected, and on finding them touch them on the shoulder and ask them to go to their rooms, whither they are followed and given a formal offer of election, which is practically always accepted. Those of the men elected who are popular among their associates are heartily cheered and congratulated by their classmates and friends, as an election to the society is looked upon as one of the greatest student honors in the entire course. As a rule, of the fifteen members chosen, two are editors of the Yale Literary Magazine, one or two are chosen from each of the three great athletic interests—base-ball, foot-ball and boating—one from the staff of each of the Yale newspapers, one or more for high scholarship, and so on, the intention being, apparently, to secure representative men from all the leading student interests in the class.[36]

Simeon's fame as a speaker and writer spread during his senior year beyond the fences of the Yale campus. A letter came from Newark, New Jersey, in December, 1860, in which the writer said that he had seen by the Yale catalogue that Mr. Baldwin had won many prizes for composition and speaking. He then offered to purchase essays and speeches to be used in another New England college.[37]

Complementing Simeon's scholarly and extracurricular activities was his awakening interest in the social world. In February of 1861, shortly after his twenty-first birthday, he attended a fancy costume party.[38] Not long afterwards Mrs. Baldwin thanked her husband for a check

which has come in good time, for myself and Sim, whose wants increase with his years and with his disposition to enter more into society.[39]

In April the final rupture between the North and South occurred, and the nation became locked in civil war. The conflict affected Simeon's life relatively little, although he was deeply moved by the tragedies he saw the nation and his friends suffer. He graduated from Yale on July 25 in a blaze of glory, giving the salutatory oration and winning the Berkeley Scholarship and the Townsend Premiums for English Composition.[40]

During his last weeks in college Simeon and his friends exchanged farewell notes. To his friend, Alexander Root of Texas, Simeon wrote a most sincere goodbye:

Dear Sandy,

The most unwilling goodbye that I have spoken or written yet is this to you. The rest of us part we may say but for 3 yrs at farthest but where you and your state will be in 1864 is a harder question than you or I can answer. One can hardly blame a man for following his father & his state. . . . Well Sandy individually we shall feel the same at last, and I only hope we shall meet again at some future time under better auspices—and still belonging to the same country—I suppose that I am not committing treason in rendering aid & comfort to the enemy when I write myself down most sincerely your friend.

S. E. B.[41]

In spite of the war life went on quite as usual for the Baldwins during the first summer of hostilities. Early in August Mr. Baldwin entertained his Yale class at dinner on the occasion of its fiftieth reunion. The Whitneys went to the Connecticut hills for the summer. The Fosters spent their vacation at Saratoga. Simeon and some friends left New Haven in their boat for a long rowing trip in Long Island Sound to the Connecticut River and thence upstream.[42] They camped overnight as they proceeded and in several days reached Springfield, Massachusetts.[43]

Back in New Haven in the fall Simeon entered the Law Department at Yale, where he studied for a year, spending part of his time in his father's law office.[44]

In addition to his law studies he took a lively interest in public affairs during 1861 and 1862, particularly the conduct of the war. In a letter published in the New York *Times* Simeon opposed strenuously the secession of the western counties of Virginia to form a new state. By recognizing a rump Virginia legislature, he maintained, the President and Senate were supporting a government which only fifteen or eighteen out of the more than one hundred counties of the state claimed as their legal government.

It is a matter of the plainest justice, then, to the thousands of loyal Virginians who would vote down this project if an advance—of our army gave them the power to vote, that Congress should refuse to be made a cat's-paw in carrying out this scheme, which is only a new form of secession, and which has its only hope of success in being hurried through in a time of civil disorder and confusion.[45]

Throughout his first year at law school Simeon maintained a correspondence with several of his closest college friends. Many of these found it possible to pursue their careers in spite of the war. Anthony Higgins was studying law alone at his home in Delaware and missed the esprit de corps of college life.[46] Francis Kernochan was attending the newly founded Columbia Law

School and tried to persuade Simeon to join him.[47] William Park reported that he was not studying theology, as Simeon thought, and indeed was determined to have nothing to do with it.[48] Sextus Shearer and Edward Sill had sailed together for California. Both deplored the time wasted on the long voyage around South America, and Shearer told Simeon to be thankful that he was doing something worth-while and was not like himself a "miserable cuss." [49] Still another friend, Hubert S. Brown, wrote that he was puzzled by the problem of what to do in life and observed to Simeon that

> . . . the niche which I am to fill wasn't by nature pointed out with the same unquestionable clearness that it was in your own case.[50]

Not all of Simeon's associates were unaffected by the war. From Edward F. Blake, one of his oldest and closest New Haven friends, Simeon received firsthand accounts of the fighting.[51] The war was brought still closer home when in November, 1861, his brother, George, also entered the army as adjutant of the 15th Regiment, Massachusetts Volunteers.[52]

Having two sons of military age did not deter the Baldwin family from vigorously supporting the cause of the North both before and after the conflict erupted into open warfare. As a delegate to the peace conference held in Washington in February of 1861, Senator Baldwin had refused to support the compromises for which most of the commissioners voted in a final attempt to prevent war. In their father's position both George and Simeon had whole-heartedly concurred.[53] Mrs. Baldwin likewise felt strongly about the war as can be illustrated by a letter written to her son on the battlefield.

> Great purposes are being worked out through great sufferings and blood—
>
> But for this cause was this generation raised up—. And once more am I thankful to God that I have a son whose heart and *hand* is in this work—.[54]

In June, 1862, George was prostrated by ague and fever and was ordered out of his regiment. He was evacuated on a hospital ship to Philadelphia, where Simeon met him and escorted him safely to New Haven.[55] By the fourth of July George was well enough to go to Worcester, and Mrs. Baldwin was free again to turn her attention to the wounded who were pouring into New Haven for hospitalization.[56]

Even her son's illness and the suffering and anguish she saw at the hospital did not alter Mrs. Baldwin's feelings regarding the righteousness of the cause and the necessity of pressing to a decisive conclusion. She wrote to her daughter:

> I presume he [George] will wish to return to the Army at the earliest moment he is considered sufficiently recovered to be useful.
>
> I cannot hold him back—and if Sim even, should risk eyes for life I should not object—not that he speaks of it—. But I have the feeling that the time has come for all our young men to go—.[57]

While in Worcester George's fever returned, and as soon as he was able his parents removed him to Saratoga in hopes that the mineral waters would help him recuperate. In the meantime Simeon was home alone and informed his mother that he had given a dinner party for five of his New Haven friends.[58] He had hoped to organize a boating trip that summer but his friends were too scattered, and he was not able to do so. Early in August his mother summoned him to Saratoga to help her escort George, who remained very weak, back to New Haven.[59]

The crowds of gay people enjoying themselves at the watering place seemed to Simeon in rather poor taste at a time when men were being slaughtered a few hundred miles away. This feeling was deepened almost to revulsion when Simeon heard that two of his friends, Edward Blake and Henry M. Dutton, had been struck down in the fighting at Cedar Mountain. Both were killed on August 9, 1862.[60] Blake's death was an especially great sorrow to Simeon, for the two boys had grown up together. Both had gone on the long boating excursion up the Connecticut River the previous summer and on a camping trip in Maine the year before.

Late August saw the family together again in New Haven. Simeon was busy making his final preparations to leave for Cambridge, where he planned to attend the Harvard Law School. In addition to letters of introduction he took with him a certificate of exemption from enrollment in the state militia because of defective vision.

By mid-September Simeon was settled in Cambridge. This was the first time he had ever lived away from home, and it proved to be the last. He obtained a room for $1.75 a week and board for $4.[61] Another expense was the express charge on his laundry case which he sent home regularly. Learning that the rate from Boston to New Haven was twelve cents cheaper than from Cambridge to New Haven, thrifty Simeon made a trip to Boston each week to send his laundry home. He missed the gymnastics and rowing in which he had participated in New Haven and soon bought a rowboat which he used regularly on the Charles River.[62]

Simeon's impression of the Harvard Law School was generally favorable. Whereas Yale had only one professor of law, there were several in Cambridge. The library was so much larger than the one in New Haven that he found it more difficult to prepare cases. Moreover, the spirit of study prevailing at Harvard seemed better to him than at Yale. The quality of students Simeon found to be generally below what he had expected. There were about sixty students in residence—half the normal number. Probably a majority of them had never graduated from college, and many, Simeon thought, were on a par with college freshmen in intellectual maturity.[63]

At Harvard Simeon approached the study of law from several directions. He attended the law lectures regularly; he spent many hours daily pouring over Kent's *Commentaries;* he belonged to two moot court clubs, where he acted in turn as judge and lawyer; and in addition, along with his classmates, he took his turn participating in public moot cases.[64]

A few weeks after he had begun his studies in Cambridge, President Lincoln issued the Emancipation Proclamation. Towards this Simeon adopted a cautious attitude. Whereas he had opposed the extension of slavery, he had no great desire to uproot it suddenly. To his father he wrote:

Greely must grow fairly crazy with joy over the President's Proclamation. It was a very unexpected move to me, and, I presume, to the country. I am afraid that it will work trouble in Kentucky and Maryland. Though their slaves are excepted, the system will be shaken everywhere. I don't think the President would have issued it, had he not thought it would bring back most of the Seceders before the first of January. But in any event, it is a terrible assumption of power in a republican executive.[65]

As fall blended into winter bad news came from George, who had returned to the battlefront in September.[66] While riding, his horse slipped and fell, breaking George's leg.[67] After a stay in a Washington hospital, he was able to go home for a slow convalescence.

In January of 1863 Mr. Baldwin, who had scarcely known a day of sickness, became seriously ill. He had a dull pain in his head and a constant wearied and tired feeling. The doctor's diagnosis was nervous prostration complicated by influenza. The gravity of his illness led Mrs. Baldwin to summon Simeon home in mid-January.[68] Henrietta came from Worcester to see her father later in the month, and early in February, after her departure, Mrs. Baldwin wrote her that Mr. Baldwin was about the same. He seemed to prefer to sit or lie quietly and talked little.[69]

Soon after this it became apparent that Mr. Baldwin was dying. As one friend of the family wrote, probably in February:

It is with sincere sorrow I have to say that from all the information I can gather, there is very little, if any, ground to expect the recovery of Gov Baldwin. He is said to have entirely broken down, his system being completely prostrated. I have talked with his two sons, the wounded officer & the law student—but they do not appear so much discouraged as others, probably from the instinctive filial affection which shrinks from the idea of losing a beloved parent—. . . . His intense application without any relaxation from year to year, has overtasked his mental faculties, & he is thus suddenly arrested, although blessed with a very vigorous constitution— Every one feels regret at the condition of the greatest lawyer in the State & one by talents & character commanding universal respect I shall rejoice if our fears for him are not realised.[70]

On the 19th of February Mr. Baldwin died.

Perhaps the finest letter of condolence received by Mrs.

Baldwin was from the committee which retained Mr. Baldwin to defend the Amistad captives more than two decades before:

Dear Madam,

Permit us to mingle our sympathies with the numerous friends of your departed husband who express to you their sense of the exalted virtues, and your irreparable loss.

It is now upwards of twenty three years since we, in the capacity of a committee representing thousands of benevolent persons, employed him as counsel of the Amistad Africans, whose cause he readily undertook and prosecuted with untiring vigilance and consummate ability while many in his profession, from political or professional reasons, shrunk from the unpopularity of vindicating those who were incarcerated under a charge of crime deserving, in the opinion of a large portion of the community, to be expiated only by an ignominious death on the scaffold.

The cause thus manfully & heroically undertaken was carried through the various courts until it came for final decision before the Supreme Court of the United States at Washington. There the poor Africans were defended by your husband, as associate counsel with the Honorable John Quincy Adams, who had shrunk from the arduous labor involved in an acceptance of the urgent request of the committee on account of his great age, and the loss of familiarity with legal proceedings, but who, on being assured that Mr. Baldwin's services had been secured, and that he would prepare his Brief, replied with great animation, "If he will do that I will undertake."

Mr. Baldwin's able argument before the Supreme Court was published, and read not only by the profession generally, but by the leading minds of the country. It was deemed unanswerable, and it settled the question that the negroes were entitled to their liberty. Mr. Adams said of it, "The rights of my clients to their lives and liberties have already been defended by my learned friend and colleague in so able and complete a manner as leaves me scarcely anything to say."

Mr. Baldwin's feelings, as well as his intellectual and legal powers, were deeply enlisted on behalf of the much injured Africans of the Amistad; he greatly rejoiced in their deliverance and restoration to their native land; and he has left a record for the instruction of posterity not only evidence of his distinguished ability in this case as a legal advocate, but proofs of his philanthropy in efforts for his deeply-wronged and oppressed fellow-men.

With the highest veneration for the character of your departed husband, and our most cordial sympathy with you and your children in this time of bereavement, we remain, dear Madam,

Very respectfully and truly, your friends

Lewis Tappan
Joshua Leavitt
S. S. Jocelyn [71]

With his father's death a new life began for Simeon. He withdrew from the Harvard Law School and spent the spring and summer of 1863 preparing himself for admission to the bar. He lived with his mother and took his father's place as head of the household. His days of school life had ended; those of a promising young professional man were about to begin.

EXPANDING HORIZONS

DURING THE FIRST ELEVEN YEARS of his professional life, Baldwin made promising beginnings in nearly every sphere of activity for which he is remembered. He became one of the prominent young men of the Connecticut bar; his career as a legal educator was launched; several scholarly articles and one book came from his pen; in politics he met defeat and victory at the polls and became a figure of promise in Connecticut Republican circles; and as a public speaker he gained experience. In many of these activities he had little to guide him except confidence in himself and the knowledge that much of what he was doing had long been neglected. Among his contemporaries his industry and accomplishments were constant sources of wonder and admiration.

I

After his father's death in February, 1863, Baldwin's formal law training ended, and he studied independently in New Haven until the following fall. By early September Simeon was ready to begin practice and was admitted to the bar in that month.[1] As a young lawyer his chances of succeeding were better than average. From his father he inherited a small fortune [2] and the mantle of one of the state's most eminent attorneys. The Baldwin name had been synonymous with legal preeminence and high political office in Connecticut since before 1800. He was well acquainted with the local legal fraternity and with the family and business inter-relationships which existed in the city of New Haven.

Although business at first might be slower, Simeon decided to open an office himself rather than join a more experienced lawyer. By so doing he believed he would grow to rely more on his own judgment. He came to the bar with no ready-made clientele, and his early cases were the type most young attorneys obtained. They involved bill collecting, minor criminal cases, serving legal papers and taking depositions for lawyers in other localities, and small civil actions. His earliest known legal task—and one reflecting his customary prudence—was the drawing up of his own will in the spring of 1863. In this document he overlooked the possibility that he might some day marry, but two weeks later this oversight was corrected in a second will which made provisions for a wife and family.[3]

As might be expected, the early months at the bar were discouraging ones. His college classmate, Anthony Higgins, wrote late in 1863 that he hoped Simeon would soon have twenty cases instead of two.[4] Later in the winter Baldwin gave Higgins a full account of his early practice. If this letter could be found, it would undoubtedly illuminate this period of his life,[5] for when replying, Higgins said:

> I shall try to preserve the letter so that when you or your descendants write your biography, some data on this interesting & critical portion of your life may be had.[6]

Higgins was not the only one of Baldwin's friends to whom it was a certainty that he would attain prominence. During the same month another classmate, Edward Rowland Sill, wrote from California:

> I have been very glad to hear, from various occasional sources, (though you didn't say much about it yourself) that you are getting on prosperously as a lawyer. We have all, I believe, taken it very much as a matter of course, that you were to be an able lawyer, and there seems no prospect of your disappointing us.[7]

An unusual case tried by Baldwin in his early years involved the suspension of the writ of *habeas corpus* during the Civil War.[8] An army captain on orders from General Dix had arrested a colonel on duty as recruiter of colored troops in Connecticut for alleged irregularities. The colonel obtained a writ of *habeas corpus*, but the captain refused to obey it on the ground that federal authority was involved and superseded state jurisdiction. Baldwin argued the case for the colonel but was overruled. One of his friends expressed regret that General Dix had deprived him of an opportunity of pleading such an interesting case and added:

> . . . but I am inclined to believe that General Dix's sense of justice and indignation at injustice is not far wrong in leading him to check your bright Connecticutters from swindling the poor darkies out of a third or a half of their bounty money. Surely your law does not contemplate such a percentage.[9]

Having practiced less than a year, Baldwin received a fee of one hundred dollars. This was a gigantic sum to one of his professional contemporaries, who was more accustomed to "tens."[10]

As the first years at the bar passed his practice grew reasonably quickly. His advance was apparently more rapid than that of any of his classmates who were lawyers. Anthony Higgins wrote in May, 1866, that Baldwin's increase in practice only answered his expectations for him.[11] Some months later another friend congratulated him on his success and hoped he might end the year with an even thousand dollars from his practice.[12]

From time to time Baldwin gathered together the printed briefs of his cases and had them bound in volumes. The earliest of these covers his practice from 1865 to 1874.[13] A survey of this volume indicates the types of cases Simeon was handling during his early years at the bar.

An 1867 case involved the right of a student to vote.[14] The action was brought against the Selectmen of New Haven by a Yale student who had been denied the voting privilege on the grounds that he had come to the city to attend college and not to reside there permanently. Baldwin represented the student and carried the case to the Connecticut Supreme Court of Errors. Another case concerned the attempt of the heirs of a man killed by a train to collect damages from the Hartford and New Haven Railroad Company.[15] In still another suit a woman sought to obtain redress from the city of New Haven for injuries caused by a branch which fell on her while on a public road.[16]

Baldwin's political activities aided him more than once in his legal career. His friendship with State Senator George A

Fay prompted the latter to turn over two cases to him in 1871.[17] One involved a client whose lawyer was attempting to charge an outrageous fee. The other concerned a newspaper publisher who was trying to collect an advertising bill.

During these years Baldwin's practice contained many commissions from out-of-state lawyers. These included serving legal papers, taking depositions, collecting bills, and giving opinions as to local business firms' reputations. Many of these assignments came through various legal directories in which lawyers in different sections of the country advertised their availability.

Baldwin's career shifted sharply in 1871 when he joined the legal staff of the New York and New England Railroad to represent the company's affairs in Connecticut. With this commission Baldwin entered the field of corporation law, and for the next twenty years this proved to be his principal type of professional work.

Part of his responsibility for the New York and New England involved obtaining desired legislation from the Connecticut General Assembly. In 1873 he helped secure the passage of a bill [18] ratifying the proceedings by which some of the security holders of the defunct Boston, Hartford & Erie Railroad Company had formed a new corporation, the New York & New England Railroad Company. This recognized the New York & New England as a legal corporation and enabled it to do business under the laws of Connecticut.[19]

Soon after beginning his work with the New York & New England, his brother wrote:

> I hear golden opinions of you on every side. I also hear incidentally that your charges are lower than those of any other of the counsel employed.[20]

II

Second only to his legal practice was Baldwin's political activity during this early period of his career. While in college, he had been active in Republican affairs, and soon after returning to New Haven in January, 1863, he engaged once more in politics. In the spring of that year he ran for his first public office, town clerk.[21] He failed to win the election, but as a friend wrote:

. . . though your brief though glorious career ended in temporary defeat, I doubt not it will still farther follow its resemblance to Joe Hookers late campaign, by using repulse only as a rest for another spring at the enemy.[22]

A year later Baldwin was more successful and was elected a justice of the peace for a two-year term.[23]

In July of 1864 he was again active politically, eddying around the margin of the political whirlpool, he told a friend,[24] as secretary of the Union Lincoln Association of New Haven. This was the local organization working for the President's re-election.

In September the presidential campaign was in full swing, and Baldwin took an active part in it. He was prominent in the local Red, White and Blue Club,[25] and as a member of the sixth ward committee of the New Haven Republican organization he reserved rooms in the State House for use in connection with a mass meeting. Delegations from the surrounding towns had been invited and were to be fed by the various wards. Baldwin was in charge of this for the sixth ward.[26]

Campaigning in the state and local electoral contests became an annual affair for Baldwin. In the spring of 1866 he spoke in the town of Prospect in behalf of Hawley's candidacy for governor. Baldwin emphasized presidential affairs and Morris, the other speaker, dwelt on congressional policies, but the two joined in vituperating the Democrats.

Our campaign speeches this year all run that way, like the sermons of the minister, who used to "give it to the Jews," whenever he was afraid of hurting anybody's feelings by striking nearer home.

Morris and I both thought we had spoken fairly well, but on returning to our lodging-place, our host only remarked, Well, Mr. Morris, I think you have improved very much since you spoke here before. I was congratulating myself on having escaped such a left handed compliment, when his eldest son broke in with my portion: Well, one of the young ladies told me that she liked Mr. Baldwin's speech very well, and hoped he would come there again, particularly if he wasn't married. If, you see, any of our wedding cards had travelled as far as Prospect, I should have been denied even that commendation, so ungrateful are republics.[27]

Baldwin delivered other addresses in the campaign at Centerville and North Madison.[28]

Simeon Baldwin's period of political apprenticeship was rewarded in 1867 when he was nominated and elected to the Board of Councilmen of New Haven, the lower house of the city's bicameral legislative body.[29] In the same election he was an unsuccessful candidate for the Connecticut Senate.[30] His influence in party circles was growing, and in May of 1867 John M. Morris, the clerk of the state Senate and member of the Republican State Committee, asked him to draft a law dividing the board of selectmen of the towns between the two major political parties.[31] In turn, Baldwin suggested to Morris that county courts be instituted. The latter approved of this idea, but believed it had no chance of becoming law.[32]

In 1867, probably because of his membership on the Common Council, Baldwin was appointed to a committee of three to revise the New Haven city charter. This was the first of many similar public commissions on which Baldwin served during the next fifty years. The new charter was adopted in 1869.[33]

In the spring of 1868 local political affairs engrossed Baldwin once more. Writing to his mother in late March, he said:

I am quite busy over political matters, of course, this week, and have had one long interruption since I began this letter, from a Registrar of Votes, who wanted information as to his rights and duties in cases of fraudulent attempts to vote by those not qualified. We have nominated William Fitch as our candidate for Mayor this year. I was offered a re-nomination for Senator, but declined in favor of a Hamden man.[34]

Baldwin ran again for the Common Council and was re-elected.[35]

In 1869 Baldwin desired the position of United States District Attorney for Connecticut and received assurance from United States Senator Buckingham that should the position come vacant, he would be glad to use his influence in Baldwin's behalf.[36] Some months later the incumbent District Attorney informed Baldwin that a move was under way to relieve him of the position when his term expired. If this should occur, he offered to assist Baldwin in securing the office.[37] Upon learning this Baldwin made a determined bid for the position. It soon became apparent, however, that both Connecticut Senators were committed to Calvin G. Child, who was the secretary to Senator Buckingham when the latter was Connecticut's governor during the Civil War.[38] Another stumbling block was Baldwin's kinship to United States Attorney General Hoar, who would probably scruple at appointing a relative to a position in his command.[39] Early in 1870, Child was appointed and thereupon proposed to make Baldwin his unofficial assistant for the New Haven area.[40] Baldwin accepted,[41] and this association endured for several years.

As Baldwin's acquaintance and influence in the Republican party grew his imprint was seen more and more frequently in legislative proposals. For a number of years he supported unsuccessfully bills to establish county courts. In 1871 he suggested to State Senator George A. Fay that the Superior Court be enlarged. Fay agreed that something needed to be done and asked Baldwin to draw up a set of resolutions on court reform, which he would submit to the lawyers in the legislature.[42] Shortly thereafter Fay introduced a bill Baldwin had drafted increasing the number of judges in the Superior Court.[43] Nothing, however, resulted from these efforts at this time.

In the spring of 1873 Simeon Baldwin, then only thirty-three, was proposed by prominent members of the New Haven Bar for judge of the United States District Court—a notable recognition of the esteem in which he was held by the older members of the profession. Having apparently sought his brother's advice, George wrote:

> I have talked over the matter with Dwight [Dwight Foster, their brother-in-law] and we are both of opinion that if the appointment were *sure* it would be worth your while to make the pecuniary sacrifice and accept it. . . .
>
> I should not wish to put myself in the position of a seeker for office and be disappointed at the end.

But if your friends choose to take this matter in hand and can secure the appointment without any solicitation on your part, I should accept it without hesitation.[44]

Shortly thereafter it appeared that Baldwin would not receive the position. His brother reminded him, however, that:

. . . whatever the result the honor is still yours of having been solicited to permit the use of your name as a candidate by the leaders of your own bar.

Your position in this matter is exactly what it should be. There are offices, recognised as rewards for party services, which may, perhaps, be personally solicited without loss of self respect. But a judge should be appointed upon consideration of personal merit only and the office should seek the man not the man the office. This is just your case. Your merits have been recognised by those who know them best, and if the President chooses to appoint some other man you have all the honor without the sacrifice.[45]

When the position finally went to a Hartford lawyer, Governor Marshall Jewell wrote to Baldwin expressing his regret that he had felt obliged to support the successful candidate.[46]

The need for constitutional reform in Connecticut had by 1873 become pressing. The main problem was one of reapportioning the electoral districts so that the growing industrial cities would be more adequately represented in the legislature. Under the Constitution of 1818 no town or city, however large, had more than two seats in the House of Representatives. In his characteristically forthright manner Simeon Baldwin set about to correct this situation. He was one of the active members of the New Haven County Constitutional Reform Association [47] and wrote two of a series of pamphlets on various aspects of the subject. When in the fall of 1873 the Association developed third party aspirations, its president [48] and vice-president [49] resigned. That the letters of resignation came to Baldwin indicates he was a prime mover in the group. Early the next year Baldwin offered the presidency of the organization to former Governor Cleveland, who, in declining, said he sincerely hoped that Baldwin would succeed in his praiseworthy efforts to give the people of Connecticut a better constitution.[50] Unfortunately the movement failed, and in spite of many later attempts at change, today the same archaic system of representation prevails.

III

Perhaps the activity of this period Simeon Baldwin enjoyed most was his association with the Yale Law School. In the late 1860s ex-Governor Henry Dutton was the sole remaining professor at the Law School and became concerned about its future. Yale's professional schools at the time were treated as stepchildren and generally lagged behind the development of the undergraduate college. Dutton sent petitions and appeals to President Woolsey, committees were appointed to investigate the "neglected and declining condition of the Law School," but little came of this activity.

Dutton was also busy in other directions. In March, 1868, he obtained the adoption of a resolution by the New Haven bar allowing graduates of the school to apply for admission to the bar without studying in a law office. In addition he assisted the growth of the library by securing passage of an act by the Connecticut General Assembly in July, 1868, providing that copies of the General Statutes and Session Laws be supplied each year to the Yale Law School. These were to be exchanged for the statutes of other states and kept in New Haven for the use of the Yale Law School and of the state officers and members of the General Assembly.[51] At that time the General Assembly met in Hartford and New Haven on alternate years.

In the spring of 1869 Dutton suddenly became ill and soon thereafter died. With no time for preparation Baldwin was called upon to substitute for him. He was then only twenty-nine years of age and had been a practicing lawyer for less than six years. "It was with fear and trembling," he later wrote that he undertook the task, for

> It was then not long since I had been one of the students there myself, and one or two of the men who recited to me were of almost my own age. However, it is always easier to ask questions than to answer them, and by hard work I believe I contrived to keep a little ahead of my class from day to day.[52]

Following Dutton's death in 1869 Yale considered discontinuing the Law School. The closer contacts Dutton had established between the school and the local bar, however, prevented this calamity. When rumors of the proposed action reached the New Haven lawyers, they exerted their influence to save the institution. This intervention was timely, and when a committee of the New Haven bar offered to carry on the law instruction, the college, after due consideration, accepted.

The four members of the bar who volunteered to assume responsibility for the school's operation were Simeon E. Baldwin, Louis H. Bristol, Johnson T. Platt, and William C. Robinson. Their youth—the oldest of them was thirty-five—was in marked contrast to the advanced ages of previous professors. Bristol soon dropped out as a sponsor of the new regime, and when the school reopened Baldwin, Platt and Robinson were in command. Robinson acted as secretary of the school for the year 1869–70 and as dean for the following three years. So successful was the new management in operating the school that the Corporation of Yale repeatedly requested that it continue to conduct the school. Some thirty years later Robinson wrote of these years:

To any but three sanquine youths, with an ardent love for their profession, the prospect would have been discouraging. There was no money, not even to pay for necessary advertising. . . . But with three students already on the ground, with the great reputation which the school had gained during its fourscore years, and with the magic name of Yale to conjure by, we could not despair. With what means we could command, the school was advertised. The curriculum was remodelled and enlarged. The number of daily exercises was doubled. Eminent lecturers were employed to give instruction upon special subjects. Students were held up to a rigid fulfillment of their scholastic duties. And when we counted up results in 1872 we found that we had gathered more than fifty scholars, of whom twenty-five had been completely trained and graduated and admitted to the bar.[53]

Besides their everyday teaching and administrative work the triumvirate devoted considerable time to long-range plans. They envisioned a building for the school some time in the future. For the present, however, arrangements were made for the school to use one floor of the new county courthouse which was about to be built. These quarters were commodious compared to the single room formerly used. Equally pressing was the need for a substantial improvement in the library facilities and for the endowment of chairs and lectureships so that full-time professors could be maintained. Four professorships and four lectureships were recommended, as follows:

Professor of Real Property, the History of the Common Law and Equity Jurisprudence
Professor of Commercial Law, Wills and Administration
Professor of Domestic Relations and of Public & Private Wrongs
Professor of Pleading and Evidence, including Admiralty Procedure

Lecturer on International Law
Lecturer on Constitutional Law
Lecturer on Civil Law
Lecturer on Medical Jurisprudence [54]

As practicing attorneys Baldwin, Platt, and Robinson realized that the school needed an administrator to give more time to its guidance and development. In looking for such a person Baldwin suggested the Honorable Francis Wayland,[55] and the latter joined the faculty in the fall of 1871. Wayland had practiced law in New Haven, had been judge of probate there and in 1869 served as lieutenant governor of Connecticut. His independent means enabled him to accept the token salary the Law School could pay him. With Wayland's appointment many of the school's plans moved ahead. In addition to his teaching duties he was made a member of the committee to solicit funds for the school, and in this work he was notably successful.

In July, 1872, Wayland, Baldwin, Platt, and Robinson were promoted to professorships. The faculty then chose Wayland as dean, a position he held for thirty years. As Robinson years later said, the school needed and found in Wayland "a leader who could multiply its resources, extend its fame, and be an acceptable medium of communication between it and the outside world." [56] In addition to the teaching of Wayland and the triumvirate a number of prominent men gave lecture series on various aspects of law during the early years of the reorganization.

Simeon Baldwin's teaching consisted of courses in constitutional law, contracts, and wills. In addition he served as a member of the controlling trio and as treasurer of the school for over four decades. For all of these services Baldwin and his colleagues received practically no compensation.[57]

By 1874, when the school celebrated its fiftieth anniversary, the faculty felt a sense of great achievement. In the words of the historian of the Law School, Frederick C. Hicks:

> The event which, in the minds of those interested in the welfare of the school, marked the conclusion of the preliminary stage of its rehabilitation, was the celebration of the semi-centennial of the school's connection with the University—fifty years having elapsed since the names of law students were first included in the college catalogue. It was the one outstanding ceremonial event in the whole history of the school up to that time, and it was the occasion for setting up ideals to which to aspire—ideals then thought to be only possible, not probable, of attainment, but which a half century later were largely to be realized.[58]

IV

Simeon Baldwin's career as a writer began in his college days when he contributed to the *University Quarterly*. Shortly after graduation, he commenced writing legal articles, and in time he turned to history, government and the affairs of the day.

His first article in the field of law was published in May, 1865, in the *American Law Register*. Entitled "The Authority of the 'Provisional Court' of Louisiana," [59] it was suggested by two accounts Baldwin had read in previous issues of this journal on the judicial arrangements made by the Union forces in conquered Louisiana. Baldwin maintained that the all-powerful provisional court authorized by President Lincoln was probably unconstitutional and that its decisions would not be binding when the regular state courts of Louisiana were again functioning.

Two years later a second article appeared in the same publication, and in this Baldwin questioned the constitutionality of the final exemption clause of the federal bankruptcy law of 1867.[60] The argument was clear and well-reasoned, and Baldwin concluded that this section of the act was unconstitutional.

In 1866 he assisted in editing the first of many volumes on the law. This was entitled *Connecticut Reports* [61] and was the official printed record of judicial decisions rendered by the Supreme Court of Errors. The task involved assembling and preparing the year's law cases for publication. A year later Baldwin began negotiations for the preparation of a more ambitious work, a digest of Connecticut court decisions from the state's earliest days to the present time. Such volumes were very useful to lawyers in referring to previous decisions. The most recent digest was out-of-date, and a new one was clearly needed. For a man of twenty-seven, with less than four years at the bar, to attempt such a work was decidedly venturesome. It also was indicative of the self-confidence and initiative with which Baldwin was liberally supplied. His editing the *Connecticut Reports* had given him some experience and perhaps led Little, Brown & Company to encourage him.[62] The reaction of Baldwin's friends to his assuming this task is perhaps an indication of how his contemporaries viewed it. One wrote:

> I wonder at the magnificent audacity with which you are "walking into" the law. The idea of compiling a Digest of Reports, after three or four years practice! Simmuns, how did you dare to undertake it? But I have no doubt you will do it—thoroughly and well—as you always have done everything; from a Pow-Wow Song, to a Salutatory. When does the first volume appear? [63]

Baldwin's political experience and friends served him well in 1868 when he was attempting to secure the passage of a law by which the state would purchase a certain number of copies of his digest. He drew up a petition to the effect that the utility of the sets of *Connecticut Reports* which were furnished by the state to the towns would be materially increased if each set were accompanied by a digest of reports brought down to the present time.[64] The desired effect was accomplished, and the legislature passed a law in 1868 purchasing 183 copies of Baldwin's digest.[65]

By the summer of 1870 the work was completed except for incorporating the decisions of the last session of the courts,[66] and in March, 1871, the volume at last appeared.[67] It included an alphabetical index of all the cases reported as having been decided by the Supreme Court of Errors and the Superior Court of Connecticut and the United States Courts for the district of Connecticut from earliest times to the present. The digest was arranged by subject, and under each heading were references to and explanatory remarks about the pertinent cases. Over four thousand cases were indexed, and the volume was nearly seven hundred pages in length.

The final appearance of the digest was a triumph of persistence on Baldwin's part and was received by the bar of Connecticut enthusiastically.[68] Since the title, following the custom of the day in similar legal works, was *Baldwin's Connecticut Digest*, and since the nature of the work was such as to make it almost a daily reference book for Connecticut lawyers, its author soon became a well-known name throughout the state. It would be difficult to overestimate the effect this work had upon Baldwin's legal career. It established him at once as superior to the average young lawyer.

The appearance of the digest at this time was probably partially responsible for Baldwin's appointment in 1871 to a committee to revise the educational statutes of Connecticut.[69] A year later he was placed upon a similar group to revise all the statutes of the state. The revision, known as the *General Statutes of 1875*, was an important task, and the honor of being so appointed was increased by Baldwin's youth, he then being only thirty-two. The state compensated the committee for its work, Baldwin receiving a check for two thousand dollars in 1874.[70] Two years later he received a like sum. At the same time the other commissioners received sums ranging from six hundred to fifteen hundred dollars. This was perhaps an indication of the major share of the load Baldwin carried.[71]

His final publications during this period were two pamphlets on the reform of Connecticut's constitution. Baldwin wrote these as part of his campaign to arouse sentiment for revision of the state's antiquated fundamental law. In the first of them, *Constitutional Reform. A Discussion of the Present Inequalities of Representation in the General Assembly*, one is impressed by the clarity of statement, the well-reasoned arguments, and the logical conclusions. Baldwin observed that the cardinal principle of American constitutional law is that the majority must rule. He pointed out that in Connecticut, because of grossly unequal electoral districts, the majority does not rule and called for a constitutional convention to remedy these inequalities. Various plans and their probable effects were outlined. Baldwin concluded with a plea for a constitutional convention to make moderate changes immediately rather than wait until a political revolution perhaps brings a completely remodelled political system.

The second pamphlet, *Considerations on Constitutional Reform in Connecticut* [72] also published in 1873, presented the problem for the special benefit of the state legislators. He traced the factors which had caused Connecticut's constitution to be outmoded and suggested the changes he believed necessary to provide an efficient, representative government. Whereas in the first pamphlet he had concentrated on changes in the Senate, in this he suggested more representation in the House for larger towns, a two-thirds vote to override the governor's veto, and tenure for judges during good behavior. A plurality vote should be enough to elect state officers, and better regulation of caucuses and nominating conventions should be instituted.

V

It would be difficult to imagine anyone taking part in more organizational activity during a lifetime than did Simeon Baldwin. This is the more remarkable because he was highly studious and introverted, and he appeared not to be the type to enjoy the sociability of conventions and committee meetings.

In 1864 Baldwin joined the Connecticut National Guard. During the summer of that year there is a reference to Simeon's depositing money for a substitute for the army. This was done before he left town, presumably for a vacation.[73] Whether he was actually drafted or was merely preparing for that contingency while away is not clear. He had apparently decided that his poor eyesight would not permit him to serve actively, and his enlistment in the National Guard may have been his way of rendering service to the limit of his capacity. He served in this organization four years, receiving his discharge in 1868. Each summer he spent a week in training camp.

In the fall of 1864 he entered more intimately into the affairs of the New Haven community by accepting membership in two venerable organizations, the Connecticut Academy of Arts and Sciences and the New Haven Grays. The former,[74] chartered in 1790, was a local society of the learned patterned on the American Philosophical Society and American Academy of Arts and Sciences. It held periodic meetings at which scientific and other scholarly papers were read and discussed. During the latter decades of the nineteenth century its *Transactions* contained valuable contributions to knowledge—the papers of Josiah Willard Gibbs, for example, one of America's foremost physicists.

The Grays was an honorary military company. Founded in 1815, its members wore elaborate uniforms and paraded on holidays and at such ceremonies of state as the inauguration of the governor. Both groups still exist today.

Two years later, in 1866, Baldwin extended his activity to yet other New Haven organizations. In the spring he was elected a director of the General Hospital Society of Connecticut, a post he retained all his life. In the fall he became a member of the Young Men's Christian Association, of which he later was president.

Throughout his life Baldwin took great interest in the United Church (Congregational), the most northerly of the three churches on the New Haven green, and never was he busier in church affairs than in this period. He taught a Sunday School class and was a member of the committee to supply the pulpit.[75]

In 1869 Baldwin was elected a trustee of his Alma Mater, Hopkins Grammar School, a position he held the rest of his life.[76] Late in the nineteenth and early in the twentieth centuries he helped the school weather some nearly fatal storms.

In the sixties Baldwin also served as one of the incorporators of the Trumbull Trust Association, which held the property of Psi Upsilon, Baldwin's junior society at Yale. A rival organization had erected a new chapter house, and it became apparent that Psi Upsilon would have to meet this competition if it was to retain its place on campus. As a consequence a drive for funds was made in the late sixties, in which Baldwin took an active part, and in 1870 a new building was erected.[77]

VI

The years from 1863 to 1874 brought to Simeon Baldwin's personal life the highest happiness and the most profound sorrow. During these eleven years Baldwin married, had three children, saw one of them die, watched his wife sink into lifelong invalidism, and lost his mother, his greatest source of strength.

The promising young lawyer met the beautiful girl he was to marry in 1865. Miss Susan Winchester was at the time giving foreign language lessons to young ladies of New Haven. Her home had originally been Boston, but shortly after her father's death in 1845, Susy's mother took her four small daughters to Italy. Susy lived for about a decade in Florence, returning to America in 1856, when she was sixteen. She lived with her grandparents in Boston for two years until her mother and stepfather came to the United States in 1858. The family resided in Vermont for a time, but in 1861 returned to Florence. Susy's younger sister and two half sisters went with their parents, while the three eldest girls remained in America. Susy completed her education in Boston and by 1865 had come to New Haven to tutor.[78]

In June Simeon and Susy announced their engagement [79] and made plans to be married in the fall. Mrs. Baldwin commented in July that she had been occupied getting to know Miss Susan Winchester and liked her very much.[80] Later in the month Baldwin spent a week in Boston becoming acquainted with his fiancée's relatives.[81]

The marriage took place on October 19, 1865. After their

wedding trip Susy and Simeon resided at the Baldwin home for the first years of their married life. Their first child, Florence, was born on January 10, 1868. A son, Roger Sherman, made his appearance the following year on January 17.

The spring of 1869 saw the Baldwins preparing to occupy a house of their own.[82] There were many delays but finally in May they moved.[83] The burden of two small babies, moving, and becoming the mistress of a household apparently were too much for Mrs. Baldwin, and she was nervously ill for some time thereafter. Baldwin's mother became concerned about her daughter-in-law's health and wrote her son regarding it.

> I have had Susy and her state of health on my mind very often since I have been here—having more time to think than when at home.
>
> And the result is that I think it of the utmost importance to her, that she should be kept away from home and all family care for some weeks to come—. Elizabeth wrote me that Susy had gone to Boston with her aunt—and that is all right—for a time—. But it seems to me, that the wisest and best thing you can do is—and the most hopeful for the future to supply sufficient funds for Miss Mears [Mrs. Susan Baldwin's aunt] to go with Susy to some sea side place near Boston—where they will meet some pleasant people, and all will be new and fresh—. There is always something to interest and amuse in the water and rocks and beach & bathing and the thoughts are taken from oneself. . . .
>
> I hope and believe that Miss Winchester [Mrs. Susan Baldwin's sister, Miss Charlotte Winchester] will remain with the children—and give Susy time to regain her usual health. If the right measures are taken now it will save you untold trouble in the future—. And you must not allow the added expense to influence you—for you know and I know that it cannot be counted against life . . . [and health].[84]

In 1871 the Baldwins decided to build a larger house on a plot of land adjoining the family homestead. This location was more central—just a block from the New Haven green.[85] When Simeon Baldwin occupied this house in April, 1872, it was the last move he was ever to make; he lived here for the remaining fifty-six years of his life.

On January 27, 1872, Helen Harriet, the last of the Baldwin children, was born. Following the birth of her third child Mrs.

Baldwin again suffered from nervous disorders and was obliged to go away for an extended rest. Slowly she was sinking into the invalidism which was soon to isolate her completely from her family. To have watched the center of his life ebbing away must have been a devastating experience to a man in his thirties who had known little but success and triumph. To have been powerless to stay the course of his wife's malady must have indeed been maddening to a man who had been able to force himself to great feats of accomplishment. The slowness of Mrs. Baldwin's decline, however, partially softened the stroke. Baldwin unbared something of the depth of anguish his wife's incapacity brought him in a letter to his sister, Henrietta, at the time of his mother's death.

> The telegrams that brought me home from Lake George, on Wednesday evening, were the heaviest blows I have ever known, save one, and that came so gradually that the suffering was never concentrated into any single moment, like this.[86]

In the summer of 1872 Florence, then four years old, became seriously ill. Her aunt took her away to the country where for a time she seemed to recuperate. Her improvement was only temporary, however, and on September 16, 1872, she died.

After this disaster Baldwin completely submerged himself in his work, which as time passed and sorrows multiplied became increasingly a refuge from the trials of life. Years later he said:

> There are those to whom hard work brings its daily blessing as a banisher of sorrow. Melancholy is a foe to be expelled at any cost, and pre-occupation is often the only thing that avails to shut it out.[87]

In the summer of 1874 one more tragedy befell Simeon Baldwin. His mother and trusted friend during the years of family illnesses died without warning. She had been a widow for eleven years and had devoted herself largely to the care of the families of her three married children. Active until the last she passed away on July 29, 1874.[88]

The Baldwin family received scores of letters of condolence, and perhaps one of the most sincere tributes to their mother came from Anthony Higgins, Simeon Baldwin's college classmate.

You do not need words from me to know how warm was my regard or how high my admiration for her. I always felt, & often said that she was the one woman it had been my fortune to know, who could truly be said to be "great"—but so she always impressed me, & her loss is one of the few we mourn as one which can not be replaced.[89]

To his sister Henrietta, who was in Europe when their mother died, Simeon Baldwin wrote with deep feeling:

To me, though, . . . [her death] brings a most crushing and deadening sense of desolation; to me, far more than to any of you, for she had continued to be the centre of my home and daily life.[90]

With the death of Mrs. Baldwin an era ended in the life of Simeon Baldwin. As his wife had become increasingly unwell, he had leaned more and more upon his mother. When she died, therefore, a great support was suddenly removed. By this time, also, to compound his sorrows, Baldwin's wife had become completely incapable of assuming the duties of her household and spent the remainder of her long life a helpless invalid.

PROFESSIONAL SUCCESS

During the two decades from 1874 to 1893 Simeon Baldwin developed from a promising young lawyer to a master in his profession. His interest in legal education continued, and he made significant contributions to its advancement. Perhaps his outstanding feat during these years was his successful attempt at founding a national association of lawyers. The taste he developed for research and writing in this period led him later to devote a considerable portion of his time to these pursuits. By 1893 he had achieved recognition in the form of the presidency of the American Bar Association and an honorary degree from Harvard University.

I

During the years between Simeon Baldwin's thirty-fourth and fifty-third birthdays he attained an eminence at the Connecticut bar equalled by few and surpassed by none.[1] While Baldwin's principal legal activity was that of a practicing lawyer in this period, he was concurrently teaching law at Yale and writing on legal subjects. At the peak of his reputation as an attorney, he resigned his extensive and lucrative practice in 1893 to become a Connecticut Supreme Court justice.

Baldwin's law cases during these years increased in number and importance. He was employed in the early seventies as Connecticut counsel for the New York and New England Railroad, a post he retained until 1893. In this position he was influential in obtaining a reduction in the rate of taxation for railroads in Connecticut, exerted pressure to secure favorable and deter unfavorable legislation, and conducted suits in the company's behalf. Since the New York and New England had emerged from the Boston, Hartford and Erie, a bankrupt railroad, the amount of litigation in which the new road was involved was substantial.

Baldwin was highly regarded by his employers and in 1881, when his brother, George, resigned the position, was offered the general counselship of the railroad.[2] Baldwin was sufficiently interested in this opportunity to be willing to curtail his other work in order to accept it. He wanted a ten-year contract at $10,000 a year and planned to spend three or four days a week in Boston, the railroad's headquarters. He refused, however, to be uprooted from New Haven entirely.[3] These terms were apparently not satisfactory to the railroad, for he did not receive the appointment.

Baldwin did become general counsel and a director of the Boston and New York Air Line Railroad.[4] This enterprise was attempting to build an inland route competing with the shore-line road between New York and Boston. In this undertaking it encountered the opposition of the New York, New Haven and Hartford Railroad, operators of the shore-line, and was eventually absorbed by the latter. Baldwin also served as general counsel for the Housatonic Railroad, a small line which operated in Western Connecticut.

Baldwin's railroad law work involved him in the affairs of the New England Transfer Company, which operated a boat carrying railroad cars between New York City and New Jersey. This company was established in the seventies by the New York and New England Railroad, and Baldwin was named its secretary. An intimate picture of the vicissitudes of a new business is contained in the correspondence between Baldwin and Charles P. Clark, the Transfer Company's head. Seasonal traffic fluctuations affected its operation, as the amounts of freight entering and leaving New England rose and fell. In 1876, by means of the transfer boat, through passenger service from Boston to Washington was established.[5] Later in the year a controversy developed over the boat's franchise. New York City claimed it was a ferry, while the company maintained it was a transfer boat.[6] Finally in the summer of 1879 the New York, New Haven and Hartford, the dominant railroad of southern New England, forced the weaker New York and New England to share control of the New England Transfer Company.

In 1883 Baldwin worked to obtain a reduction of state taxes on railroads. To this end he prepared a pamphlet entitled *Railroad Taxation. Facts Submitted to the Joint Standing Committee on Finance in Support of the Bill for an Act to Reduce the Rate of Railroad Taxation.*[7] In this Baldwin stated clearly and simply the reasons why railroads deserved lower taxes: less than one-half the capital invested in Connecticut railroads was earning dividends; the Connecticut rates were high in comparison with neighboring states; every other state tax which had been raised during the Civil War had subsequently been lowered except that on railroads. Baldwin's arguments may have helped to convince the legislature, for it enacted the desired reduction.[8]

Baldwin's railroad activities did not constitute all of his legal work. In addition, he had many individual clients. During this period he argued at least three cases before the Supreme Court of the United States: one in 1875,[9] another in 1884,[10] and a third a year later.[11] In 1875 Baldwin also represented the State of Connecticut in a notable insurance suit, which he lost. There was apparently some collusion between the court and the insurance interests, an example of the loose political and business morals pervading much of the nation in the second half of the nineteenth century. That there was connivance between the judges and the insurance companies is revealed by a letter to Baldwin from the Connecticut Insurance Commissioner.

> Since the close of the trial I have been told so many things concerning the relations of the judges with the insurance ring that I have ceased to wonder at their decision. The disgrace of it falls not upon them but upon the state.[12]

Another phase of Baldwin's law work was his role in revising the laws and legal system of Connecticut. In the seventies, as we have seen, he served on the commission to codify and revise the statutes of the state. Soon after the appearance of these a colleague wrote to him:

> Now that we are possessed of a thoroughly revised edition of the General Statutes of this State, I trust you will excuse me for taking the liberty to suggest that you use your efforts to induce the judges to revise the Rules of Practice in the Courts.[13]

Baldwin agreed that the rules of practice needed revision.

> No rules, however, [he declared] are worth much unless they are fearlessly administered, and I never expect to see that done in this State, until Judges are appointed for life, or until seventy.
>
> So long as their re-election depends on the influence of counsel practicing before them, so long will they be easy in granting postponements, admitting irrelevant evidence, etc., etc.[14]

A more fundamental change in Connecticut legal procedure was advocated in 1877, which, when finally accomplished, also brought a new set of rules of practice with it. This was the movement to simplify legal procedure by substituting a single form of action for the several different forms of judicial proceedings then in use in the state. The most radical change proposed was the abolition of the distinction between suits at law and suits at equity. Baldwin strongly advocated this change in a report to the State Bar Association of Connecticut.[15] New York many years before had begun the movement to simplify legal procedure, and sixteen states and six territories had adopted it by 1877.

These changes were discussed within the legal profession and moved an important step towards fulfillment when Governor R. D. Hubbard asked Baldwin whether a committee of prominent lawyers could be selected to report without charge to the state a plan for the simplification of Connecticut's legal procedure.[16] Baldwin replied that such a committee could be assembled to draft a bill abolishing the distinction between legal and equitable actions and making the necessary provisions as to the new forms of pleading. A more detailed measure, however, would be the work of a year and would not be well done unless paid for.[17]

In the spring of 1878 the General Assembly passed a resolution providing for such a committee, and Baldwin was appointed a member by the Governor.[18] The committee worked throughout the summer and fall and by December had drawn up the necessary legislation. This recommended the abolition of the various forms of civil action and permitted the suitor to enter a simple statement of complaint. It also recommended allowing the concurrent exercise of law and equity jurisdiction by one court and in one course of proceedings. The commissioners also prepared a set of forms adapted to practice under the proposed bill and planned to present them to the judges for approval if the bill became law.[19]

The consensus of opinion among the lawyers was favorable to the proposed change.[20] In February Baldwin appeared before the legislative committees in the bill's behalf,[21] and soon thereafter it became law. The commission thereupon presented its set of rules and forms of procedure under the new Practice Act to the judges of the Superior Court. After several drafts the judges accepted them in the summer of 1879.

In addition to the Practice Act and the forms and rules to implement it, the Chief Justice of the Supreme Court of Errors requested the commission to revise the "General Rules of Practice for the Superior and Supreme Courts" so that they would be accommodated to the new Practice Act. This task completed the revamping of the entire system of judicial procedure of Connecticut, and in this undertaking Simeon Baldwin played a major role. When he complained to another committeeman that he was having headaches, the latter was not surprised.

> Such an astounding & continuous power of work & that of the most tedious description of detail and minutiae made you seem to me like a calculating machine. You took altogether too much of the whole burden & hard work of the Rules & forms everything in fact of the Rules & with all your other work I don't wonder at the "code headache." [22]

The Practice Act, the code of procedure and the new General Rules of Practice for the Superior and Supreme Courts all went into effect on January 1, 1880. In February Baldwin received a check from the State of Connecticut for his services in the amount of $68![23]

The aspect of Simeon Baldwin's legal career most likely to bring him enduring fame was his part in founding the great guild of the legal profession, the American Bar Association. City, county, and state bar associations had long existed in the United States. Baldwin saw the need, however, for a national association of lawyers to work for uniform laws in the various states, to raise and make more equal the standards for admission to the bar, and to promote in general the interests of the profession.

The first indication that Baldwin was thinking of such an association appeared in the fall of 1877 when he asked the opinion of his college classmate, Anthony Higgins, a practicing attorney in Wilmington, Delaware, as to the need for a national association. Higgins replied that such an organization would serve a most useful purpose, especially with regard to law reform.[24]

Soon thereafter Baldwin proceeded with great dexterity to establish the organization. He placed his ideas before the Connecticut Bar Association, and in February, 1878, was appointed with Governor Hubbard and William Hamersley, a prominent Hartford attorney, to correspond with other state bar associations regarding the formation of a national society.[25] The results of their inquiries were sufficiently encouraging for them to issue on June 1 a printed letter signed by fourteen prominent lawyers from various parts of the country. This called for an informal meeting at Saratoga, New York, in August, 1878, to discuss the feasibility of establishing an American bar association. This letter of invitation was sent to a selected group of lawyers in each state, and the recipients were requested to send their views to Simeon E. Baldwin.

The Saratoga meeting was held, and the American Bar Association was successfully organized. As Professor James Grafton Rogers said many years later of Baldwin's relations with the new organization:

> The Bar Association was his individual creation. He enlisted the fourteen leaders who signed the call for its initial session, selected the names to whom the call was sent, mailed it and received the replies. He drafted the Constitution, guided the first steps, selected the first officers, saw to its routine on the Executive Committee, and until his presidency thirteen years later, and even afterwards, was the chief source of its projects. Its printed records are full of reports and papers from his busy hands. America owes a vast amount of designing to a grave little man from New Haven consumed with a passion for work.[26]

All did not go well with the Association in its early years. There was indifference in some quarters and open hostility in others. An abortive effort was made to establish a rival national association in 1888.[27]

Some of the most significant contributions of the American Bar Association in its early years were made by the Committee on Jurisprudence and Law Reform, of which Baldwin was chairman until 1887.[28] Under his leadership the Committee studied and made reports on a number of subjects. Among them were the treatment of professional criminals (1885), arbitration in federal courts (1888), consular marriages (1888), divorce and marriage (1888), and forms of verdicts in criminal proceedings (1890).[29] Usually the subjects were referred to the Committee by the Association, discussed and studied there, and reported to the next annual meeting. Recommendations were considered by the full conference, and if favorable action was taken, frequently representatives of the Association were requested to secure the introduction of bills in the state legislatures to accomplish the desired ends.

Another branch of the Association's work in which Baldwin was a prime mover was the section on Legal Education. This was organized under the temporary chairmanship of Simeon Baldwin at Milwaukee in August, 1893, and Henry Wade Rogers, later Dean of the Yale Law School, became its first permanent chairman.[30]

Baldwin's labors in behalf of the legal guild as well as his by this time wide reputation as a lawyer, legal educator, and scholar were recognized in 1890 by his election to the presidency of the American Bar Association.[31] This was his first major national honor, and it was followed the next June by an LL.D. from Harvard University.[32]

At the age of fifty-one Simeon Baldwin had arrived in the legal profession. He was respected among lawyers at home and throughout the land. He was active politically, and the law being an important gateway to political preferment in America, he should have been able soon to occupy a governmental position of high rank. The course Baldwin was to pursue in the next few years would probably determine his future irrevocably.

II

During the years from 1874 to 1893 Simeon Baldwin continued to play an active role in political affairs. Although he had held no important public offices, he wielded increasing weight in Connecticut politics. In addition, he abandoned his heritage by leaving the Republican fold. By the end of the period he was one of the leaders of the Democratic party in his state.

In September, 1875, Simeon Baldwin accepted the nomination for alderman of New Haven's first ward.[33] He was elected to this office on October 4, 1875,[34] and served two years.

Baldwin participated in backstage maneuvers on numerous occasions aimed at favoring the candidacy of one man or opposing another. In the spring of 1880, for example, he corresponded with the Honorable George F. Edmunds, United States Senator from Vermont, regarding the latter's availability for the presidential nomination. Baldwin informed Edmunds that many Republicans in Connecticut would like to see him the party's standard bearer.[35] This move was aimed against such a regular and unsavory politician as James G. Blaine, who was a prominent contender. Edmunds, however, declared himself unavailable.[36]

During the early eighties Baldwin participated in the movement for the establishment of a civil service system in the federal government. Interest in such a program was shared by many reform-minded people throughout the country. In 1881 resolutions drawn up by Baldwin calling for action on civil service reform were introduced in the Connecticut Senate. Similar resolutions were presented to the House of Representatives, and Baldwin was asked to testify at committee hearings.[37] During the year he corresponded throughout the state in behalf of this movement. In August he drafted a petition calling for the organization of a Civil Service Reform Association in Connecticut, and in the fall the organization held its first meetings.[38]

Another political reform program which claimed Baldwin's attention during this decade was revision of Connecticut's constitution. This movement had not completely lapsed since Baldwin's first efforts in 1873 to arouse public interest in it. At that time he advocated modifying the basis of representation of senators from districts to at large but suggested no change in the composition of the House of Representatives.

In 1881, however, in addition to the change in the senatorial apportionment, Baldwin proposed an amendment giving cities of 10,000 or more three representatives (instead of one or two) and one extra for each added 5,000 population.[39]

By 1884 Baldwin was calling for a constitutional convention. His program had broadened considerably more by this time, and he listed five main problems for the convention to consider: (1) a plurality rather than a majority should elect state officers; (2) population should be the basis of representation in the House of Representatives; (3) there should be a provision against special legislation; (4) means should be found to abolish lobbying; (5) a system of nominating candidates should be adopted which would do away with caucus tyranny.[40]

The only concrete result of this agitation was the approval in 1884 of a constitutional amendment giving all towns of 5,000 and more inhabitants two representatives in the lower house of the General Assembly. This satisfied the more moderate advocates of reform, and the movement temporarily lapsed.[41]

Four years later Baldwin once more attempted to revive the fight for constitutional revision by urging the governor-elect late in 1888 to press the matter in his message to the General Assembly.[42] The governor replied that he doubted that the people were prepared for extension of representation at that time.[43]

By early 1889 Baldwin's views on this subject had altered considerably. Regarding the apportionment of senate seats, he advocated continuing the twenty-four districts and adding fifteen senators at large. No one would vote for more than eight of the latter. This plan would not upset the balance of power between the parties, but it would attract better men and give all localities an equal chance to present them. In the House he proposed giving all towns of 20,000 or over three representatives with two more for every additional 20,000. These would be elected like the senators at large, no one voting for more than a bare majority.[44] Baldwin put his ideas into the form of a bill and had a member of the legislature introduce it.[45] This, however, met the fate of all his earlier efforts.

In 1884 Simeon Baldwin made the most significant political decision of his life. For over twenty years he had worked faithfully in the Republican party and, although holding no important public office, had risen to a place of some influence in state party circles. He was nearing a position where he could soon have expected an important post. When, in 1884, James G. Blaine was nominated for president by his party, however, many Republicans refused to support him because of the corruption associated with his name. These revolters were called Mugwumps, and Baldwin was their leader in Connecticut.

In October, as president of the Connecticut Independent Republicans, Baldwin drew up and circulated copies of a petition entitled "To Republican Voters of Connecticut." The signers of this document pledged the following key sentence: "We all unite in calling upon our fellow republicans in this state to give no vote for Mr. Blaine."

Baldwin's bold step produced varied reactions. Former president Woolsey of Yale wrote him that either Senator John Sherman or Senator George F. Edmunds had been his choice for the nomination rather than Blaine.

> But it was easy to decide to accept the republican party with its candidate against so worthless a party on the whole as a democratic one. And then as one thing began to appear after another, moral stains, apparent subserviency to very base men, in the democratic candidate, as well as want of ability I must confess I should have been ashamed, if I had decided to vote for Mr. Cleveland, even if he had been the candidate of the republicans. The men whom he has trusted and helped in their iniquity seem to have no character at all.
>
> As for Mr. Blaine I rely especially on Mr. Hoar's defence of him, and on the good opinion of Messrs. Hoar Edmunds & Hawley. . . .
>
> The independents who have broken away from the party have lost part of my respect. I cannot but feel that the imposing array of men in N. York and Boston, who have risen up within the party, has had too

much personal weight. If they had staid in the party, whatever danger now befalls it from a low class of men inclined to enter it would have been counteracted.[46]

In sharp contrast to Woolsey's position was that of Baldwin's college friend, Daniel H. Chamberlain, former governor of South Carolina:

I have read with satisfaction . . . the address of the Independent Republicans of Connecticut. I am truly delighted to see your name formost [*sic*] in the work with those of so many others whom I know. Dr. Woolsey's and Dr. Porter's [president of Yale] positions seem altogether inexplicable to me. If they have not read the evidence, their position is not creditable. If they have read it, it is less so. It seems necessary to think them, as well as Mr. Harrison, capable of conduct and views of duty which I abhor and which I never imagined such men could be guilty of. My loyalty to Yale is deeply offended by such conduct, and my happiness in your honorable stand is proportionably increased.[47]

On October 13, 1884, the manifesto of the Independent Republicans was published in the New Haven *Evening Register*. This summarized the position taken by the anti-Blaine faction and urged all Republicans to vote for Cleveland.

Baldwin was congratulated by many for his work in the 1884 election. One letter from a prominent Vermont lawyer and Democrat, Judge Edward J. Phelps, indicated something of the role Baldwin played in this movement:

I have been minded before to write and congratulate you on the splendid fight and gratifying success you made in Connecticut, one which I attribute largely to your personal exertions. Its effects will be most salutary. You have done a great work for the Republican Party if they would be content to take the benefit and credit of what their best men have done. But I hope they will read you all out [of the party]—since you never ought to have been in.[48]

In September, 1885, the feud between the regular and the Independent Republicans was still smoldering in Connecticut. To a letter from Lynde Harrison, Republican State Chairman, asking whether the Independent Republicans would now return to the fold and work for Republican victory in the local elections of that year, Baldwin replied that his organization would withhold its decision until the candidates and platform of the Republicans had been made public.[49]

Although in 1886 a Republican was governor, and Simeon Baldwin was still an Independent, he was nevertheless appointed to a special commission to consider and report to the General Assembly a comprehensive plan for providing revenue for the state.[50] This commission studied the system of taxation in Connecticut and made recommendations in 1887 for its overhaul. The committee's report was not well received, and many amendments were inserted before it was accepted by the legislature.

By 1888 Baldwin had decided to cast his lot with the Democratic party. In the summer of that year he was elected an honorary member of the Mitchell Democratic Association of New Haven.[51] His letter of acceptance contained a clear statement of Baldwin's political principles at that time:

> I accept the election with pleasure. Four years ago, I cast my first vote for a Democratic administration, and I have never regretted it. When I voted then for President Cleveland it was as an Independent Republican. I shall vote for him this fall, as a Democrat, proud to belong to the great party which, under his lead, has proved itself true to its best traditions, and dared to reassert those strict and simple rules of government under which Jefferson and Madison first brought it into power. The questions of today are again those out of the discussion of which the Democratic party arose, to express the will of the American people. Then as now there were no party differences as to slavery, as to secession, as to the supremacy of the national government within its sphere. Then, as now, there were differences as to how far that sphere extended, as to what true republicanism meant, as to what revenue should be collected and how it should be spent.
>
> On these main questions, I have found myself now for years in sympathy with the Democratic party. It has promoted economy in the public service; it has sought to reduce our revenue to the measure of our wants, not to create wants to the measure of our revenue; it has returned to the foreign policy of Washington; it has respected the rights of the states, and solidified the American people.[52]

Two years later Baldwin's organizing talents were thrown behind the establishment of a state Democratic club. In January of 1890 he circulated a petition seeking support for such a venture. The group was formed in that year, and Baldwin was elected its first president.

That same year saw one of the most bitterly contested elections in Connecticut's political history. The Democratic candidate for governor received a questionable majority, although he had secured a 3,000 vote plurality. Under the Connecticut constitution, when no candidate for a state office received a majority of the votes cast, the election was determined by the General Assembly, both houses sitting together. Although the Senate was controlled by the Democratic party and the House by the Republicans, the number of Republican legislators in the two bodies was greater than the total of the Democrats. Knowing that the Republicans would outvote them if the election were thrown to the legislature, the Democrats were anxious to substantiate their candidate's claim to a positive majority. The Republican House of Representatives, on the other hand, refused to declare the Democratic candidate elected, contending that alleged voting irregularities might well reduce his majority to a plurality.

The chief question at issue came to be whether the legislature should accept the electoral returns as certified to it by the Secretary of State, or whether it could investigate the alleged fraudulent voting. The Democrats favored the former policy and the Republicans the latter.

A variety of attempts was made to break the deadlock. Baldwin suggested allowing the Supreme Court and three Superior Court judges sitting together to decide the matter.[53] In March, 1891, he proposed another plan which, he believed, would resolve the gubernatorial crisis and seat the Democratic candidate.[54] William Hamersley, a Hartford Democratic leader, thought that Baldwin's "ingenious bill," as he termed it, would result in seating the Republican contender.[55] As with all previous proposals the "ingenious" one failed to provide the hoped-for solution.

The *New Englander and Yale Review* for April, 1891, published able articles by Lynde Harrison [56] and Simeon Baldwin presenting the respective views of the Republican and Democratic parties. Baldwin argued from historical precedent that the legislature could not under the constitution go behind the electoral returns and determine whether votes should or should not be admitted.[57]

In spite of the variety of plans advocated for its solution, the gubernatorial contest remained deadlocked. As a result the incumbent governor, Morgan G. Bulkeley, who had been elected in 1888, served for another two years. During this period the legislature appropriated no money for the operation of the state. Governor Bulkeley quite opportunely was also the president of the Aetna Insurance Company, which advanced the necessary funds! After the election of 1892, the legislature reimbursed the Aetna.

The gubernatorial deadlock led Baldwin to hope that constitutional revision might finally be forced, for one of his proposed changes would permit a plurality instead of a majority to elect state officers. The impasse in 1890 had certainly shown the need for this alteration. Baldwin hoped that at the same time his primary aim—revision of the system of apportionment—might also be realized. In the past the House of Representatives had been controlled by a minority of the voting population since each small rural town frequently had as many representatives as the largest cities. This state of affairs worked to the disadvantage of the Democratic party, whose strength was concentrated in the more populous areas. Hitherto, regardless of how great a popular majority the Democrats secured, the Republicans still were able to control the lower house.

In order to take advantage of this opportune situation, Baldwin influenced the State Democratic Club to pass resolutions favoring a constitutional convention. As a practical politician he would now be satisfied with a few changes. If a plurality rather than a majority would be sufficient to elect the state ticket and if a few more representatives from the cities were added in the House, the Democratic party might soon control both houses of the legislature as well as the executive branch.

To publicize his views Baldwin wrote a tract which was distributed through the Democratic town committees. This called for a constitutional convention to provide for plurality elections, rework the thirty-four amendments into the constitution, and abolish special legislation where general laws would serve. In order to allay the suspicions of the small towns Baldwin expressly stated that their power in the legislature would not be taken away.[58]

In the fall of 1891 Baldwin again urged the Democratic party to take a forthright stand on the question of revising the constitution.[59] Largely because of his persistence, the Democratic party platform of 1892 included a plank calling for constitutional revision.[60] The party was victorious in Connecticut, and a few days later Baldwin was actively working towards constitutional reform. Although his party controlled the Senate, the votes of ten Republicans in the House were needed to pass a bill submitting to the people the question of calling a constitutional convention. Baldwin wrote to several Republicans whom he hoped to persuade to join the Democrats in pressing the measure.[61]

Before he had time to carry this movement to completion,[62] however, Baldwin made a decision which removed him from political activities for nearly twenty years. Governor-elect Morris offered him a place on the Connecticut Supreme Court of Errors, and after careful consideration Baldwin decided to accept it. The position had a hereditary attraction for him, because his grandfather had held it and it had been offered to his father.[63]

On January 13 the appointment was announced, and the nomination sent to the legislature for confirmation. Letters of congratulations flooded in upon Baldwin, and in many of them the hope was expressed that this position would prove to be a steppingstone to something higher. Several mentioned the Supreme Court in Washington as Baldwin's natural resting place, and a few the Cabinet. His sister, Henrietta, wrote that the announcement brought back memories of the old Judge Simeon Baldwin, their grandfather.

. . . and as I laid down the paper—visions of the old office with the garden beyond—and the old farmers coming in & out to consult "the Judge"—so sure all was wisdom which fell from his lips—drowned for a few moments everything else in my mind.[64]

Baldwin wrote to his sister, Lizzie:

My nomination was to be kept a secret till publicly announced, but it was offered me last November, and accepted then. As you conjectured, I hesitated most on account of its preventing me from starting Roger as my partner in business. He could, however, have kept very little of the business I had. It is not of the kind that people give to a young man, if they can help it, nor of a kind to which he could do justice. Ten years hence, it might have been different, but ten years hence neither of us may be here, nor would there be likely to be just a similar opportunity, which now makes me from the outset not the fifth but the *fourth in seniority on the bench*.[65]

Baldwin's confirmation by the General Assembly was not secured without some difficulty. Being Republican the House was reluctant to approve a candidate who was a member of the opposing party. A faction of the Democrats, on the other hand, opposed Baldwin because they thought he had been a party member too short a time to warrant such a high appointment. Many members of both parties were dismayed when the House on January 25 refused to confirm Baldwin's nomination.[66]

One of Baldwin's colleagues, Professor William C. Robinson of Yale Law School, was pleased that the nomination was not confirmed.

I congratulate you on your so-called "defeat." The idea that you should bury yourself in the Connecticut bench has never been even tolerable to me, and if the Providence which has interfered to rescue you, is not altogether a pleasant one, I believe you will hereafter be grateful for the interposition. So far as you are willing to relinquish practice, the Law School and the law publisher has [*sic*] need of you, and if you wish to enter public life there are positions which would better crown your days than the one which it has now surprised all your friends that you would be willing to accept.[67]

Baldwin's friends and admirers rallied to his support, however, and enough Republicans refused to vote with their party to bring about the confirmation on February 2.[68]

Baldwin's method of handling this affair provides an interesting contrast to the position his father would have taken fifty years before. The elder Baldwin believed that the office should seek the man, and as a candidate he would never raise a hand to secure any position for himself. When his son found he was in danger of losing the judgeship, on the other hand, he rallied his friends and openly solicited their assistance. He went as far as to place $150 at the disposal of his sponsors to pay for travel about the state to round up support for him. Many of them refused any payment, and most of the money was returned to him. Such a step was in no sense dishonorable, but it illustrates the difference between the political idealism of Roger Sherman Baldwin in the 1840s and the political realism of his son in the 1890s.[69]

With his confirmation a new life lay before Baldwin. Many past activities, including politics, law practice, and business connections were left behind; ahead was the quieter life of judge, scholar, and professor.

III

During the period under review Simeon Baldwin labored diligently for the Yale Law School. These years were characterized by a steady growth in the school's facilities, faculty, curriculum, and student body.

The efforts of Dean Wayland to increase the school's assets were first successful in the library. When the triumvirate assumed control in 1869, the library had about 2,000 volumes and no funds with which to keep collections up to date. By 1874 $20,000 had been raised, and with this sum the collection was increased to over 7,000 volumes. Another gift of $10,000 provided the library with an income from which to keep its holdings current.[70]

Adequate housing for the school had already been acquired in the new county courthouse. Rent, heat, and light were furnished at public expense, so that tuition could now be used more extensively towards creating the ideal law school former

President Woolsey had envisioned in his *Historical Discourse* at the school's fiftieth anniversary in 1874.

Let the school, then, be regarded no longer as simply the place for training men to plead causes, to give advice to clients, to defend criminals; but let it be regarded as the place of instruction in all sound learning relating to the foundations of justice, the history of law, the doctrine of government, to all those branches of knowledge which the most finished statesman and legislator ought to know. First of all I would have the training essential to the lawyer by profession as complete and thorough as possible. Let that be still the main thing, and let the examinations together with appropriate theses be a proof that every graduate has fairly earned his degree. But with this let there be ample opportunity for those who wish the aid of teachers in studying the constitution and political history of our country to pursue their studies in a special course by the side of or after the preparation for the bar. Let the law of nations, the doctrine of finance and taxation, the general doctrine of rights and the State, the relation of politics and morals, be within the reach of such as wish to prepare themselves for public life, and of those young men of wealth, of whom there is an increasing number, who wish to cultivate themselves and take their appropriate place of influence in society. Let there be the amplest opportunity for the study of English institutions, even far back into the middle ages, for that of Roman history and Roman law, for that of comparative legislation, and even for less immediately practical subjects, such as feudal and canon law. Let the plan of the library be expanded, so that it shall furnish the best books on all branches and topics connected with law, legislation and government. Can it be doubted that such an institution, of which I have sketched a faint outline, would be of vast service; that its influence would reach into the halls of Congress, into the departments of government, that it might become a fountain of light through the whole land.[71]

The conviction that the Law School should prepare men for public service and intellectual leadership through a broad legal education had been in the air for some time. President Porter of Yale in his inaugural address in 1871 had pointed out the advantages to the Law School of being closely associated with scholars in such fields as ethics, politics, and sociology. He hoped that the school might avail itself of the wisdom and learning of the professors who taught these subjects in Yale College.[72]

One way in which the Law School tried to realize the hopes of former President Woolsey and of President Porter was by utilizing special lecturers who devoted a few hours a week to the school. During the first years under the triumvirate almost all of the lecturers were from the Yale faculty.[73]

It was these supplementary lectures which set the Yale Law School apart from its sister institutions during this period. Former President Woolsey was able to say in the *Historical Discourse* in 1874 that:

> . . . nowhere in the United States are these subsidiary branches of knowledge . . . , these handmaids to a finished legal education, brought more effectively into the service of legal studies and made more useful than in the Yale Law School. . . . By carrying out this plan, it is made apparent how much more comprehensive and finished a legal education ought to be, when it is pursued as a department of a university, than when it stands alone.[74]

Shortly after the semicentennial exercises in 1874, the Law School embarked upon a new departure which went still further towards realizing the broad type of legal preparation envisioned by Woolsey. It introduced a program of graduate work in law and offered the degrees of Master of Laws and Doctor of Civil Law for one and two years, respectively, of advanced study. In this venture Yale was a pioneer. As Simeon Baldwin wrote many years later, Yale was the first university of any English-speaking country to offer a four-year course leading to the D.C.L. It was the first university in the United States to offer any degree in law except the baccalaureate.[75]

The chief responsibility for the introduction of graduate work in law rests with Simeon E. Baldwin. His colleague, Professor William C. Robinson, went even further in assessing Baldwin's contribution to legal education:

> He who controlled its [Yale Law School's] academic progress, and directed its development, was Professor Baldwin,—the man who has done more to elevate the general standard of legal education than any other person in this country, and who was the projector and progenitor of the entire system of graduate law instruction in the United States.[76]

Although the intellectual climate was ripe at Yale for such a development, the impetus which set the program in motion was the desire of a few students for it. Their request fell upon Professor Baldwin's eager ears, and he bent his efforts toward setting up a full-fledged graduate program.

In June, 1875, the four members of the law faculty presented a letter to the Yale Corporation requesting that the Master's and Doctor's degrees be awarded. A year of consideration was given to the proposal, and in May, 1876, the Corporation formally approved it. The catalogue for that year announced that the plan would go into full effect in September, 1876. It boasted that greater advantages were then offered at Yale for the study of public law, Roman law, comparative jurisprudence, style in oratory and composition, constitutional history, and political science than had ever been offered before at an American law school.[77] During the first year of the program there were ten candidates for the M.L. degree.

In September, 1877, Baldwin explained the Yale plan for graduate study in law to the American Social Science Association at its annual meeting in Saratoga, New York. The object of the advanced courses was to make available facilities for the study of law beyond the minimums required in the conventional one- or two-year courses. Such a program was not, however, for the average lawyer.

> Law schools are not for the many, but for the few; not so much for those who are content to follow the law merely as a money-getting trade, as for those who seek it as a liberal and liberalizing profession. To such, the mastery of the science, to which they have devoted their lives, is a sufficient object, of itself. The possession of knowledge is not necessarily less precious, less felt to be a power within one, because in the drudgery of daily toil it gives no help. It lifts the man above the plane of his drudgery, and makes him respect himself.[78]

Another of Baldwin's contributions to legal education during this period was the lengthening of the baccalaureate course of study at Yale from two to three years. In the above-mentioned address before the American Social Science Association in 1877 Baldwin discussed the need for more time for regular law courses and the difficulty of arranging it.[79] The plan for graduate study was in one sense a means of lengthening the professional course for those who could afford it.[80]

In 1885 Baldwin advocated the three-year course for the LL.B. in the *Columbia Jurist*. He pointed out that the American Bar Association had recommended this in 1881. A large part of a student's first year was spent in becoming acquainted with the language of the law. Then came a growing familiarity with legal principles and finally some facility in their application to particular cases.

> I regard the second year of a legal education as much more fruitful than the first, and the third as worth more still than the second. The third year finds the student prepared to conquer. Difficulties which may before have darkened his way, now vanish at his touch. He has the conditions of intelligent acquisition.[81]

Three years later Baldwin formally presented his plan to the Governing Board of the Law School, and a committee was appointed to investigate. The proposals were tabled by the Governing Board that year and the next and were not considered again until 1894. The reluctance of the Board to act was understandable since very few law schools at that time required three years for an LL.B.[82]

Finally in 1894 the Governing Board recommended and the Yale Corporation approved a plan by which the baccalaureate law course would be three years in length. At the discretion of the faculty, however, holders of an A.B. (which was not required for admission to law schools at that time) and others who gave evidence of satisfactory ability could complete the course in two years. This rule became effective in the fall of 1896. In 1902 the exception was removed and the three-year course fully established.[83]

During the half century Simeon Baldwin was a member of the Law School faculty the variety of courses he offered was very wide. From 1874 to 1893 these included contracts, nature and history of American law, wills, corporations, American constitutional law, Roman law, practice in United States courts, railroad law, American constitutional history, comparative jurisprudence, conflict of laws, Code Napoleon, mercantile law, modern European legislation, and political history. Some of these courses he taught all through the period and a few were given only once or twice.[84]

One other service of Simeon Baldwin to the Law School during this period should be mentioned. This was the compilation of an alumni record which was published in the school announcements for 1881–1882, 1884–1885, and 1887–1888. Baldwin served the school in many ways, and not the least of them was in personally undertaking tasks such as this, which he thought might help the school and which otherwise would not have been done.

Never a man to seek popularity Baldwin was genuinely respected by his students. Many letters and personal testimonies from those who attended his classes affirm their high regard for him. One such letter in 1883 from a former student thanked him for his excellent instruction and for the patient spirit he manifested towards his students.[85] Some years later another student wrote to commend Baldwin's teaching methods. He liked the presentation of concrete cases on which the students could apply general rules or abstract principles.[86]

IV

In the late nineteenth century a movement to wrest control of Yale University from clerical hands gained momentum, and in this undertaking Simeon Baldwin soon became one of those most actively engaged. From colonial days the college's governing body had been firmly in the hands of the Congregational ministry. Its corporation consisted of the president and ten fellows, all of whom were Congregational ministers residing in the state of Connecticut. In 1792, in return for a grant of money from the state of Connecticut, the governor, lieutenant governor and the six senior assistants in the council were made ex-officio members of the Board of Fellows. In 1819, after the council had become the state senate, the six senior senators replaced the assistants. As the nineteenth century moved on and a majority of the graduates went into business and professions other than the ministry,[87] the alumni increasingly desired a share in the control of the university. The Young Yale movement, as it was called, reached a climax in 1869–70. As a result the Connecticut General Assembly, at the university's request, voted to permit the substitution of six fellows to be elected by the alumni from among their numbers to replace the six senior state senators. This concession placated the alumni for a time, but the majority of the corporation was still made up of Congregational ministers, and the president was still a clergyman. The corporation rested peacefully in the belief that it was powerless to alter its composition because of restrictions in the college charter.

On April 25, 1881, Simeon E. Baldwin jolted these gentlemen out of their complacency by delivering an address before the New Haven Colony Historical Society,[88] in which he reexamined the Yale charter and made the startling statement that neither the fellows nor the president need be clergymen. In contrasting the original charter with the revised one of 1745 Baldwin said that in the former the

> . . . qualifications of the successors of the original Trustees had been expressly laid down: they must be "ministers of the gospel, inhabiting within this Colony," and thirty years of age. The new charter does not specify any limitations upon the power of appointment.[89]

After surveying the numerous changes in the makeup of the Yale Corporation down through the substitution of six alumni fellows for state senators in 1872, Baldwin concluded:

> No qualifications, as respects eligibility to the presidency, are, so far as I can see, imposed by the existing laws, nor any for the position of Fellow, except as to the six elected by the graduates of the university, who must themselves be graduates of one of its departments.[90] . . .
>
> If the present ministerial Fellows should elect a layman of suitable qualifications as one of their associates, or a clergyman of another denomination, or another State, they would deviate far less from ancient precedent than did their predecessors in 1792, when they opened their doors to the representatives of the State government.[91]

The address brought repercussions almost immediately. The editor of the New York *Evening Post* asked Baldwin to write an article for his paper on the subject in order that it might receive wider publicity. This he did, and it was published on May 7.[92] Former Governor R. D. Hubbard commented on Baldwin's position in the following words:

I was right glad to see your paper in print. I thank you for having broken ground in that direction. The commons of the University are with you. The House of Lords has to give way to the Commons in the long run. I think 'twill be so in the matter of this old prescription. Hurrah for the Commons![93]

A few years later, in 1885, two vacancies occurred on the Yale Corporation. Henry C. Robinson, a prominent Hartford attorney and Yale alumnus, wrote an open letter, a copy of which he sent to Baldwin, urging that they be filled by ministers residing outside the state. He also proposed that another denomination, the Episcopal, for example, be represented.[94]

In order perhaps to head off more drastic proposals, some of the clerical members of the corporation showed interest in Mr. Robinson's suggestion. One of them, Reverend J. H. Twichell, wrote to Baldwin asking for a copy of his discussion of the Yale College Corporation question.[95] Another, when asked his opinion by Baldwin regarding the appointment of non-Connecticut men, replied that he saw no objection to it. He had not known, however, until he had read Baldwin's article that it was possible to do so. Reverend Anderson further said that he inferred from Baldwin's note that President Porter would oppose a change. If this were so, it would make a difference in the action of the fellows.[96] President Porter's sentiments were apparently heeded, and no changes were made at this time.

It is beyond question that Baldwin's paper created quite a stir both in alumni and corporation circles at Yale. But in spite of these and other efforts, the several vacancies among the clerical fellows during the 1880s continued to be filled by Congregational ministers resident in Connecticut.

In the fall of 1885 it was announced that President Noah Porter would resign the following June. Once more the contest between the old guard and the moderns for the control of Yale was joined with renewed vigor. An editorial in the *Nation* in

November, 1885, aptly summed up the two opposing bodies of ideas regarding the nature and purpose of Yale which were contending for mastery in the choice of the new president. The first of these stemmed from Yale's origin as a training school for ministers. The curriculum was designed to train clergymen, and the college had been primarily a theological seminary.

The modern theory, on the other hand, held that a college should ground young men in the elements of an education which would prepare them for any pursuit. Harvard with its elective system represented the new; Yale with its fairly rigid curriculum leaned toward the old. In the *Nation's* words:

Yale College has greatly modified its course, and has given considerable scope to the elective principle; but it has clung pretty stoutly to the original theory of its establishment. It is still an institution practically governed by a few clergymen of a single denomination in a single State. It is still insisted by the believers in the old theory that the first requisite for a President is that he shall be a clergyman of the "orthodox" church. The conservative party may carry their point in the election of a new President, but they will only postpone the inevitable. A great modern college cannot be permanently conducted upon the same lines as a colonial divinity school.[97]

The author of this editorial proved correct in his surmise that the conservatives would win the contest for the presidency in 1886. Timothy Dwight succeeded Noah Porter, and the unbroken line of Congregational minister-presidents continued until the turn of the century. Dwight, however, proved to be the last of the clerical heads of Yale. Commenting on the corporation's decision in 1886, Morris Hadley, son of the next president and the first layman to head Yale, said:

It was once again not a case of the Corporation choosing an inferior candidate as against a better one, for the new president was an outstanding man of great ability. It was a case of a choice between two different futures for Yale. The new president was Timothy Dwight, Yale 1849, grandson of the Timothy Dwight who had built so wisely in 1795. Nearly sixty when elected, he had been professor of New Testament criticism and interpretation. Like his grandfather, he was a Congregational minister. He worthily carried on the traditions established by that grandfather, but the direction which Yale took was once more determined by the wisdom of the past rather than by the possibilities of the future.[98]

The pressure of the proponents of change continued and grew stronger as the passing years diminished the number and the strength of the aging conservatives. The occurrence of a vacancy among the clerical fellows in 1889 provided the occasion for a resurgence of alumni effort to fill it with someone other than a Connecticut Congregational minister. Buchanan Winthrop, Yale 1862, a New York attorney who served from 1891 until his death in 1900 as an alumni fellow,[99] wanted to make a test case at once regarding the legality of having a layman sit upon the Yale Corporation in place of a clerical fellow. His plan was to persuade the corporation to appoint a layman, have the latter's right to his seat challenged, and then carry the question up through the courts until a definitive answer was obtained. Winthrop suggested that Baldwin was the man most suitable to be the challenged layman.

> Your high standing—your legal ability and the fact that you could not fail to be a persona grata to the old fossils all mark you for the place—but at the same time I want you to argue our case—so I wish you would suggest some citizen of New Haven of high standing honor and integrity as much like a Congregational clergyman without being one as possible and tell me who is the best man to nominate him at the May [alumni] meeting.[100]

Baldwin rejected this plan, however, and proposed a more moderate one. First, the corporation should be persuaded to elect a Congregational minister from outside of Connecticut. Even this could not be done, Baldwin believed, unless President Dwight were convinced that the material interests of the university demanded it. If he led the way, the rest of the corporation would follow.[101]

Criticism of the university's conservatism and proposals for change reached the editorial pages of two important metropolitan dailies at this time. The New York *Times* printed on April 14, 1889, and the Boston *Herald* on April 20, editorials very similar in tone and content. Both were written by Julius H. Ward, Yale 1860, an editorial writer for the Boston *Herald*,[102] and were suggested by an article in a Hartford paper [103] which represented Baldwin as the head and front of the movement to reform the Yale Corporation.[104]

Pointing to the substitution of the alumni fellows for the senators as a step in the right direction, the *Herald* lamented that this was not sufficient:

> The hitch is in the corporation, whose ten self-appointed ministers have a controlling vote and are able to keep the alumni from ever having a representative majority in the board. Yale has always been loaded down with its conservatism, and this is the source from which it comes. Its trustees should be fairly representative of the position of the institution in the educational direction of the country.[105]

That the editorials were written to arouse support among the Yale alumni of Boston and New York for corporation reform was made clear by the recommendation in both that the next vacancy among the ministerial fellows be filled by a layman or an out-of-state minister. Following such action a friendly suit should be brought to determine whether the corporation had exceeded its powers. The situation would thus be clarified and possibly a more representative board be secured.[106]

The time had not come in 1889, however, for the conservative forces to yield. President Dwight was apparently unconvinced that the material welfare of the university was suffering under the present dispensation, and not until after his retirement in 1899 did changes come.

As late as 1898 a prominent Yale alumnus, Daniel H. Chamberlain, one-time governor of South Carolina, who had earlier been active in the movement to liberalize Yale's Corporation, added this paragraph to a note to Baldwin:

> I suppose Yale is following the even tenor of her way, undisturbed and unaffected by anybody's criticisms, strong in her self-complacency, and firm in her rejection of all *outside* advice and sudgestion [*sic*]! [107]

That fall the announcement was made that President Dwight would retire the following June. Baldwin's nephew, Roger

Foster, a New York attorney, thereupon wrote his uncle that Judge Henry E. Howland, an elected fellow of Yale from 1892 to 1910, had told him that no clergyman would be chosen to replace Dwight.[108] This proved to be a correct prediction, for Dwight's successor was Arthur T. Hadley, a professor of political economy at Yale and a layman. Even then, as Hadley's son has pointed out,

> . . . it was not easy for the Yale Corporation to bring itself to entrust a forty-three-year-old professor of political economy with the charge of a college that had been governed by venerable clergymen . . . and it was not offered to him until the Corporation had considered several ministers, none of whom was willing to stand.[109]

Control of Yale's governing body continued in clerical hands a few years longer. Following Hadley's election, however, the corporation took deliberate steps toward liberalizing its composition. When the next vacancy among the permanent fellows occurred in 1902, it was filled with a Congregational minister, but one from outside Connecticut. A bolder step was taken in 1905 when another ministerial fellow resigned. He was replaced by a layman. In the following year still another precedent was established with the election of a Presbyterian clergyman. Finally, in 1910 the next two vacancies were filled with laymen, and the clergymen lost their majority.[110] There were then ten laymen to seven clergymen on the corporation (not counting the governor and lieutenant governor, who were prohibited from voting for successors to the clerical fellows).

With these appointments the revolution which had begun in 1872 with the replacement of the six state senators by elected graduates was complete. Yale had now joined the lengthening list of institutions which had made or were making similar changes during the past several decades. Every president since Hadley has been a layman, and the number of clerical fellows has continued to decline until in 1954 there are only three.

V

During this period of Simeon Baldwin's life the output of his pen shared the expansion common to his other activities.

Whereas in his earliest years of practice much of the time he gave to writing had been devoted to the preparation of the first volume of his *Connecticut Digest*, in the period under review he wrote on a variety of subjects. The principal categories in which they may be grouped are history and government, law and legal education, civic problems, politics, and religion. In a large number of instances the articles were prepared first as addresses and later published in periodicals, journals of learned societies, or issued as pamphlets. So voluminous do Baldwin's writings become henceforth that only a sampling can be presented in this study.

Baldwin's association with the New Haven Colony Historical Society, of which he was president for many years, gave him a ready sounding board and publication outlet for his early historical investigations. Practically all of these were published by the society.

When Baldwin began writing in this field, there was no place in America to learn scientific historical investigation, and he was completely self-taught. In spite of this he made use of the techniques of research which were coming to America from Germany during the latter part of the nineteenth century. Especially he appreciated the need for going to the sources, and in all of his historical writings his use of original documents was notable.[111]

Baldwin's awareness of the changing currents of historiographical thought is apparent from a comment in one of his essays.

> The historian of the present day spends less time than his great predecessors in the records of battles and seiges, of the doings of courts and the contests of diplomacy. It is perhaps his highest aim to paint in vivid colors the social conditions of the community with which he has to deal, the spirit of its life, the principles that govern the common acts of the common people, and the influences brought to bear upon them from the side of education and the higher civilization of the age.[112]

Baldwin was in the advance guard of the social history movement. But he was exaggerating when he implied that the average historian in 1884 was interested in social history. John Bach

McMaster and a few others were pioneering in this field, but their fellow workers were not numerous.

Baldwin's historical writings concerned principally New England during the colonial and early national periods and the development of democratic government in America. The range of these writings is revealed by their titles: "The New Haven Convention of 1778," a history of anti-inflationary efforts during the Revolution; "New England Secessionists," inspired by the appearance in 1877 of Henry Adams' *Documents Relating to New England Federalism, 1800–1815*; "The Boundary Line Between Connecticut and New York," a prosaic account of a provincial dispute; "Recent Changes in our State Constitutions," a history of constitutional development on the state level; "A Young Man's Journal of a Hundred Years Ago," comments from the diary of a New England school teacher on Dutch life in Albany shortly after the Revolution; "The Captives of the Amistad," the most complete account of Connecticut's most famous law case in which Baldwin's father played the leading role; "The Early History of the Ballot in Connecticut," a somewhat technical account of voting procedures in colonial Connecticut; and "The Three Constitutions of Connecticut," a review of constitutional development from the Fundamental Orders of 1639 and the royal charter of 1662 to the state constitution of 1818.

One of the essays in this division deserves special comment. In contrast to Baldwin's frequent practice of investigating a narrow topic of local history, this dealt with a grand theme. It was a survey of the accomplishments of the American republican government during the first century. Baldwin entitled it "The Centenary of Modern Government," and presented it originally as the annual address before the American Bar Association in 1889.[113] In this remarkable essay Baldwin showed something of his breadth as well as his depth of knowledge and understanding of the workings of modern government. He traced with clarity the chief trends of American government since the adoption of the federal Constitution in 1788. Pointing out how under modern conditions new countries become conservative and old ones unsettled, he observed that nowhere was property more secure than in the young United States. Baldwin noted the division of powers, judicial review, the combination of a strong central authority with local home rule, religious freedom, the extension of the franchise, education at public cost, and the right of labor to protection at the expense of capital as some of the principal features of modern government. His skill in eliciting the implications of some of these policies was indeed remarkable, and this essay will probably rank as one of his most able.

The second major division of Simeon Baldwin's writings is that group concerned with problems of law and legal education. These vary from one-page notes to lengthy essays, the latter frequently being addresses before bar associations.

Brief mention of some of these will indicate the variety of Baldwin's legal writings. He wrote the preface to the *Revision of 1875. The General Statutes of the State of Connecticut* and also the report of the Commission on Revision of the Statutes on a proposed bill to introduce cumulative voting in public elections. In 1875 he published a pamphlet edition of the United States Constitution with references to judicial decisions involving its interpretation. This he used in his constitutional law course. In 1877 he composed the report of the Committee of Jurisprudence to the State Bar Association of Connecticut on the expediency of writing legal and equitable remedies in a single form of action.[114] And in that year he also explained the newly introduced graduate courses at the Yale Law School in an article for the *Journal of Social Science*.[115]

In the summer of 1880 Baldwin accepted the invitation of the International Code Committee of America to be its delegate at the conference of the Association for the Reform and Codification of the Law of Nations at Berne, Switzerland.[116] Baldwin's account of this meeting, which appeared in the *American Law Review*,[117] is the earliest evidence of his interest in international law, a field in which he later wrote considerably.

The second volume of Baldwin's *Connecticut Digest* appeared in 1882. This followed the plan of the first volume and brought it up to date.

Simeon Baldwin believed the educated lawyer should be acquainted with the legal systems of other lands as well as that of his own. To this end he established and taught for many years a course in comparative jurisprudence. In an 1883 paper entitled "Preliminary Examinations in Criminal Proceedings" [118] Baldwin showed his wide knowledge of European judicial practices. No other nation in the western world, he pointed out, went as far as America in protecting the rights of an accused person. Baldwin made a strong case for the preliminary examination of an accused person by a magistrate immediately upon arrest in order to lessen the suspect's opportunities for fabricating an alibi.

Baldwin gave one of his most significant addresses of this period on July 3, 1884, before the State Bar Association of Tennessee. Entitled "Insanity as a Legal Fiction," [119] it urged the legal profession to shed the inherited fabrications of the law. Baldwin pointed out that for three centuries the courts had set aside wills of unreasonable men by calling them insane and argued that a sounder approach would be to guarantee legally a share of an estate to close relatives, as some states were then doing. Similarly the plea of temporary insanity in criminal proceedings developed because the common law allowed in capital cases an all or nothing sentence, death or freedom. Baldwin advocated additional choices for the jury other than guilty and not guilty, such as continental justice permitted. This, he believed, would effectively end the temporary insanity plea.

In the middle eighties Baldwin wrote three short articles on aspects of legal education. In "The Time Necessary to Get a Legal Education" [120] he advocated that three instead of two years be required to earn an LL.B. In "Law Latin and Roman Law" [121] he sketched the history of the study of Roman law in America and suggested that every accomplished lawyer should have some knowledge of it. "The Recitation System" [122] was Baldwin's first contribution to the vehement pedagogical arguments on teaching methods which flourished in the American law schools of the late nineteenth century. Baldwin contended that the recitation system was far superior to the lecture method of teaching law. By going to the books under the professor's guidance and endeavoring to discover the logic behind the author's propositions, the student could best learn to reason on questions of law. In later articles, as we shall note, Baldwin paid his respects to the case method of instruction.

Yet another field to which Baldwin made contributions during the 1880s was penology. He was for several years chairman of the Committee on Jurisprudence and Law Reform of the American Bar Association. In 1885 Baldwin wrote the report of the committee recommending that criminals convicted a second time be placed under police supervision upon their release for from five years to life.[123]

A paper elaborating on this problem—the disposition of habitual criminals—was read by Baldwin on September 9, 1886, before the American Social Science Association.[124] In this he first traced the history of past methods of correction. The most common of these was imprisonment for life on the second or third offense. He opposed life imprisonment on the grounds it was too expensive and tended to dissuade juries from convicting. Some hope of starting anew also should be left to the prisoner. Baldwin called attention to the recommendation of the American Bar Association committee—prolonged police supervision upon release—and advocated its adoption. More police would be needed under this plan, but prison costs would be decreased.

In 1891 Baldwin was president of the American Bar Association, and for his presidential address performed the constitutional requirement of reviewing the year's legislation in the United States.[125] Baldwin summarized the laws of the year on both federal and state levels in his customarily efficient and orderly manner. A few items mentioned have a familiar sound to the present-day reader. One was the avalanche of legislation at the end of the congressional session. The other was a notation that the war on oleomargarine was continuing with unabated vigor.

A fruit of Baldwin's association as one of the counsel in the Andover heresy trials was an article in 1891 entitled "The Visitorial Statutes of Andover Seminary." [126] He traced the institution of visitors back to medieval universities as a device to insure that the provisions of a bequest were followed by its administrators. Such a group of visitors was provided for by the men who organized and endowed the theological foundation at Andover to insure that the rigid Congregationalism adhered to by the founders would always be taught. When the visitors attempted in the 1880s to remove a professor for heretical views, they became involved in a legal contest with the trustees, who were the active managers of the school. The Supreme Judicial Court of Massachusetts decided that the visitors could inspect the school at any time but should give advance notice of such visitations, and must take no action without first hearing the trustees.

In 1892 Baldwin produced one of his finest essays of this period which he delivered as the annual address before the Ohio State Bar Association. Speaking on "American Jurisprudence" [127] he set forth the contributions America had thus far made towards developing a distinctive jurisprudence. Among the principles and practices which Baldwin enumerated as being peculiar to America were: voluntary expatriation; the raising of treaty obligations to a position equal to the supreme law of the land; the establishment of distinctive civil and criminal procedures; the evolution of a system of code pleading; the introduction of reformatories; the overprotection of accused persons by permitting no preliminary examination in criminal cases and allowing appeals on trivial points; the early relaxation of laws against debtors; the practice of electing judges; the recognition of the rights of women to own property regardless of their marital status; the function of the judiciary not only as an administrator but also as an interpreter of the constitutionality of the law; and finally the fact that in America both the executive and legislative branches of the government were in some ways subject to the judicial.

Along with his varied civic and political activities Baldwin occasionally wrote reports and tracts aimed to give information or plead a cause. One of the earliest advocates of public parks for New Haven, he delivered a lecture in 1881 in which he sketched the spread of parks in foreign lands and in other American cities and then chronicled the twenty-year struggle to establish a year previously the first park in New Haven.[128] As chairman of a commission of citizens appointed by the New Haven City Council in 1881 to determine whether the city should purchase the waterworks, Baldwin wrote the group's report which mildly favored city ownership.[129] Another civic problem on which Baldwin wrote at this time was the desirability of consolidating the overlapping city and town governments of New Haven.[130]

Under Baldwin's political writings should be listed his 1883 article mentioned previously entitled "Railroad Taxation,"[131] a plea for lower taxes for Connecticut railroads, and two in a series he called "Tracts for the Times."[132] The latter were issued by the State Democratic Club in the early nineties. One urged the election in 1892 of the Democratic candidates for state offices, and the other answered affirmatively its title, "Is there any need of a constitutional convention?" In this category also was Baldwin's article on the disputed election of 1890 in Connecticut, which appeared in the April, 1891, *New Englander*.[133]

A final group of Simeon Baldwin's writings concerned religion. Baldwin's interest in religion and its power to ameliorate human relations was strong all his life. He spoke before various Congregational Clubs throughout Connecticut and to other religious groups and through these talks revealed the main currents of his religious thought.

In 1884 he addressed the New Haven Congregational Club on *Judaic Christianity*,[134] tracing the various influences of the Hebrew cultural and religious patterns upon early Christianity. The doctrine of atonement he emphasized as an important Christian tenet borrowed from Judaism. Two years later he spoke before the same group on *The Genius of Congregationalism*.[135] Here Baldwin pointed out that Congregationalists believed their type of church organization, in which the individual congregation was completely independent, was most like that of the first Christian assemblies. Congregationalism had begun to differ with the older Christian churches in that it was beginning to realize that life in heaven was not separate from life on earth. While the ancient churches asserted that life was to be endured here with the only reward being in heaven, the Congregational church, according to Baldwin, was trying to make earth more heaven-like. This change in attitude on the part of the Congregational Church Baldwin cited as an example of the great elasticity of its doctrines.

Baldwin's most forthright pronouncement on the state of religion in this period was contained in a paper read before the annual meeting of his church in New Haven on January 21, 1883.[136] Baldwin noted the decrease in membership of the North Church and attributed it not so much to a decline of spirituality as to theological barriers to admission in the form of creeds made by an older generation but still in force. These, Baldwin believed, ought to be removed, so that anyone endeavoring to follow Christ's way of life according to his own interpretation of it could be admitted to membership. In this address as in others he drew a distinction between theology and religion. The former was for the ministers primarily, and even they were not in agreement on many fundamentals. Baldwin's view was extremely pragmatic:

> Religion is to live the life of Christ. He who best does that, has all of theology that need be asked, of one who only asks to be enrolled among Christ's followers.[137]

Since his boyhood, Baldwin pointed out, there had been many changes in theological beliefs. Then it was thought that the creation was the work of a week. Ministers hesitated to admit that any of the apostolic writers could be mistaken in any points of fact, however clearly they might appear to differ from each other in telling the same incident. They also feared that infants who died unbaptized might be damned eternally. The emphasis at that time was on God's wrath against sin and not on his mercy towards sinners.

> I am thankful that there has been a steady progress in this ancient church towards what seems to most of us a clearer view of truth. The view of Christian life as actuated less by a dread of future punish-

ment for evil done or good undone, than by a loyal and generous desire to follow the example of our Master's life, a love for His teachings, a wish to do right, because it is right. [*sic*] To lead a religious life from these motives of love, and trust, and discipleship, appeals to a higher sense and feeling than did the old arguments of the old New England—the old Calvinistic theology.[138]

Regarding the conduct of Christians Baldwin noted as great changes in it as in theological views. Dancing, card playing, a quiet walk on Sunday, attendance at the opera, theater, or circus a generation ago would have been condoned by very few who professed to be Christians. In the 1880s many felt free to indulge in any of these activities without violating their religious beliefs, and Baldwin saw nothing to regret in these innovations.

Among the many letters Baldwin received in response to this address, one from his brother reflected a common reaction:

. . . I received and read with great interest, some amusement and much amazement your very frank utterances at the annual meeting of the North Church. I find no fault with your platform which is broad enough to include all who are not Jews or Mahometans but I am not surprised that it should have failed to meet with general acquiescence in a congregation which professes a faith not very far removed from Calvinism.

But it shows how fast and far the world has moved that you should have been permitted to read so bold a paper to the end. Fifty years ago you would have been excommunicated for such heretical sentiments and two hundred years ago you would have been burnt at the stake. As it is the opposition seems to have confined itself to your suggestions with respect to dancing and theatres and to pay no regard to your very liberal views with respect to the rigid creed to which a blind and unreasoning adherence was formerly exacted.

But I think your paper will do good and that you are not much in advance of the time. Indeed I dare say that some of those who considered it their duty to protest would support you now if they had the courage of their convictions.[139]

Baldwin's attitude towards the Roman Catholic Church was always very cordial. He regarded it as a co-laborer in the Lord's vineyard and believed the Lord needed all the help obtainable.

When a minister asked him to contribute in 1889 to the *Evangelical Alliance*, a religious publication, Baldwin refused because of its strong anti-Catholic bias.

> I regard the Romish church as a true as well as a large part of the Christian Church, and I think its aid and cooperation should be invited by all who are endeavoring to promote social reforms or religious progress.[140]

The production of Baldwin's pen increased in quantity, quality, and variety during the twenty years under review. He devoted an ever larger proportion of his time to writing as these years passed. Baldwin's strong liking for this type of activity and the hearty encouragement his friends gave it were undoubtedly factors in his acceptance of a Connecticut Supreme Court judgeship in 1892. One of these supporters urged him in 1888, for example, to give up the drudgery of the law, please himself and benefit society to a far greater extent by putting into imperishable form the information with which he was so saturated.[141] As a member of the bench these goals could be realized because his law practice and political activities would have to be abandoned, thus leaving more time for research and writing.

VI

Simeon Baldwin loved his native city and devoted large amounts of time, effort and money to its welfare. Soon after he established himself in his profession, he became associated with several of the philanthropic and cultural organizations of New Haven. His early connection with the New Haven Grays, the Connecticut Academy of Arts and Sciences and the Young Men's Christian Association have already been noted. His activities as a member of United Church and as a director of both the General Hospital Society of Connecticut and of Hopkins Grammar School also dated from the 1860s.

In the middle portion of his life Baldwin continued his affiliation with most of these organizations, held offices in many, and added several new ones to his expanding interests.

First among his New Haven activities Baldwin maintained a life-long interest in his church. He taught Sunday School there for a number of years and was urged by his class to continue when in 1876 he tried to resign.[142] He served on the committee to supply the pulpit and corresponded widely to bring both temporary and permanent pastors to the church. He was a faithful member of the New Haven Congregational Club, delivered several lectures before it, and was its president in 1886.[143] Baldwin was moderator at the annual meeting of the General Conference of Congregational Churches of Connecticut in 1881 and two years later a state delegate to the National Council of Congregational Churches.[144] Closely allied to his church interests was the Young Men's Christian Association. Maintaining his membership over a long period of years, he was president from 1884 to 1886 [145] and was requested to continue longer in office.[146]

As a director of the Hospital Society of Connecticut nearly all of his adult life, Baldwin was a loyal and diligent worker, serving on the prudential committee in the 1880s.[147] In a similar role as a member of the board of trustees of Hopkins Grammar School, he endeavored to raise money for the institution in the early eighties.[148] Because of repeated annual deficits he voted in 1887 with a majority of the board members to give the school to the city of New Haven [149] This plan was not then consummated, and the school continued its precarious existence until more adequately financed many years later.

Baldwin's concern for the past as well as the present of his city made it natural that the New Haven Colony Historical Society should engage his attentions. This organization was founded in 1863 to foster interest in the history of the area contained in the original colony of New Haven. Baldwin became its president in 1884, a post he held until 1896. Although an extremely busy man Baldwin made time for research, principally on aspects of Connecticut history. He read the results of his investigations before the New Haven Colony Historical Society, and as noted previously many of these essays were printed in its *Papers*.[150]

Perhaps the most tangible of Baldwin's many services to New Haven was his crusade for a park system for the city. He was one of the civic leaders who for years had urged the acquisition of East Rock, one of New Haven's twin hills, as a public park. This was finally accomplished in 1880, and Baldwin was appointed to the first Board of Park Commissioners, a position he did not relinquish until the last years of his life. Under his guidance East Rock, West Rock, and more than a score of smaller parks were added and developed during the forty-odd years he served.[151]

Besides the local groups Baldwin constantly extended his organizational range to state, regional and national associations of various kinds. Some of these were the American Social Science Association, the New England Tariff Reform League, the American Historical Association, the American Economic Association, the American Academy of Political and Social Science, and the American Antiquarian Society. He also held membership in temperance, divorce reform and prisoners' aid associations.

After he became a judge in 1893, Baldwin's preoccupation with research and writing attracted him to the national scholarly societies, and he became president of several of these. With his shift of interest his role in the local civic and reform groups became correspondingly smaller.

VII

During these years Baldwin's family life was for the most part serene. His wife's sister, Miss Charlotte Winchester, had become the very capable head of the household and supervised the rearing of his children, Helen and Roger.

Although most of Baldwin's contemporaries saw only the formal and reserved aspects of his personality, his intimate associates caught glimpses of his humor.[152] A friend of his daughter said of him:

> Mr. Baldwin to his children's friends would seem at first stern, and always very controlled and rather ascetic; but before one had been there for supper many times one would begin to be fond of him, to

watch for a sympathetic glance, to desire greatly his good opinion, and to be delighted if one could make him laugh. If you could, his laughter was most spontaneous, his head thrown back, his whole self relaxed.[153]

Baldwin's fondness for humorous versifying appeared on a Christmas card to an intimate friend, Mrs. Ellen Gifford, whose father's estate he was administering.

> Lo, the poor lawyer! See his brow profound,
> His modest glance, bent low upon the ground,
> The unobtrusive step, with which he steals,
> As one who all another's troubles feels,
> Between those angry clients, and without
> A moment's hesitation or a doubt,
> Withdraws all cause of strife, and asks no fee
> Save what the trifle he removes may be.
> You never need quarrel,
> (This is the moral),
> If only a lawyer is near.
> Your burdens he'll bear
> Away, for his share,
> And what use of dispute, after they disappear?
> A much abused creature,
> (Like Henry Ward Beecher)
> I'd like to know who calls his services dear.[154]

Few among Baldwin's associates would have guessed that the serious, reserved and sometimes frosty-appearing attorney was the author of this verse.

Beginning in 1877 Simeon Baldwin began computing annually his monetary worth.[155] By inheritance he had received $64,711—it was very characteristic that he should list the amount to the last dollar—and in fourteen years of practice to 1877 had saved enough of his earnings and income from investments to increase this to $104,788. During the remaining sixteen years of Baldwin's career as a practicing lawyer the amount tripled. This was made possible by his tremendous energy, his renowned ability which brought him lucrative cases, and by his shrewd investments.

One of Baldwin's nonproductive investments was the New Haven *Morning News*, of which he became one of the owners and treasurer in the early eighties. This was the only two-cent daily paper in New Haven at the time and was to some extent a Democratic party organ aimed at winning the working class vote.

An old account book giving the *News*' financial position indicates that it was by no means a profitable venture. The paper showed a deficit every year from 1885 to 1896, and its owners were constantly making loans to it in order to keep the *News* afloat.[156] Although it was commonly believed that Baldwin was the principal owner of the paper, he denied this in 1890, saying that he had sold considerable of his stock to the managing editor.[157] Three years later the latter indicated that Baldwin at that time controlled the paper.[158] After a reorganization in 1897, Baldwin withdrew from the enterprise entirely.

Although the Baldwins lived comfortably, they did not indulge in ostentatious displays. Many years later when he was Governor of Connecticut, Baldwin regularly carried his lunch to the capitol—a sandwich which he ate in his office. He was exceedingly generous with his means, and as his income rose, so did his benefactions.

During the summers of 1874 through 1879 Baldwin vacationed with his children and Miss Winchester usually on the lakes of northern New York. They chose resorts where life was quiet, the food excellent, and swimming and rowing facilities favorable. Baldwin's passion for rowing, which dated back to his school days, continued during this middle period.

In the summer of 1880 Baldwin made his second trip to Europe. He traveled in Holland and Belgium and along the Rhine to Switzerland,[159] where he attended the sessions of the Association for the Reform and Codification of the Law of Nations at Berne in August.[160]

Similarly to former summers, the Baldwins vacationed during the 1880s at resorts in New York, New Hampshire, or Maine. In 1883 Simeon Baldwin was too busy to take any vacation but commuted to and from Pine Orchard, a beach colony near New

Haven. In 1887 he took his son, then an undergraduate at Yale, to Europe, where they spent several weeks in London and Paris.[161] While in London the Baldwins were entertained at breakfast by Lord Bryce.[162] Their acquaintanceship dated back to 1885, when Bryce wrote to Baldwin requesting information [163] on aspects of law in America for his *American Commonwealth*, which was then in preparation. At Bryce's request Baldwin read and criticized his chapter on state finance.[164]

By the late eighties his children were grown, and the family no longer vacationed together. Miss Winchester and Helen usually went for a shore or mountain sojourn, Roger visited with his friends, and Baldwin frequently stayed in New Haven alone until it was time for his annual trek to the Bar Association meetings.

In 1890 Roger graduated from Yale and entered the Law School that fall. Before the first semester was over, however, he withdrew because of illness and went to California for the remainder of the year.[165] After several months on a ranch his health improved, and by May he felt well again.[166] In the fall of 1891 Roger returned to Law School and completed his work for the LL.B. in 1893 and LL.M. in 1894.

The years from 1874 to 1893 were those when the high promise of Baldwin's youth was fully realized. Professionally he reached the first rank. His civic and reform activities made him a pillar of the community. In leaving the Republican party he demonstrated his political courage and independence. His organizational talents brought about the founding of the great guild of the legal profession. And what sometimes appeared to his contemporaries as his superhuman powers of concentration enabled him all the while to carry on both a university teaching and a research career. The names of men who accomplished as much in so many directions are indeed not numerous.

As the period closed the dividends of a quarter century of ceaseless toil began to appear in his election to the presidency of the American Bar Association, his receipt from Harvard of his first honorary degree, and his appointment to the supreme bench of his native state.

MR. JUSTICE BALDWIN

I

When Simeon Baldwin's nomination to the bench of the Supreme Court of Errors was confirmed early in February, 1893, several changes in his way of life ensued. First there was new, and as it proved, pleasant work as judge—hearing cases, discussing them with the other members of the court, and writing opinions. Along with this gain came two significant losses; his law practice and his political career. The net result was more time for other pursuits, chiefly research, writing, speaking, and work with scholarly organizations.

Baldwin was well qualified to be a judge of his state's Supreme Court. By temperament he was fair, judicious, and scrupulously honest. He was the type of man who would weigh the evidence presented by both sides, make appropriate allowances for the partisan zeal of attorneys, and as closely as any man render a fair decision. His written opinions were noted for stating clearly and simply the points at issue and for logically and inexorably drawing the conclusions from them. As a judge he was respected by all segments of the population.

This universal regard for Baldwin's judicial capacity was promptly recognized as early as the summer of 1893, when a vacancy occurred on the United States Supreme Court. Immediately his name appeared in the news as Connecticut's candidate for the position. One of his friends declared that the Connecticut press, regardless of party affiliations, was unanimous for him.[1] Dean Wayland wrote:

> Meanwhile, Connecticut newspapers and some outside the state are clamoring for you as successor to Judge Blatchford—And the Law Faculty are [*sic*] torn by conflicting emotions—a sincere desire to see you where you belong, judicially—and a sickening conviction that your promotion would take Hamlet out of the play.[2]

Since the Democratic party had been returned to power in Washington in March of 1893, the likelihood of Baldwin's receiving the appointment was enhanced. His friends rallied to his support, circulated petitions among the lawyers, and wrote in his behalf to the President. Early in September the Connecticut congressional delegation called upon President Cleveland to urge Judge Baldwin's candidacy, but the Chief Executive said he inclined toward a New York man,[3] William B. Hornblower. Later in the month the latter's name was presented to the Senate for confirmation, and because of the opposition of Senator David B. Hill of New York, the nomination was rejected.

Upon receipt of this news Baldwin's friends supported his candidacy more vigorously than ever. Judge Charles B. Andrews, Chief Justice of the Connecticut Supreme Court of Errors, wrote to President Cleveland in most flattering terms, saying that Baldwin had had as large a practice and dealt with as many legal problems as any man in the country and, in addition, had a wide knowledge of affairs and of history.[4]

Baldwin was anxious to have the position and encouraged the steps his friends were taking in his behalf. He went as far as to ask a Connecticut Democrat in the Patent Office to use his influence with President Cleveland. The latter replied that:

> It is a very delicate matter to go to the President about this. It might probably do more harm than good. I am certain that he knows personally all about you and your distinguished career. Judge Wheeler will be down here to-morrow morning, and I will confer with him about it. To me the prospect looks exceedingly bright.[5]

The next few days were suspense-laden ones for Baldwin. He was at one of the most crucial points in his life. Had he been appointed, his career on the national stage might have brought him to such revered positions as Chief Justice or even President.[6] Such speculations are idle, however, for again Baldwin did not receive the appointment. And thus ended one of a series of exciting but unfulfilled possibilities which could have placed Baldwin among the foremost figures of his time.

It was not until thirteen years later that Baldwin's caliber as a judge was successfully recognized. On September 5, 1906, Chief Justice Torrance of the Connecticut Supreme Court died. On the basis of seniority Baldwin was his logical successor. His appointment as a justice in 1893 had been made by a Democratic governor, however, whereas the state's chief executive in 1906 was a Republican. In spite of this the press of both parties joined in endorsing Judge Baldwin for the chief justiceship. The Springfield *Republican*, for example, said:

> The vacancy in the chief justiceship of the Connecticut supreme court, caused by the death of Judge Torrance, will be filled by the next Legislature, the prospect being that the choice will be Judge Simeon E. Baldwin of New Haven. Although Judge Baldwin was originally chosen to the supreme court bench as a democrat, all are agreed that his long service, high standing in the profession and national reputation as a jurist and publicist entitle him to the honor of promotion by a republican General Assembly. Judge Baldwin is now the senior member of the court and has not many more years of judicial service. [Judges must resign at seventy in Connecticut; Baldwin was then sixty-six.] He eminently merits the crowning recognition of the chief justiceship.[7]

There was universal satisfaction when in January, 1907, the Governor nominated and the General Assembly confirmed Baldwin in the position. In congratulating him, Baldwin's brother said:

> . . . the honour is the greater because it has been conferred by a Governor who is not of your own party and who has been bold enough to recognize in his selection that merit has sometimes superior claims to political allegiance.[8]

The year 1907 also marked the centennial of the establishment of the Connecticut Supreme Court of Errors. Among the first judges to sit upon this court when it was constituted in 1807 was Simeon Baldwin. One hundred years later his grandson was its presiding judge. Perhaps it was this rather remarkable family relationship which determined Baldwin to give a luncheon for the judges of the Supreme and Superior Courts and for the members of the Connecticut Bar Association commemorating the centennial of the state's highest court.[9] On this occasion the Chief Justice delivered a short address tracing the development of the Court during its first century.

The Supreme Court of Errors, as its name suggests, is the final court of appeal in Connecticut. Only cases of some importance, therefore, came before Baldwin and his colleagues. The majority of the Court's decisions applied to intrastate affairs. Rarely were matters decided the implications of which reached beyond Connecticut's borders.

Undoubtedly Baldwin's most far-reaching decision was *William H. Hoxie* v. *The New York, New Haven and Hartford Railroad*, handed down in the summer of 1909. In this case he declared unconstitutional a section of the Federal Employers' Liability Act of 1908, which enlarged the United States government's control over interstate commerce. The precedent established by this decision was appealed in another case through the federal courts and ultimately reversed, but not before it had involved Baldwin in a controversy with former President Theodore Roosevelt during the campaign of 1910. The latter had urged passage of the law to which Baldwin took exception and attacked the Connecticut judge for his "retrogressive" stand.

The Federal Employers' Liability Act of 1908 introduced a radical change in the common-law liability of railroad corporations for injuries to their employees. Under the long-standing fellow-servant rule of the common law, an employer was not held responsible for injuries to a worker caused by the negligence of a fellow employee. The Act of 1908 reversed this rule and placed liability for such accidents directly on the employer.[10]

William H. Hoxie, an injured employee of the New York, New Haven and Hartford Railroad, brought suit under this law in the Connecticut courts. Upon appeal from the Superior Court the case came before the Supreme Court of Errors in 1909. Baldwin and his colleagues unanimously upheld the decision of the lower court in an opinion written by the Chief Justice. He concluded:

1. Congress did not intend by the Act of April 22d, 1908, to authorize the institution of an action under it in the courts of the States.

2. It had no power to make it incumbent on the State courts to assume jurisdiction of such an action.

3. The issues before the Superior Court involved the consideration of these points, which justified, of themselves, the dismissal of the plaintiff's action; but further,

4. The Act, so far as it concerns this cause, is wholly void by reason of certain of its provisions which cannot be separated from the rest.[11]

The Hoxie decision was not appealed, but another case, *Edgar G. Mondou* v. *The New York, New Haven and Hartford Railroad Co.*,[12] which the Connecticut Supreme Court of Errors decided on the same grounds as the Hoxie case, was carried to the federal courts. The October, 1911, term of the United States Supreme Court heard this case along with several similar ones and (1) reversed the decision of the Connecticut Supreme Court of Errors and (2) declared the Federal Employers' Liability Act of 1908 to be constitutional.[13]

The disparity of opinion between the state and federal courts was in large measure a question of the limits to the power of the federal government over interstate commerce. Baldwin and his colleagues favored keeping the national authority out of former state preserves. The Supreme Court, representing the national interest in a period of expanding federal power, found that the commerce clause could be extended to cover relations between an interstate corporation and its employees and reversed the state court.

Although most of the work of the Supreme Court of Errors was of a serious nature, life on the bench was not without its humorous touches. A letter from a sheriff protesting Judge Baldwin's meager allowance for his services provides an example of such comic relief.

Mr. Baldwin

Dr Sir

I wish to make a statement to you in regard to the Easton Horse Thief case, I was the officer that made the arrest and in which you cut my fees down to less than I paid out, I will tell you what I did and you can judge whether any of it was unnessessary or not. I hired a horse and buggy for which I paid $3 Dollars for went to Bport [Bridgeport] arrested the man brought him to Easton for trial which was over 20 miles I then hired two keepers because I could not get one to stay with him alone for which I paid $2 Dollars. I then hired another team for which I paid $2 Dollars for and went to summons witnesses which took me all the afternoon I then hired a pair of horses and two seated carrige for which I paid $4 Dollars and an assistant $2 Dollars because everyone said he was a bad man and would get away from me it being dark. I fed two teams in Raymonds stalls one single one double for which I paid $1.50. I paid for two suppers assistant and myself .50 cts about half-past nine the first mouthfull I had since four oclock in the morning I did an awfull hard days work and what did I get for it. You claim the law does not require you to pay horse hire, now was it nessessary that I should have those teams or not,

Yours Truly,

Henry W. Osborn, Easton Conn [14]

The years passed during Baldwin's period on the bench, one quite like another. Although he was nearing three score and ten, his vigor was unabated, and his capacity for work unimpaired. He hewed to a narrow line, keeping himself completely occupied at all times. This for him was the tried and tested way, if not to attain happiness, at least to avoid sorrow and morosity.

In February, 1910, Baldwin celebrated his seventieth birthday, the mandatory retirement age in the Connecticut courts. He looked forward to his withdrawal cheerfully, however, writing to his sister:

I should not wonder if I enjoyed my decade from seventy to eighty, should I live it out, as much as any of its predecessors. Leisure to choose the occupation I like is a gift not to be despised. If well used, there are few better.[15]

The Chief Justice was given a dinner by the Connecticut bar in February in honor of his retirement. The senior class at the Law School also commemorated this event with the following testimonial:

To Simeon E. Baldwin, Chief Justice of the Connecticut Supreme Court of Errors,

A tribute of respect and affection from the members of the Senior Class of the Yale Law School who have learned to appreciate your worth as a man and the lofty ideals your service on the bench have so fittingly exemplified.

To you as a teacher we are indebted for the inspiration of a noble life. Our school owes its existence in a large measure to your early efforts. Your constant and unselfish active interest has contributed to its growth and progress.

On this occasion of your retirement as Chief Justice of the State, we desire to express the heartfelt hope that many years yet lie before you during which we will continue to have the benefit of your guidance and your teaching.[16]

Few judges have left office with as much genuine public regard as Simeon E. Baldwin enjoyed in 1910. He was Connecticut's first citizen, and before the year was over the people gave him the highest elective honor their state could bestow, the governorship. In professional circles Baldwin's withdrawal from the judiciary brought many sincere tributes to his ability as a judge. The *Green Bag*, a magazine of the legal profession, displayed the judge's picture on the first page of its April issue and said in part:

Judge Baldwin's retirement has been marked as is not often the case when the leader of a state judiciary leaves the bench by general recognition, from all parts of the state, of the loss the Commonwealth has thus sustained and of his many virtues of character and personality. He evidently has the affection of the people not less than of the bar.[17]

Seventeen years later, when Baldwin died, his professional colleagues once again attested to his reputation as a judge. The Chief Justice of the Supreme Court of Errors, George W. Wheeler, said:

Certainly there has been no man who has lived among us for the past half century comparable to him in national repute or in achieving work. He was beyond question the greatest man Connecticut has produced in that time. He was among the foremost lawyers of the State and nation, his 17 years of service as a justice and chief justice of our State in a court, perhaps never excelled in its history and ability and accomplishment, stamped him as a jurist who possessed not only a very wide knowledge and understanding of the law, but also those indispensable qualities of a truly great judge, good judgment, sound sense, fairness and impartiality of view which would on no occasion sacrifice the public for the private interest, and a steadiness of purpose and courage which would not deviate from the course his conviction and conscience pointed out.[18]

Judge John Kimberly Beach had the following to say regarding Baldwin's judicial ability:

As judge and chief justice he was courteous, patient, alert and wise in administering the rules of the court. His opinions are marked for learning, brevity, clarity, accuracy of thought and diction, literary finish and finality of decision. They justly won for him the title of a great judge.[19]

II

Second only to Baldwin's judicial duties were his associations with Yale University from 1893 to 1910. He continued to teach, acted as treasurer of the Law School, and was influential in committing the institution to several new departures. In recognition of his eminence as a jurist and scholar and of his valuable contributions to the university, Baldwin was among those mentioned for the presidency of Yale in 1898.

As a member of the Law School faculty he taught a variety of subjects. These included outlines of American law, agency, wills, constitutional law, railroad law, legal ethics, conflict of laws, and private international law. Some of the courses consisted of as few as five lectures; the majority, however, met one hour a week for a whole semester. As the years passed new instructors relieved Baldwin of several courses, so that by 1909 his schedule consisted of outlines of American law (seven lectures); constitutional law (one lecture a week); railroad law (one lecture a week); legal ethics (five lectures); and private international law (one lecture a week).[20] When Professor Baldwin ceased to conduct his class in wills after June, 1904, many students requested that he offer it optionally during the current term. Their petition stated that the course was considered one of the most valuable in the curriculum.[21]

Baldwin's ability as a teacher was attested by his students generally. In fact, no unfavorable reflections on this aspect of his career have been discovered by this writer. Early in 1894 an anonymous member of the senior class wrote to ask him to reduce his assignments, saying that he gave more than fifty pages while the other professors assigned only twenty. The student assured Professor Baldwin that he was "esteemed and favored by your audience as a kind and skillful tutor, and I, for one, am very grateful to you." [22] The manner in which the writer expressed himself indicated that he was probably one of the many Japanese students who came to Yale in the late nineteenth century. Baldwin's oriental scholars were especially loyal to him. Frequently when he departed from New Haven by train, they would bid him farewell at the station with bouquets and bows. These marks of respect embarrassed the reserved and dignified professor exceedingly![23]

Two of the finest tributes Baldwin ever received came from former students:

> . . . the pleasantest recollection I have of classroom work either in Yale College or Yale Law School, is of the hours spent in your recitations. It has always seemed to me that the most marked characteristic of your instruction was not merely your willingness to let the student think for himself, which of itself set you apart from many instructors, but your ability to *help* him think for himself.[24]
>
> . . . .
>
> Judge Baldwin was the most learned all-around man in the law that I have ever met. He was a wizard in jurisprudence. Two of his courses, *American Constitutional Law* and *Railroad Law*, were among the star courses of the law school's curriculum.[25]

A brief portrait of Baldwin, the teacher, then in his middle fifties, is contained in the autobiography of a former pupil and colleague:

> In the latter part of the spring term of my senior year in college . . . I met for the first time another Yale Law school professor, who was destined to play an important part in my after-life. He was of medium height and physique, wore thick spectacles—evidently quite nearsighted, had a longish, auburn beard—and, notwithstanding his quiet and gentlemanly demeanor on the platform, how very fast he could talk and how large was the quantity of verbal substance he could pack into a few sentences! He was Judge Simeon E. Baldwin of the Supreme Court of the State of Connecticut. . . .

With the advent of good spring weather I often saw this latest addition to my Yale Law School professorial acquaintances coursing up and down Elm Street on his bicycle, his longish beard cleaving the breeze and his long coat-tails flying to the wind.[26]

In addition to his teaching Baldwin had since 1874 served as treasurer of the Law School. This duty he fulfilled until 1910, when the finances of the university and of the law school were merged.[27]

This period witnessed a remarkable transformation of the Yale Law School. The nineteenth century semi-proprietary status of the school was abandoned, and its budget became an integral part of the university budget. The school moved far in the direction of a postgraduate institution during these years.[28] Resources were expanded many fold. The school's progress can be measured by a variety of criteria—strength of faculty, physical plant, admission policies, and monetary resources.

The Law School faculty at the beginning of this period was composed principally of part-time instructors. In 1895 Professor William C. Robinson wrote to Baldwin that the time had come, he believed, when the faculty should be composed of permanent, full-time professors. Far too many of the teaching staff at that time had something other than the Law School as their chief interest. In the past the professors had been recruited almost exclusively from Connecticut lawyers, pleasant fellows, alumni, or those willing to come cheaply. Such appointees had been acceptable when the Law School was poor and weak, but now it should aim for men who had made their marks as professors of law. The school now could and should command the best talent in the country.[29] By the end of the period Robinson's hopes had been realized, and the dean's report for 1911–12 indicated that instruction was almost solely in the hands of full-time faculty members.

Likewise the physical plant was being improved and expanded. The Law School had been housed in the county courthouse from 1872 to 1895 and in the latter year moved to the newly completed rear section of Hendrie Hall. As his crowning achievement of three decades as dean, Francis Wayland singlehandedly raised the money for the front portion of the building shortly before his retirement.[30] The dedication of Hendrie Hall was combined with the celebration on February 4, 1901, of the one hundredth anniversary of John Marshall's inauguration as Chief Justice of the United States. Both events were commemorated by a series of addresses, one of which was by Simeon Baldwin.[31]

Dean Wayland's resignation became effective in 1903, and he was succeeded by Henry Wade Rogers, whose selection had been urged by Simeon Baldwin. Baldwin and Rogers had become well acquainted while they served together in the section on Legal Education of the American Bar Association. Rogers had previously been professor and dean of the Law School of the University of Michigan and President of Northwestern University.

In his annual report for 1911–12 Rogers listed the major changes in the Law School since 1900. In addition to instruction having passed almost completely from part-time to full-time professors, a bachelor's degree was required for admission except for Yale students. Another significant innovation was the substitution of the case system for the lecture-textbook method.

With the first of these policies Baldwin was in complete accord. The second he came to regard as a doubtful improvement since it lengthened the time required to complete a legal education. Toward the third he was entirely out of sympathy and repeatedly expressed his opposition to the policy in his writings.[32] When the faculty voted in 1912 to allow an instructor to use the case system if he so desired, Baldwin suffered the severest defeat of all the years he had been associated with the Law School.[33] Yet he accepted the decision and continued his loyal and generous support of the school. Indeed, as Professor George D. Watrous said, the school was closer to Baldwin's heart than any other institution with which he was connected.[34]

Another significant change in the first decade of the twentieth century was the permitting of Yale students to apply some credits towards both an A.B. and an LL.B. Several years before Baldwin had urged Chauncey M. Depew, then a member of the Yale Corporation, to support his plan for combining the senior year of college and the first year of professional school, a step which Harvard and Columbia had already taken. Baldwin deplored that boys had to spend so much time in preparation for their careers that they were nearly thirty or older before they could marry.[35] Depew agreed with Baldwin and promised to do all he could to bring about this much-needed reform at Yale.[36]

Impetus was given to the movement for closer relations between the Law School and the college by the annual exodus of graduates of Yale to Harvard Law School. Seeking to halt this drain the faculty recommended that Yale seniors be allowed to take some law work which would count both towards an A.B. and an LL.B. Baldwin warmly supported this move and served on the committee which in 1900 reported in favor of allowing seniors to take five hours in the Law School with dual credit. This was approved and in 1903 increased to six hours.[37] Partly due to pressure applied by Dean Rogers and Baldwin upon the prudential committee of the corporation, the dominant undergraduate college made further concessions. Beginning in 1904 juniors and seniors were permitted to take as much as fourteen hours of law work and to receive credit for it towards both an A.B. and an LL.B. Still more steps in this direction were taken in later years, and the Law School secured increasing control over the law offerings in the College.[38] The net effect of these changes was that students were able to complete the work for both degrees in six instead of seven years.

In emphasizing the need for reducing the amount of time necessary to complete a professional education, Baldwin did not intend to minimize the importance of a liberal arts background, especially for the law. In reply to a request from the chairman of the American Bar Association's Committee on Legal Education and Admission to the Bar,[39] Baldwin recommended mathematics, English composition and literature, history (especially English and American), Latin, French and German, logic, rhetoric, political economy, and physics as the subjects most helpful to a student intending to be a lawyer. To require an A.B. for admission to law school, however, he thought undesirable, for some students could get their preparation in high school, while others would need considerably more formal instruction. Stressing the desirability of a background based on the liberal arts, he said:

The lawyer who has an education in law and nothing else is a dangerous man in the community. He will be one-sided. He will lack real comprehension of the science he professes. He will not see things in their right relations, nor weigh things in their due proportion.[40]

A substantial portion of the Yale Law School's ultimate financial strength came from gifts made by Simeon E. Baldwin, some of them during these years. His professional salary was always a nominal one, and his benefactions to the Law School far exceeded his remuneration for teaching. In 1896 Baldwin presented anonymously to the school one hundred and twenty-six shares of New York and New England Railroad preferred stock with a par value of $12,600 [41] to be used as an endowment.[42] President Timothy Dwight in thanking him for this gift said:

May I be allowed also, as one of the brotherhood of Yale men and one who has long lived in and for the University, to bear testimony to you of my estimate of the generous service which you and your colleagues have rendered to the Law School during these many years, and of the satisfaction and pleasure which the remarkable success of the School has given to me, as it must have given to all true lovers of our Alma Mater.[43]

In 1909 Baldwin gave the Law School securities valued at $112,626 with the condition that he was to receive the income during his lifetime. After his death the fund was to form the endowment of a law professorship.[44]

All his life Baldwin gave generously of his time, energy and financial resources. The tradition in which he was reared demanded hard work, unostentatious living, thriftiness, charity, and adherence to the Golden Rule. From earliest manhood Baldwin practiced these precepts.

Yale did not audibly admit it had been listening to the rumblings of discontent,[45] but when President Timothy Dwight announced in 1898 that he would resign the next year, Yale was about to lose its last clergyman president. Word drifted about that his successor would be a layman, and there was much speculation as to the choice.[46]

One of the potential candidates was Judge Simeon E. Baldwin. Several admirers and former students wrote to him expressing their hope that he would be the next president and offering their support. Some wrote to the newspapers urging his selection. One such letter, dated March 18, 1899, and published probably in the Springfield (Massachusetts) *Republican*, said this in advancing Baldwin's candidacy:

To the Editor of the *Republican:*

. . . . Mr. Baldwin is in a direct unbroken line of distinguished ancestry of New Haven, who have honored the college, the city, state and nation by distinguished service. He is a graduate of the college, long one of its able professors in the law department, judge of the highest court of the state, a man of broad culture, a sound theologian, whose opinions are quoted on denominational controversies as the end of the law and the end of controversial discussions, an able jurist on all questions of national and international matters, the prime mover in and the one who arranged the transition of the college to the university, and one who has ever had, and now has, a keen, lively interest in the life and prosperity of the university. Mr. Baldwin was long a practitioner at the bar, a successful business man, and his efforts in a financial way would undoubtedly lead up to a conspicuous revelation in financial matters for the university. He is a man of classical attainments, and possesses more requisite points for the presidency of the university than any other name yet suggested. He has a clean record, is of undoubted capacity, of pre-eminent fitness in qualification for the office, with legal acumen to look out for the financial interest of the great university.

L. E. M.

Writing to his sister early in 1899, Baldwin took note of the rumors of his becoming President of Yale:

As to the College Presidency, I have told two or three who have come to talk to me about it, that I didn't know what I would say, if it were offered me, further than this:—that I should give the offer very careful consideration. As you know, I find my present position a very pleasant one, and all the duties are agreeable to me. To be at the head of a great University would present greater opportunities, particularly to one who has felt restless under the binding sway of old traditions at Yale, which have no part or lot in the twentieth century. It would also bring greater risks and probably greater cares.[47]

It is doubtful that Baldwin was considered seriously for the position. His most obvious drawback was his age, which was fifty-nine on February 5, 1899. Another liability was his active share in the movement to wrest control of the Yale Corporation from the ministers. This unquestionably lost him friends in that body. At all events the position went to a younger man, the able and brilliant Professor Arthur T. Hadley.

In June, 1908, Baldwin reminded President Hadley that he was sixty-eight, the mandatory retirement age for professors. Hadley asked him to continue his teaching, however, saying that the rule applied only to full-time faculty members.

I see that if we followed the letter of the rule your services would be lost to us—which in the opinion of all who know anything about it would be a great and irreparable misfortune to the School.[48]

At President Hadley's request Baldwin postponed his retirement for another decade. He conducted a course even during the crowded years when he occupied the governor's chair. Finally in June, 1919, following his seventy-ninth birthday, he dismissed his last class.

III

Much of the time released by Simeon E. Baldwin's withdrawal from private legal practice and politics in 1893 was devoted to a variety of national and international professional and scholarly societies. Chief among these were the American Bar Association, the American Social Science Association, the American Historical Association, the International Law Association, the American Political Science Association, and the Association of American Law Schools. Between 1890 and 1910 he was president of every one of these organizations, an accomplishment few, if any, of his contemporaries achieved.

Baldwin's first honor of this sort had come in 1891, when he became head of the American Bar Association. As founder and past president of the latter, he was frequently invited to address the annual conventions of state bar associations. In June, 1897, he journeyed south to Warm Springs to deliver the principal speech before the Georgia Bar Association.[49] This was one of Baldwin's great addresses. Entitled "Absolute Power, an American Institution," he analyzed skillfully the tremendous authority of the American president. This speech reflected Baldwin's growing interest in political science and won him the plaudits of Albert Bushnell Hart, professor of government at Harvard:

It puts into concrete form a conviction which has long been forming itself in my mind that the salvation and only safeguard of great democracies is in the entrusting of large powers to individuals. To give power and in the same breath to take it away is to leave civilization powerless. Responsible leadership is the only way out of our present ills; and that includes the right to choose inferior leaders and to make mistakes. Your address is one of the healthful lookings in the face of our difficulties; it goes past the form and into the substance of political power.[50]

So well accepted was this speech that Baldwin recast it and delivered it as the annual address of the American Social Science Association late that summer at Saratoga.[51]

At this session of the Association Baldwin was elected to the presidency. The American Social Science Association, founded in the 1860s, had met annually at Saratoga Springs and provided a common meeting ground for members of various fields of the social sciences—law, history, and political science among them. One by one these subjects founded their own national professional societies, and the older organization was faced with a dwindling membership. In the late nineties, to remedy this situation, Baldwin assisted in formulating plans to revivify the Association by the addition of sections of arts and letters.[52]

At the 1897 meeting of the American Bar Association in Cleveland,[53] Baldwin was influential in persuading the group to invite the International Law Association to convene jointly with them in America the next year.[54] The latter organization accepted the invitation, and Baldwin began at once to correspond with its London headquarters to complete arrangements for the convention. Originally scheduled for 1898, the joint meetings took place the following year at Buffalo. When, in August of 1899, the two associations convened, Simeon E. Baldwin was the official link between them. He was then vice-president for the United States of the International Law Association, and later in the year he was named its president.[55]

At Saratoga soon afterwards Baldwin, retiring from his second year as president, delivered a major address before the American Social Science Association. He spoke on "The Natural Right to a Natural Death," [56] which was one of his most widely acclaimed and most controversial addresses. In it Baldwin advocated the passage of laws prohibiting physicians from prolonging the lives of persons mortally ill.

In December of 1898 the American Historical Association met in New Haven, and Baldwin, who had become a recognized authority in the field of constitutional law, spoke on that aspect of America's acquiring the Philippines. In the address Baldwin referred to the constitutional difficulties in the way of permanent control,[57] mentioning, for example, the necessity of guaranteeing the Philippines trial by jury and the practical impossibility of so doing.[58] In the discussion which followed, Professor Albert Bushnell Hart, the Harvard government professor, and James Schouler, one of the distinguished historians of the day, opposed Baldwin's legalistic argument, pointing out that the scholars sat and talked while events marched on. The Louisiana Purchase, they contended, was precedent enough for the acquisition of the Philippines. The newspapers reported that the audience was with Hart and Schouler.[59] Nevertheless, Senator O. H. Platt, one of the foreign affairs chiefs in the United States Senate, was sufficiently interested in Baldwin's point of view to request a copy of his paper.[60]

Baldwin went abroad in 1900 to attend a number of conferences, and from his letters he apparently enjoyed his trip more than any previous one. The bench and bar of England had invited representatives of the legal profession in the United States to a grand banquet in the Middle Temple on July 27, and Baldwin was to be a guest.[61] As President of the International Law Association he was to preside at the annual meeting to be held at Rouen, France. He also planned to attend the sessions of the Congrès de Droit Comparée [62] and the meetings of the Association Permanente du Congrès Scientifique Universel des Institutions de Prévoyance,[63] both of which were to meet in Paris.

Crossing the Atlantic in July the first event was the great banquet at the Middle Temple. Baldwin's thorough enjoyment of the evening was evident from his description of it to Miss Winchester:

I got my speech typewritten also, and well in my head, and had five minutes to spare after that before I drove over to Middle Temple all arrayed in a fashionable London style of dress suit and high collar. They had seated me at the left of the Lord Chancellor, his right being given to our ambassador. The hall was filled with some 200 lawyers, comprising most of the leading judges and barristers of England, and . . . forty Americans, two of them United States Senators—Depew and Wetmore. I had a good deal of pleasant chat with my neighbors, Lord Justice Smith being on my left—a very agreeable man, as was the Chancellor. . . . Choate spoke first: then Lord Halsbury, and then I. What I said was well received. I gave about what I had intended to say, but forgot some things and put in others which occurred as I went along. One of the English barristers afterwards told me that he was told by a Boston lawyer or law publisher (I didn't understand which) that he put me among the list of four out of which to name the first lawyers in the United States. The speaking kept up till near midnight, and at nine this morning I was in the Calais train.[64]

Baldwin was not without his share of human weaknesses as this touch of vanity indicates!

At the annual meeting of the International Law Association at Rouen Baldwin as president was wined and dined even more than in London. Describing one day's proceedings at the conference he said:

Day before yesterday I began the day's work by presiding at a meeting of the executive council at half past nine at the Palais des Consuls. At ten I opened the meeting of the association. At half past twelve I lunched with one of our Vice Presidents, M. Marais, a very able lawyer of Rouen with a son of Roger's age, also a lawyer. At three I was at a garden party at a villa three miles from town. . . . At seven I was dining with the Prefect of the Department, and at half past nine attending a grand reception and garden party at the prefecture. It is all very fine, but hard on the eyes and does not have much of real vacation in it.[65]

After a brief stay in Paris, where he attended other conventions, Baldwin spent a week resting and sightseeing in Normandy and Brittany.[66]

In August of 1901 Baldwin traveled to Denver for the meetings of the American Association for the Advancement of Science, the American Bar Association, and the second annual meeting of the Association of American Law Schools. While there he was elected a fellow of the American Association for the Advancement of Science and three years later became one of its vice-presidents.[67]

Baldwin was also appointed at this time to the executive committee of the Association of American Law Schools. This organization developed from an invitation for a meeting authorized in 1899 [68] by the section on legal education of the American Bar Association to the law schools of the country. Their representatives met in August, 1900, and organized the Association of American Law Schools. In 1902 Simeon Baldwin was chosen president of the new organization.[69]

As his presidential address before the Association of American Law Schools in August, 1903, Baldwin spoke on "The Study of Elementary Law, the Proper Beginning of a Legal Education." In this talk, published in the *Yale Law Journal*, he protested strongly against the exclusive use of the case system in law school instruction.[70] Writing shortly thereafter to a man who had sympathized with his point of view, Baldwin said:

It seemed to me time to speak out, in regard to this fad of exclusive case instruction. A young Harvard Law School graduate was arguing before me the other day that an abutter on a highway who was building on his lot had the right to block up the entire street with his materials, as long as he might find it necessary for his purposes. I asked him if this could be done to the exclusion of the public right of travel during the time. He said it could be for he had found no authority to the contrary. This kind of clinging to authority and decided cases, makes a man after a while almost incapable of reasoning with his eyes open to the actual world about him.[71]

In January, 1903, Baldwin was consulted regarding the establishment of a national political science association. Professor J. W. Jenks of Cornell asked him to serve on a committee to discuss the need of founding such an organization.[72] In May Professor W. W. Willoughby of Johns Hopkins pressed Baldwin further on the matter, and he replied that the best course in his opinion would be to graft the proposed society onto the American Social Science Association, at least at the beginning.[73] An independent American Political Science Association was organized, however, by the spring of 1904. Simeon E. Baldwin was one of its two vice-presidents and six years later became president.[74]

Interested in international affairs during all of these years, Baldwin played a prominent role in a gathering of lawyers from many nations held in conjunction with the St. Louis Exposition in 1904. This Universal Congress of Lawyers and Jurists was sponsored jointly by the Louisiana Purchase Exposition Company and by the American Bar Association, and Baldwin was named by President Roosevelt as one of the American delegates.[75] As a member of the planning committee he went to St. Louis in December, 1903, to formulate rules and a program for the meetings.[76]

At the sessions of the Universal Congress in September Baldwin gave one of the key addresses. The long series of dinners was a bit wearisome, he wrote, but he was gratified that everything went off so well. Thirteen nations were represented, and Baldwin felt amply repaid for his long stretch of committee work in preparation for the sessions. He believed many American lawyers received a new notion of what Europe had been doing in recent years to advance private international law.[77]

In recognition of his scholarly writings on early America, the American Historical Association elected Baldwin president in 1905. At the annual meeting in December, 1906, he delivered his presidential address, "Religion Still the Key to History," [78] a persuasive plea for the recognition by historians of the great role religion had played in the life of man.

Another phase of the work of the American Historical Association with which Baldwin was associated was the publication of an annual bibliography of American history entitled *Writings on American History*. This undertaking was commenced early in the twentieth century, and its cost was guaranteed by ten historical societies and six individuals, including Simeon E. Baldwin. Each of these agreed to give a sum each year for five years, after which it was hoped the venture would be self-sustaining.[79]

During the summer of 1908 Baldwin traveled to the West Coast for the meetings of the American Bar Association in Seattle. There he made his first annual address as director of the Comparative Law Bureau of the Association. This phase of Baldwin's Bar Association activities developed from a committee on comparative law which the 1906 meeting of the American Bar Association had authorized.[80] The committee's purpose was to survey the laws enacted in all nations and to report annually on the significant developments in world legislation. Such information would then be conveniently available to American lawyers. When the committee organized the Bureau of Comparative Law a year later, Simeon E. Baldwin was unanimously elected its director.[81] He retained this position until 1919,[82] delivering a survey of world legislation before the meeting of the American Bar Association annually for twelve years. Few men of his time had the knowledge of legislation throughout the world that Baldwin commanded during the early twentieth century.

This study of comparative law coincided with and complemented Baldwin's growing interest in international relations generally, a subject on which he wrote extensively. Throughout his life he steadily widened his horizons. In his early years his interests were principally local and state-wide with an occasional sally at something larger. Especially after 1893, national and international concerns came increasingly to dominate his thoughts and actions and local and state problems to assume a lesser place.

IV

As a responsible citizen Simeon E. Baldwin took an active part in affairs of a civic and public nature, both local and national, and frequently expressed himself on important questions of the times. He participated in the activities of many groups, both private and public, which in some way promised to produce a better community, nation or world. A substantial portion of Baldwin's energy and time was devoted to this type of activity. Variety is perhaps the only term which adequately describes these interests, which included penology, international arbitration, religion, and current political and economic affairs.

Penological problems probably attracted Baldwin's attention through the necessity of passing sentence upon convicted persons. As early as 1885, however, as chairman of the Committee of Jurisprudence and Law Reform of the American Bar Association, he had written a report on methods of punishing habitual criminals.[83] In 1897, he endorsed the principle of parole.[84] Two years later he advocated the use of the lash in minor crimes and for first offenders. Baldwin believed this form of punishment would have spared many boys and young men a life of crime if the law had permitted its use for early offences. The lash should be applied in private and in moderation.[85] Later in the year Baldwin elaborated on these remarks and went as far as to advocate castration as the punishment for rape.[86]

In 1900 the desirability of indeterminate sentences was being discussed in penological circles. This was a plan for making terms of imprisonment sufficiently flexible so that they could be adjusted to mitigating circumstances and the behavior of the prisoner. Baldwin disapproved of this proposal, however, believing that the judge was the man most capable of determining sentences.

Nor did he take an optimistic view of reformatories. The experience of Connecticut's reformatory, he affirmed, had convinced him that the state could not remake bad boys, much less grown men. Baldwin favored a free use of suspended sentences for young offenders with personal supervision by a probation officer.[87]

Appointed by the Department of State as a delegate to the Seventh International Prison Congress, Baldwin went to Budapest in September, 1905.[88] There he spoke on the question "By What Principles and in What Manner May Convicts be Given Work in the Open Air?" Since most prisoners were unskilled, Baldwin suggested that governments buy up vast tracts of poor, idle or wild land and send its convicts there to work with shovel and pickaxe, draining and irrigating. The expense of acquiring the land would be great, but the state would be able to sell it ultimately at a profit. The example of North Carolina, where such a plan was in successful operation, was cited. Where road work or other employment placing the prisoners in close contact with the public was unavoidable, Baldwin suggested allowing the better type of criminals to wear masks, dependent on their continued good behavior. Men who had lost their right to citizenship should be shackled with ball and chain and returned to their prison cells each night.[89]

Baldwin was charmed by Budapest, finding it rivaling Prague in the magnificence of its riverside terraces and buildings. He proceeded from Hungary back through Germany to Hamburg, where in mid-September he attended the sessions of the Union Internationale de Droit Penal.[90]

International arbitration first became of serious, overt concern to Simeon Baldwin in 1896. At that time a treaty on the subject was pending in the Senate, and Baldwin wrote to the Chief Justice of the Rhode Island Supreme Court to enlist the support of the judges of that state for its ratification.[91] Shortly thereafter he spoke at Yale on the practicability of a permanent court of arbitration.[92] In April of 1896 Baldwin attended a conference in Washington on international arbitration and was chosen a member of the permanent committee.[93] He also wrote an article for the *Independent* entitled "Advantages of a Permanent System of Arbitration," [94] in which he appealed urgently for the establishment of an arbitral body to settle disputes between the United States and Great Britain.

Three years later Baldwin signed a petition urging ratification of the Hague Convention, which was pending in the Senate.[95] With the adherence of most of the nations of the world, including the United States, to the Hague Convention, the organization for international arbitration which Baldwin had advocated some years previously became a reality in the Hague Tribunal.

After several years' lapse Baldwin's active participation in the international arbitration movement was revived by Professor John Bassett Moore in 1903. The latter requested Baldwin's endorsement of a call for a meeting to consider again an arbitration treaty between the United States and Great Britain. To this Baldwin consented. The draft of the call traced the history of the arbitration movement in America. As a consequence of the large conference which met at Washington in 1896, an agreement for the adjustment of all disputes between Great Britain and the United States had been reached. The Senate, however, failed to ratify it by a small margin. Meanwhile, most of the outstanding Anglo-American problems had been disposed of through traditional diplomatic means, and the time seemed opportune for a United States–British treaty requiring compulsory resort to the Hague Tribunal in certain cases. The National Arbitration Conference, as the projected meeting was named, was scheduled for January, 1904, to draft such a proposal.[96]

Early in 1905 the efforts of the National Arbitration Conference to secure a treaty between Britain and the United States came to a halt. The Senate refused to ratify the recommended treaty, and an amended version was unsatisfactory to both the President and the Secretary of State.[97]

All his life Baldwin maintained a lively interest in religious questions. During this period he strove for better relations between Protestants and Catholics, furthered the cause of religious unity among Protestant denominations, criticized tendencies in modern Congregationalism, and attempted to counter the skeptical bent of young people.

Regarding the relations between Protestant and Catholic churches, Baldwin expressed himself in the fall of 1894, when he and Professor William C. Robinson of the Law School participated in a symposium on the subject. Baldwin's remarks revealed that his cordiality towards the Roman Church was based on considerations which stemmed from his fundamentally conservative nature.

> The great danger to republican government in America now comes from two sources—the spread of anarchy and the incorporation into our society of masses of new-come foreigners, unfamiliar with our institutions and ignorant of the necessary limits of liberty. Against both these forces the Roman Catholics are our best allies. It is full time for Christian men to pull together in warfare with the bad in the world.[98]

A move towards the unification of certain Protestant denominations was made in 1906 and 1907. The Congregational, the United Brethren, and the Methodist Protestant churches held a series of meetings at which a basis for union was sought. Among the many problems the churches discussed was the disposal of the vested interests of the various bodies—their publishing societies and other denominational property. Simeon Baldwin, representing the Congregational Church, served on the Committee on Vested Interests. In February, 1907, he summarized the bases for union and the obstacles hindering it in a letter to President Alfred T. Perry of Marietta College:

> The greatest obstacle to consolidation is the fact that the Congregationalists have no official creed and do not want one, even for ministers.
>
> In the two other denominations much property is held on a tenure that might be jeopardized, should they become merged in a new denomination, having no creed.
>
> It was this more than anything else that led me to suggest the plan adopted by the committee on Vested Interests [namely, that each of the three churches retain the legal form of the church corporations, but practically merge their activities.] That does *not* contemplate an immediate consolidation into one new denomination. It does contemplate a partnership which could gradually move closer to a com-

> pleter union by a gradual process of assimilation by acquaintance and contact with community of aims and identity of spirit.
>
> In summary, to demand a common creed is to wreck the proposed union. To demand the surrender of existing creeds of the United Brethren and Methodist Protestant Churches would be to ask the impossible as things stand now. Hence, a confederated alliance working towards a future consolidation is all that seems feasible.[99]

The three groups met in Chicago in March, 1907, and agreed upon an act of union substantially the same as Baldwin presented.[100] The agreements were never ratified by the denominations, however, and each continued its separate existence.

Another prominent theme in Baldwin's religious thought was his opposition to the denominational narrowness of the Congregationalism of his day. This tendency, he believed, was driving many members of that church into Episcopalianism on the one side or agnosticism on the other. He deplored the rigidity and intolerance of many of the Congregational ministers and periodicals in insisting on old theories and creeds which were neither vital nor infallible. Baldwin said that he shuddered at the hypocrisy to be found in many Congregational pulpits.[101] One of his concrete proposals was that the severe creed for admission to church membership be relaxed. After several years of agitation within his own church, a committee on which Baldwin served was organized to study the matter. This group recommended that the only qualifications for membership should be love of Christ and a sincere desire to follow him by building up his kingdom on earth.[102]

One of Baldwin's attempts to stem the tide towards religious skepticism and disbelief among young people was his address at the Boston University commencement in June, 1902.[103] Referring to the division of opinion among Christian groups and between Christians and non-believers Baldwin maintained that:

> Education cannot be disregardful of this conflict of opinion. She must meet it in a spirit of tolerance. She must meet it as she has met every other great change of public opinion on lesser points. Her first lesson is that change may be improvement, and that without change

there can be no improvement. Her first rule is to shape her teaching by her present lights.

Put belief in God on the basis of probability, and it stands fast. Demand for it the basis of certainty, and you take the place which the agnostic occupies—a place to accept which is to deny the fundamental laws of human conduct. . . . If the young men and young women whom our universities send forth this month to take up the burden of the world, are in duty bound to set themselves against agnosticism, no less are they against a more insidious, because less repulsive, foe. It is indifferentism. Here again it is a fallacy to say that you will let the unsolved problems of the world pass by untouched because you cannot be certain how they should be met. Ask on which side probably lies the truth, and choose it for yours.[104]

Although Simeon E. Baldwin was generally conservative on political and economic questions, he gave liberal advice to Democratic Congressman James P. Pigott in 1894, when the latter asked Baldwin's views on some of the measures coming before the new Congress. The judge urged him to vote for the Wilson (low) tariff. "Its good effects will be felt by the community at large, and their [the people's] only organization for political effect is the House of Representatives." [105] He also suggested that Pigott vote for the income tax bill if it was reported favorably.

I believe the latter is one of the fairest of measures that can be devised, to fill up the treasury, without burdening the people at large. Its inquisitorial features are not much worse than those of our town tax list system, and it throws its burden on those who can bear it best.[106]

On this question Baldwin was reversing the opinion he had expressed three years previously. By 1912 he was again opposing the institution of a federal income tax because it would increase federal interference in state finances.[107]

Much of Baldwin's energy and time was devoted to such diverse causes, and he wielded considerable influence in molding policies and public opinion in some of these areas.

V

Simeon E. Baldwin's writings during his period on the Supreme Court revealed several new tendencies. As compared with the years before 1893, Baldwin's literary output was considerably greater. For the first time he was able to produce more extensive treatments than articles: three books written entirely by him appeared during these years; another was edited and written in part by him; and finally he edited a volume of law cases.

This period was also marked by some significant changes in the subjects in which Baldwin evinced interest. There was a decided increase in his writings on international affairs and international law. Two other fields which engaged Baldwin's literary efforts during these years were constitutional questions and penological problems. In all of these areas Baldwin's interest, discernible before 1893, now burgeoned forth into pronounced activity.

In addition to these large, new spheres of interest, Baldwin continued to make contributions to fields in which he had formerly written—history, government, many phases of law, legal education, and religion. His writings dealing with local civic and political affairs, however, completely disappeared, in part a reflection of his shifting interests away from local and state affairs and toward national and international concerns. The account of Baldwin's writings which follows attempts to consider some specific examples from each of the principal fields to which Baldwin contributed.

The first of Baldwin's volumes, entitled *Illustrative Cases on Railroad Law*, appeared in the fall of 1896. This collection of cases was designed to be used in courses in railroad law such as Baldwin had been teaching at Yale. His long experience as an attorney for railroads as well as his many years as a teacher of railroad law eminently qualified Baldwin to prepare this volume.

Two years later a second volume, entitled *Modern Political Institutions*, was published. Baldwin revised and brought together several essays on numerous aspects of modern government which he had delivered as addresses over many years. Taken together they represented some of Baldwin's most mature thinking in the fields of political theory and practical politics.

The collection was exceptionally well received. Oliver Wendell Holmes wrote:

> I have read your book through and every word of it has interested and pleased me. I found myself constantly admiring the ability learning and industry which it shows in such high degree. . . .[108]

Professor Jeremiah W. Jenks, reviewing the work in the *American Historical Review*,[109] stated that the most suggestive chapter was "Absolute Power: an American Institution." In it Baldwin showed that the President of the United States held a position which in emergencies gave him near-dictatorial power. Summarizing the essay, Jenks said:

> This is, perhaps, the ablest brief study that has yet been made of the gradual development of the presidency. . . .
>
> All the essays show the wide reading, the keenness of insight into customs and institutions, and the judicial temper of the author.[110]

In 1901 Yale University celebrated its 200th birthday, and as part of the commemorative activities, a series of bicentennial publications were issued by various departments of the university. The faculty of the Law School contributed a volume entitled *Two Centuries' Growth of American Law, 1701–1901*, which Simeon Baldwin edited.[111] Baldwin and Professor William K. Townsend each wrote four chapters, another contributor prepared two, and eight others, one apiece. Inevitably the chapters were of uneven quality, but the London *Times* had no hesitation in calling the contributions of Simeon Baldwin the finest in the volume.[112] Besides the introduction Baldwin wrote the chapters on "Constitutional Law," "Private Corporations," and "Pleading in Civil Actions."

In June, 1904, Baldwin's *American Railroad Law* appeared. This textbook was well received. The review in the *American Lawyer* said that the skillful arrangement of the material set forth in the volume revealed the thorough grasp of the subject which Baldwin possessed. The work contained a compact statement of railroad law as established in the United States. The citation of current cases assured the up-to-dateness of the volume.[113] The General Counsel for Michigan of the Wabash Railroad wrote Baldwin:

It is unrivalled in its brevity and clearness of statements of doctrine, and not overloaded with citations to support them. . . . Moreover, it is a *live* book! One sees in an instant, that the author is not a closet-thinker, but one who has been "through the mill" he describes.[114]

In June of 1905 Baldwin's *The American Judiciary* appeared. One of a series on aspects of American government, the volume was a concise account of the role and the functioning of the American judiciary. Divided into two main sections, the first was a treatise on the nature and scope of the judicial power in the United States; and the second described the organization and practical operation of American courts. Although reasonably well received,[115] some of Baldwin's reviewers criticized the work for its inaccuracies and its over-brief treatments of some aspects of the subject. One generally favorable review said of the final chapter, which was entitled "The Attitude of the People Toward the Judiciary":

It is our belief that this scrappy chapter is a lamentably poor ending to a worthy treatment, in brief, of the general subject. The author not only furnishes little material of value, but seems to have slight grasp of the opinion of the bulk of the people concerning the judiciary.[116]

In the field of international relations Baldwin emerged as one of America's prime authorities during the 1890s and the first decade of the twentieth century. His writings in this area were perhaps more numerous than in any other except law, and they were frequently praised by other leaders in the field.

Baldwin was especially interested in the development of international law, and several articles treated of this subject. A few of the more important were: "The Part Taken by Courts of Justice in the Development of International Law," [117] Baldwin's address as president of the International Law Association in 1901; "The Beginnings of an Official European Code of

Private International Law," [118] described by John Bassett Moore, one of America's foremost authorities on the subject, as "a most interesting and instructive contribution to the knowledge of a subject concerning which there exists little general information"; [119] "The New Code of International Family Law"; [120] "The Hague Conference of 1904 for the Advancement of Private International Law"; [121] "The Comparative Results, in the Advancement of Private International Law, of the Montevideo Congress of 1888–9 and the Hague Conferences of 1893, 1894, 1900, and 1904"; [122] "Equality Between Nations and International Conventions, as Determining Factors in Shaping Modern International Law." [123]

Many other phases of international relations were also explored in Baldwin's writings. International arbitration was one of these, and Baldwin's interest in this area has been noted before.[124] In 1896 he published "Advantages of a Permanent System of Arbitration." [125] Some years later Baldwin wrote another article on this subject, "Why the Decisions of the Hague Tribunal Are and Will be Obeyed." [126]

Among Baldwin's other significant articles on varying aspects of international affairs should be listed "The Monroe Doctrine in 1896," [127] a review of the history of the policy and an affirmation that the United States in 1896 should emphasize its position as the natural guardian of republican institutions in both North and South America; "The Mission of Governor Taft to the Vatican," [128] in which Baldwin pointed out that the assignment was not a diplomatic one, as many Protestant leaders had alleged; [129] "The New 'Association Internationale des Avocats' "; [130] "Schooling Rights under Our Treaty with Japan"; [131] "The International Congresses and Conferences of the Last Century as Forces Working Toward the Solidarity of the World," [132] which included a list of the important international conferences since 1826; "The Hague Conference of 1907"; [133] and finally "The Eleventh Convention Proposed by the Hague Conference of 1907." [134]

For many years Baldwin had taught constitutional law at Yale, and in the period under review he wrote several significant articles in this field. The first of these was "The Responsibilities of the United States, Internationally, for Acts of the States," [135] an able discussion of one of the most perplexing problems of the American federal system. A similar account was published in a French periodical under the title "De la Responsibilité du Pouvoir Fédéral aux États-Unis au Cas où les États Particuliers s'Abstiennent de Réprimer les Délits Commis sur Leur Territoire." [136] Another of Baldwin's constitutional essays was inspired by the problems arising from the spectacular growth of the American empire following the war with Spain. In "The Constitutional Questions Incident to the Acquisition and Government by the United States of Island Territory," [137] he considered some of the difficulties which would arise in incorporating the former Spanish territories in the American constitutional framework. Another article on the same subject, "The Government of our New Territory," [138] pointed out some of the problems non-Anglo-Saxon possessions presented in establishing appropriate governments for them while at the same time abiding by the constitution. "The Italian Demand," [139] an editorial in the *Independent*, urged that the federal courts be given jurisdiction over prosecutions for all offenses by foreigners who were covered by treaties between their countries and the United States. "The Supreme Court and the Insular Cases" [140] recorded Baldwin's reaction to the somewhat contradictory decisions of the United States Supreme Court in several cases growing out of the relations between America's new island possessions and the mainland. A final essay in the field of constitutional problems was "The New Reading of Due Process of Law." [141] In this essay Baldwin pointed out the new interpretation American jurisprudence had recently placed upon the phrase "due process of law." Originally interpreted as guaranteeing a fair legal procedure, its meaning shifted until it became a substantive right. The government no longer could enact laws which were not reasonably consistent with the settled maxims of Anglo-American law as it pertained to the security of life, liberty, and property. The Fourteenth Amendment, meanwhile, protected individuals (and soon corporations) from loss of life's liberty or property at the hands of the states without due process of law. As a result of the reinterpretation of due process and the ratification of the Fourteenth Amendment, in no country were life, liberty, property, and free institutions so well secured to the individual citizen as in the United States. The power of the courts in America to reinterpret the written constitution made that document flexible and accommodating to changing conditions. It also immensely enhanced the authority and prestige of the judiciary. This address, published also in an amended form as "The Courts, as Conservators of Social Justice," [142] was one of Baldwin's most stimulating essays.

Simeon Baldwin's deep interest in criminology and penology has already been noted. Among his writings in these fields several from his period on the bench deserve mention. As one of the reports in reply to submitted questions prepared for the International Prison Commission held in Brussels in 1900, Baldwin contributed *Reparation for Crime*.[143] He pointed out that in the United States redress to the individual was achieved by a proceeding separate from that taken in criminal cases by the state. Unlike the latter, proceedings for individual reparations had to be instituted by the wronged person. The state had no part in it. The difference arose from the fact that in a civil action the plaintiff recovered damages by a bare preponderance of evidence, while in a criminal action he was considered innocent until proven guilty beyond any doubt. Baldwin believed the state should pay the cost of a damage suit or at least aid in securing appropriate pecuniary indemnity.

Baldwin's thought on punishment for crime was expressed in several articles. "Whipping and Castration as Punishments for Crime" [144] and "Corporal Punishments for Crime" [145] both appeared in 1899. Perhaps the best summary of Baldwin's views on this subject was contained in "Report on Prison Reform," which the Outlook Committee of the New Haven Congregational Club printed in 1900. This paper criticized reform schools, questioned the use of reformatories for adults, urged the flogging of juveniles and ruffians, favored life imprisonment in special institutions for petty incorrigibles, advocated the employment of misdemeanants on the public highways and elsewhere outside of jail, and advised the adoption of the probation system.[146] Two other contributions to this field were made in 1901: "Flog the Kidnappers" [147] and "The Restoration of Whipping as a Punishment for Crime." [148] Four years later Baldwin attended the Budapest meetings of the Seventh International Prison Congress and spoke on the topic "D'après Quels Principes Pourrait-on Autoriser et de Quelle Manière Pourrait-on Organiser l'Occupation des Condamnés aux Travaux des Champs ou à d'Autres Travaux d'Utilité Publique en Plein Air?" [149] An English version of this talk, "Outdoor Convict Labor," [150] appeared in 1906.

Baldwin's earlier interest in historical investigation continued during the years from 1893 to 1910. Although he published more in at least two fields, international and legal affairs, his output in history was substantial, and it was during this period that Baldwin became president of the American Historical Association. One of his finest articles in this category was "The Historic Policy of the United States as to Annexation." [151] In this scholarly treatment of the history of American policy towards acquiring new territories, Baldwin made a convincing case for annexation. By quoting extensively from well-selected source documents he dispelled the notion, held by some in the 1890s, that the founding fathers did not contemplate additions to American territory. Baldwin disagreed with those who held that the American form of government made no provision for a colonial system. He conceded, however, that it would be a very different one from that of European countries.

On April 9, 1894 Baldwin gave the first of a type of address which he was to repeat many times. This was a speech commemorating the birthday of the founding of a society in the community and was entitled *An Historical Address at the Celebration of the One Hundredth Anniversary of the Organization of the Chamber of Commerce of New Haven.*[152] In 1897 he wrote a "Historical Sketch of the Supreme Court of Errors of Connecticut" for Clark Bell's *The Supreme Court of the States and Provinces of North America.*[153] In 1907, when the Court was one hundred years old, Baldwin delivered an address on the history of the

Supreme Court of Errors of Connecticut.[154] In 1899 still another of the commemorative speeches appeared as "The First Century of the Connecticut Academy of Arts and Sciences." [155]

Turning once again to his favorite field of earlier years, Baldwin delved into American colonial history and brought forth several articles. Among these was "The American Jurisdiction of the Bishop of London in Colonial Times." [156] In this article Baldwin tried to show that the Bishop of London exercised something close to episcopal authority over the colonies. He followed this a year later with "The Authorship of the 'Quatre Lettres d'un Bourgeois de New-Heaven sur l'Unité de la Législation' Published in Mazzei's 'Recherches Historiques et Politiques sur les États-Unis de l'Amerique Septentrionale.' " [157] Perhaps the most substantial of Baldwin's colonial papers was his "American Business Corporations before 1789." [158] The product of much research, it was warmly praised by contemporary historians.[159] In it Baldwin listed only six corporations as existing during the colonial period and twenty more during the years of confederation. Corporations were feared at this time because they were frequently monopolies.

Three additional articles concluded Baldwin's contributions to colonial history: "The Secession of Springfield from Connecticut," [160] "Connecticut in Pennsylvania," [161] and "Theophilus Eaton, First Governor of the Colony of New Haven." [162]

Another of Baldwin's contributions to historical writing during these years was a series of biographical sketches. In 1902 he delivered a lecture entitled "Rev. John Higginson, of Salem" before the Massachusetts Historical Society.[163] Several years later he contributed the lives of Connecticut's foremost lawyers, Zephaniah Swift, James Gould, and Baldwin's father, Roger Sherman Baldwin, to William Draper Lewis' eight-volume *Great American Lawyers*, which was published in 1908. Baldwin also delivered an address on Roger Sherman, his great-grandfather, which was published in *Two Centuries of New Milford*.[164]

Two essays treating of the development of aspects of American government were among Baldwin's most significant contributions to political science during this period. One of these was the article on the unfolding of the authority of the American presidency, "Absolute Power, an American Institution." [165] Tracing admirably the growth of the powers of the chief executive during the nineteenth century, Baldwin compared the American president's authority to that of the Russian czar. He was glad the United States had a strong chief executive, believing that the nation's danger was not the tyranny of one man but either anarchy or the tyranny of the mob. Baldwin received letters of commendation on this essay from several prominent historians and political scientists, and when it appeared in his collection, *Modern Political Institutions*, it was acclaimed as one of his most penetrating and suggestive chapters.[166]

The second was entitled "The Narrowing Circle of Individual Rights." [167] In this essay Baldwin took note of the encroachments the legislation of the Progressive Era was making on the free institutions of America. No longer was the preservation of a strong and independent individualism the object of solicitude; rather it was the augmentation of the individual's dependence upon the state. Baldwin enumerated many areas in which social regulation had restricted individual freedom: the prohibition of the manufacture and sale of cigarettes and liquor in some states; compulsory education; the forbidding of marriage among the unfit; limitations of the freedom of contract of workers. Baldwin referred to the twentieth century as the age of collectivism. He pointed out that the spirit of altruism had brought these controls, that in many fields the state had forced more humane conditions. Worried lest such encroachments on liberty go too far, Baldwin believed that in spite of the narrowing circle of individual rights, there would always remain a core of inviolable liberties.

Baldwin's contributions to legal literature continued to be substantial throughout this period. Some of the titles will indicate the type of subjects on which he wrote: "The Duty of the State, in Suits Attacking Charitable Bequests"; [168] over one hundred definitions and explanations of terms of jurisprudence for Macmillan's *Dictionary of Philosophy and Psychology;* [169] "Japanese Courts," an editorial in the *Independent* [170] on Japanese criminal procedure; "The Natural Right to a Natural Death";[171] "The American System of Supreme Courts, and What It Accomplishes";[172] "The Significance of 'John Marshall Day' ";[173] "The Objects of Criminal Procedure as They Appear to a French Prosecuting Officer";[174] "Contemplated Changes in the General Incorporation Law of France";[175] "The French Jury System";[176] "Legal Ethics,"[177] an address before the Union University Law School; "The Ideals of the American Advocate—a Symposium";[178] "The History of the Common Law,"[179] one of the principal addresses in law delivered at the Congress of Arts and Sciences of the Louisiana Purchase Exposition; "Taxation by One State of Goods in Another";[180] "Federal Taxation of Interstate Commerce";[181] "Le Pouvoir Judiciare Américain Comparé au Pouvoir Judiciare Européan";[182] and "The Law of the Air Ship."[183]

During his years as a judge Simeon Baldwin maintained his active interest in legal education, as the titles of his articles in this field reveal: "Law School Libraries, and How to Use Them";[184] "The Re-adjustment of the Collegiate to the Professional Course,"[185] the annual address before the Legal Education Section of the American Bar Association in 1898, in which Baldwin pleaded for combining the fourth year of college with the first year of professional school; "Three Years Enough for a College Course";[186] "Teaching Law by Cases";[187] "The Encroachment of the American College upon the Field of the University";[188] "The Place of Law in the Studies of a University";[189] and "The Study of Elementary Law, the Proper Beginning of a Legal Education,"[190] Baldwin's presidential address before the Association of American Law Schools in 1903.

After noting the quantity and variety of Baldwin's literary output, its quality may be called into question. Baldwin maintained a high level of accuracy. His sound judgment was reflected in his writings. His style, though not remarkable, was lucid and readable. For one who wrote as much and on as many subjects as did Baldwin, his standards were exceptional. One can only wonder what he might have accomplished had he specialized more than he did. That he did not limit his scope may have cost him the enduring fame he seemed so to desire in his younger days. The broad span of his interests, on the other hand, unquestionably made him a more truly humane and liberally educated person. With the increasing realization that twentieth-century specialization has in many instances produced narrowness and provinciality of a kind, perhaps the breadth of learning typified by Baldwin may serve as a beacon to which the present age may look.

VI

To Simeon Baldwin as to all humankind life brought its moments of joy and of sorrow. Among the joyful occasions was the engagement in 1897 of his daughter, Helen, to Dr. Warren R. Gilman, a physician of Worcester, Massachusetts. Miss Winchester was anxious for her niece's happiness, and in July wrote a long letter to her brother-in-law on the subject. She pointed out that although Dr. Gilman had great promise for the future, his finances were limited now, and he could not afford an appropriate office. She suggested that Baldwin give his daughter sufficient funds to make it possible for them to wed. If Dr. Gilman were married and had a house with an office in it, his practice would, she believed, increase, particularly in view of his specialty, women's diseases.[191] Judge Baldwin heeded his sister-in-law's advice and provided generously for the couple.[192]

The marriage of Helen and Dr. Gilman took place on March 4, 1899. For months beforehand Miss Winchester had been making the arrangements for the great day. The task was complicated by the need for furnishing Helen's home in Worcester. When, on February 12, Baldwin gave a check to Miss Winchester for her birthday, he wrote on the envelope "With a little hope that you won't choose to send off the *whole* as far as Worcester." Typical of her love and generosity towards her niece was Miss Winchester's reply: "I did use it partly to pay for the piano and glad enough I was to do it." [193] Several months after the wedding Baldwin made his first visit to his daughter's home and wrote, "Helen's house is all my fancy painted it, and I passed my Sunday there very pleasantly." [194]

Baldwin's son during these years was engaged in his law practice. One of the cases which engrossed Roger concerned a will which the relatives of a deceased man wanted to break, claiming he was not sane when he wrote it. After a long and vigorous contest, Roger won this case in June, 1896.[195] In spite of the demands of his profession Roger found opportunities to travel and spent the summer of 1899 in Europe.[196]

Roger's health, which had failed him during his Law School years, had by 1902 again declined to such an extent that he had to close his law office and go to California in the hope that outdoor life would benefit him. For a time he worked on a ranch, and later he joined the forest rangers. Finding this occupation to his liking, Roger wrote to his father that he was considering a career in forestry.[197]

In 1906 Simeon Baldwin went to California to see his son. Roger's health had become considerably worse,[198] and his father persuaded him to come home.[199] Back in the East Roger tried various occupations, spending one summer farming [200] and another roughing it in the Canadian woods.[201] In spite of his efforts and those of his medical advisers, he remained unwell during all of this period.

Now that his children were grown, an increasing share of Simeon Baldwin's time was passed alone in the house on Wall Street. From his letters to his sister-in-law, Miss Charlotte Winchester, who, though continuing to reside with Baldwin, was frequently away, glimpses of his solitary but extremely busy life can be gleaned. In the summer of 1898, for example, although nearly sixty, Baldwin arose before six every morning and rode on his bicycle several miles to Fort Hale for a prebreakfast dip.[202]

In the summer of 1902 Baldwin described his peaceful life in these terms:

> Work mornings and a country ride on my wheel in the afternoon. I rarely meet any pleasure-going bicyclists now on the country roads.

Few seem to ride except on business errands. So goes fashion her way, and I mine.

Evenings I read Goethe's *Faust*, studying out each German line. . . . In the afternoon if I have a spare hour, I read Zola's *Travail*. . . . My book grows on me, [Baldwin was preparing a volume on railroad law] and I doubt if I finish it this year.[203]

As late as 1909 this pattern of living lingered. Throughout the summer of that year the Judge continued to work on his opinions mornings, rode his bicycle in the afternoons and read widely. His reading consisted of novels interspersed with a little of Bielschowsky's *Life of Goethe* and a play of Plautus.[204] His liberal education was thus continuing as he neared his seventieth birthday.

Although Baldwin kept busy constantly, he did not neglect his social life and frequently dined at the homes of his friends. He also belonged for many years to the Social Science Club of New Haven at which the various members presented book reviews. Another local institution in which Baldwin participated over a long period was The Club.[205] This was composed of intellectually inclined individuals and had met fortnightly since 1838 or 1839. After dining together at the home of the host, one member gave a brief talk which was followed by discussion. The meetings were confidential, and the members expressed themselves without reserve.

In turn, Baldwin did his share of entertaining. In May of 1897, for example, he gave a dinner in honor of one of his legal colleagues. He decidedly preferred male to mixed company at such affairs, as his account to Miss Winchester indicated:

Last night I gave a dinner to Mr. Sharp and a couple of law students, which passed off quite to my liking. The dinner was well served, and there were no games or other nonsense to keep the young men from becoming better acquainted with their elders, and hearing something to their advantage, nor to detain them after nine, at which hour one promptly expressed an intention to retire, which—no objection being interposed, and the host rising to assist his easy exit, was safely accomplished during the next half minute, the other being also swept out with him. Mr. Sharp stayed half an hour later, and made himself very agreeable.[206]

Regarding female society Baldwin could become good-naturedly sarcastic. When Miss Winchester was away visiting with her sister in the spring of 1898 he wrote:

Golf, driving, cards and chatter; golf, driving, cards and chatter; these, I suppose are the delights which you are now enjoying to the full. I hope you will bring home a great many new facts . . . from your piazza discourse with the leisured and pleasured classes, who don't know that the apostles were Jews.[207]

Baldwin's attitude towards the female sex was further delineated when the question of women voting in church affairs arose. He was doubtful whether they should participate in the balloting since their sex was not educated in business affairs. He feared they would be likely to vote a new organ and give little attention to the financing of it.[208]

Undoubtedly the deepest personal sorrow Simeon Baldwin suffered during this period was the death of his sister-in-law in August, 1904. Miss Winchester, while visiting at her sister's summer home, fell, and died within a few days.[209] For thirty years she had presided over the Baldwin household and had reared Roger and Helen with the love of a mother. The latter recalled many years later [210] the unfaltering patience and consideration Miss Winchester exhibited to her father, reading to him evenings when his eyes would not permit their being used and seeing that his home was comfortable and well-managed. In recording her death in the family Bible Baldwin noted: "So went out what had been the light of my home, since my wife's health failed in 1872."[211] Miss Winchester's untimely death left Baldwin alone as he had never been before.

At the time of this disaster Baldwin was sixty-four, and from then until near the end of his life he lived alone in his house on Wall Street. His outward life continued as usual—the round of attendance at court sessions, meetings of local boards, teaching at the Law School, trips to the annual meetings of his associations, speeches to give, and articles and books to write. But a sense of loneliness must have weighed heavily on the aging man after 1904.

GOVERNOR BALDWIN

I

At least as early as February, 1910, the month of his retirement from the Chief Justiceship, Simeon E. Baldwin was being mentioned as a possible Democratic nominee for governor in the fall. His brother, writing at this time, said that he feared that the rumor of his nomination was too optimistic to be well founded. He suspected that the Republican machine in Connecticut, which had been in power continuously since 1895, was too entrenched to be broken by outside influences and that the day had forever passed when the office sought the man rather than the man the office.[1]

After his retirement Baldwin had reopened his law office and was beginning to practice again. Meanwhile, during the early spring the Baldwin-for-governor drive increased in momentum. By April the movement had assumed such proportions that an upstate politician wrote offering to manage Baldwin's preconvention campaign.[2] The latter's reply indicated the political independence, the refusal to bargain for place, which had always characterized his father's political life. It may have indicated also a sense of assurance that the nomination could be secured if he desired it.

> Since I resigned the Presidency of the State Democratic Club, on my nomination to the bench in 1892, I have had no active connection with politics. I am not a candidate for any public office.
>
> Whether, if I should be offered the Democratic nomination for Governor, I should accept it, is a question which there is no occasion at present for me to consider. If such a nomination should come to me, it will come unsought.[3]

The political situation in Connecticut at that time was extremely favorable to the nomination of Baldwin. The Democratic party was bankrupt; it had not won the governorship since 1892. It was badly managed and had little or no organization.[4] The prestige of the position from which Baldwin had retired, plus the additional fame he had acquired as a Yale professor, prominent public speaker and president of half a dozen learned and professional societies made him probably the most eminent man in the state and easily the most outstanding in the Democratic party. The Chief Justice's rather frigid exterior and his long abstention from any association with the party organization perhaps caused the politicos to hesitate. But Baldwin's overwhelming pre-eminence and ability to draw the independent vote plus the lack of any other suitable candidate left the party chieftains little choice except to nominate him.

There was not much doubt that the prospect of becoming the state's chief executive was attractive to Simeon Baldwin, in spite of his sincere assertions that he would not make a contest for the nomination. During the summer of 1910 he announced that if nominated, he would accept. There was, however, apparently again talk of his being appointed to the United States Supreme Court, for the temporary chairman of the Democratic State Convention, John S. Seymour, after expressing delight at Baldwin's candidacy, asked what the party would do if the Chief Justice were on the Supreme Court of the United States by convention time.[5]

In response to Seymour's request for ideas as to the party platform, Baldwin wrote:

> I am inclined to think that a short creed is always the best in church and state.
>
> The chance of the Democratic party in Connecticut this year lies, it seems to me, in getting out all its own vote, and attracting disaffected and independent Republicans enough to tip the scale. Both these elements are in accord in holding that the present tariff is too high. I should say, emphasize that issue, and express disapproval of centralization of power at Washington. As to state politics both parties seem to profess to want a public utilities bill, and economy in administration. I think we should ask for a better Corrupt Practices Act.
>
> I am inclined at present to think that the income tax constitutional amendment is a centralizing measure, that would bear hardly on the states, particularly the small and rich ones like Connecticut.[6]

The state party conventions took place in September. When the Democrats gathered in New Haven, an air of excitement and expectation pervaded the assemblage. For the first time in a decade and a half the delegates believed their party had a fighting chance to win the governorship. To begin with, they were about to nominate a candidate for whom no apologies had to be made. Another factor favoring Democratic victory was the internal dissention within the Republican party. Finally, 1910 seemed to be ushering in a national swing to the Democratic party. A few days later, the people of Maine began this movement by electing a Democratic state administration.[7] After the November elections the governors of half the states were Democratic, and the national House of Representatives had also passed into the hands of that party.

Simeon E. Baldwin was nominated by his colleague, Dean Henry Wade Rogers, of the Yale Law School. Rogers was a vigorous speaker in the tradition of the great American orators of the nineteenth century. He made a stirring appeal to the delegates in his friend's behalf, and when at the close of his brilliant peroration, he presented the name of Simeon E. Baldwin, the convention erupted in a tumultuous babel of applause and shouting. The delegates were confident that a winner had just been named and were jubilant over the prospects. The only ripple of disapproval came from Mayor Willard C. Fisher of Middletown, a Wesleyan University professor, who opposed Baldwin because of his conservatism. When the ballots were cast, 611 out of 618 votes were for Simeon E. Baldwin.[8]

The Republicans held their 1910 convention in Hartford a few days after the Democrats had adjourned. Although the spirits of the assembling delegates were dampened by the news from Maine, the convention promised to be one of the most exciting in Connecticut's political history. In complete control of the state government since 1895, the Republicans had grown corpulent and complacent in office. Party leaders marched in a *cursus honorum* from one position to another up to a term as lieutenant governor and finally governor. After one term in the highest office, it became customary for the incumbent to step aside so that those below him on the ladder of preferment might rise a step higher. During their fifteen years in power the Republicans had few doubts about winning elections, and elective positions were frequently promised for years in advance.

By 1910, however, the machinery which had been so successful was beginning to show signs of decrepitude. Factionalism had arisen, and rival leaders set out to capture control of the party. By convention time two major groups were arrayed against each other, and so evenly were they divided that few newspapers would venture to choose the winner.

One group favored the candidacy of a "regular," former Lieutenant Governor Everett J. Lake. The other supported the socially prominent Charles A. Goodwin. The latter, a young man, had become Executive Secretary to Governor Lilley in 1908 and, upon his death, to his successor, Governor Weeks. Both factions maintained their convention headquarters in Hartford's Allyn House, and a constant flow of local politicians wound in and out in the tense days preceding and during the convention.[9]

Charges were bandied back and forth that the free circulation of greenbacks was playing a decisive role in lining up delegates for the rival candidates.[10] Goodwin came from a wealthy Hartford family and was the first cousin, once removed, of J. Pierpont Morgan, whose name figured prominently in newspaper accounts of the behind-the-scenes work at the convention. Mr. Goodwin later denied that Morgan had had any connection with his nomination.[11]

In the hours immediately before the meeting both sides maintained their usual confidence, perhaps with more sincerity than customary in election-eve political predictions. For when the ballots of the delegates were cast, they proved to be nearly equally divided between the two candidates. The headlines of a New Haven newspaper screamed "Sensational Mixup on Ballot for Governorship at Hartford Meeting. First Count on First Ballot Shows One More Vote than the Total of Delegates in the State Convention Today." [12] This state of affairs brought many charges and countercharges in the hot convention hall.

Meanwhile the discovery of ballots under chairs resulted in a successful demand for a recount. A hush fell over the delegates while the tellers announced that in the second tally Mr. Goodwin had received 295 votes to Mr. Lake's 285.[13]

After the remainder of the convention's work was done and the din had died away, the expected pleas for party harmony were made, and the delegates departed. There was superficial unity among the Republicans, but the open rift at Hartford left deep scars which only time would heal. The Democrats were more nearly correct than perhaps they realized when in the convention aftermath they claimed that the Republican split assured the election of the Democratic nominee.[14] For many Republicans, sickened by the talk of purchase and sale at Hartford, were to cast their votes for Simeon E. Baldwin.

A prominent Republican newspaper admitted editorially on September 15 that the Republican convention had had its unsavory aspects and compared it perhaps a bit sourly to some past Democratic conclaves. The paper asserted, however, that the worst element had lost out.[15]

Before the Democratic campaign could get under way, it was necessary to secure the wherewithal to conduct it. Thus a meeting was held for the purpose of raising funds among the candidates. At this session the party chieftains became somewhat better acquainted with the manner of man Simeon E. Baldwin was. The various nominees stood up in turn and told how much they would give or could raise towards the party's election expenses. It was well known that the Chief Justice was a wealthy man and that he wanted to be governor. It was assumed, therefore, that his contribution would be a sizable one. When Judge Baldwin's turn came, he arose and said that in the recent controversy regarding corrupt practices legislation he had publicly stated that no candidate should spend on electioneering more than the annual stipend of the office sought. At that time the salary of the governor of Connecticut was four thousand dollars a year. Judge Baldwin went on to say that of course he planned to stump the state himself and that he estimated his expenses would be about $200. He was ready, therefore, to draw a check to the party treasurer for $3,800![16] One who was present said that the hard-bitten politicians were so disappointed by the smallness of Baldwin's contribution and so dumbfounded by his unanswerable logic that they could only look at each other in silent amazement.[17]

As a sequel to this episode, a letter in the Governor-elect's handwriting was received at party headquarters on the morning after election. The weary workers opened it and out fluttered a check which accompanied a note from Simeon E. Baldwin. The latter said that he had been tallying his personal campaign expenses (perhaps on election night) and found that he had not spent all of the two hundred dollars he had allotted to himself. He was therefore enclosing a check to the party for the balance, so that his contribution would amount to the four thousand dollars he had promised![18]

The platforms of the two parties in Connecticut showed relatively few differences. Both were committed to the establishment of a public utilities commission and to the enactment of workmen's compensation legislation. The only significant difference in the state platforms was the insistence of the Democrats on a more stringent corrupt practices law.[19] The real issues were the national ones, and Baldwin made the most of these in his electioneering speeches.

The campaign gathered momentum as October passed, and it rapidly became evident that Simeon E. Baldwin was making much the better appearance. He was an experienced politician in spite of his eighteen years away from party affairs. His knowledge of the issues was thorough, and his ability to express his political convictions was unsurpassed. Baldwin's name was the hallmark of integrity, and his age was the only factor the Republican press could find to criticize.

Mr. Goodwin, on the other hand, carried many liabilities throughout the campaign. The convention had been surrounded by intrigue and rumors of vote-buying. A Republican newspaper admitted editorially at the height of the campaign that many Republicans felt that money should wield less influence in state politics.[20] Goodwin's youth and political inexperience also told against him. A Republican journal confessed that the party's nominee was handicapped by his failure to face the real issues of the campaign, which were largely national.[21] On state issues, although he did not dodge them, the opposition had good reason to doubt his sincerity. On the question of a public utilities commission, for example, Goodwin said he favored one with teeth, but the men most active in nominating him were the most notorious utility lobbyists in the state.[22]

That Baldwin understood the significant issues of the campaign was amply revealed by his speeches. More than anything else he attacked the protective tariff, blaming it for the high cost of living. Time after time Baldwin returned to this subject, apparently believing it would have the greatest appeal to the disaffected Republicans and the independent voters. Another favorite theme of Baldwin was his opposition to the "big government" propensities of the Republicans. In his initial Hartford address, the first political speech he had delivered in that city since 1892, Baldwin made a ringing state's rights appeal. He opposed vigorously the extension of federal authority, which the Republican administrations of Roosevelt and Taft had advanced and which Roosevelt was soon to press in his New Nationalism. The Democratic party, according to Baldwin, stood on the classical statement of Thomas Jefferson that the best government was that which governed least.[23]

The Democrats in Connecticut had lost so many elections in the years before 1910 that even with by far the more illustrious candidate on their ticket and the opposition divided, they scarcely dared to hope for victory in November. The unexpected occurred, however, and Simeon E. Baldwin drew enough independent support to win the governorship by 3,600 votes. He did not have enough strength, however, to carry the rest of the Democratic ticket into office, and the other state officers and both houses of the General Assembly were again Republican. A lone Democratic congressman was elected along with Baldwin.[24] The Governor-elect termed the outcome an inspiring sign of political progress, for it showed that a majority of the people, while standing by their party in general, were ready to sacrifice its chosen leader to testify unmistakably their disapproval of its management and their conviction that the policy of that management was a departure from the true party ideals.[25]

During the campaign Simeon E. Baldwin and former President Theodore Roosevelt became engaged in a controversy which gave both of them nation-wide publicity. It all began when Roosevelt said in a speech at Concord, New Hampshire, on October 22 that Baldwin, while on the bench, had taken the most "retrogressive" possible position on the question of workmen's compensation. According to the former president, Baldwin maintained in the Hoxie case that it was competent for a workingman, when driven to accept any employment, to bind himself not to be compensated if he lost life and limb in his occupation. Baldwin replied that he had no recollection of having expressed this view and believed that such a contract as Roosevelt described would be invalid under Connecticut law.[26] He therefore asked the latter to retract his statements, if the newspaper accounts of them were correct.[27] To this Roosevelt replied that he had been misquoted and that there were two or three versions of what he had said in different papers. To clarify his position and probably to gain more publicity, he issued the following statement:

> I hold that the state has absolutely the right to enact laws refusing to permit, and that existing laws should, in accordance with the opinions of very many progressive judges, be construed as not permitting any man, directly or indirectly, by any action of his own, to estop himself from his right to have railroad or other corporation forced to compensate him for any injury done to him in the performance of his duty. If your letter is correctly quoted in the press in this matter, you hold that the acceptance of a very small benefit from the accident insu·ance company by a railroad employe would estop him from recovering the substantial amount which he otherwise would be entitled to recover for any injury received. I hold that such a view is most emphatically not progressive.[28]

Part of Baldwin's reply, as quoted in the New York *Times*, pointed out:

> The main question in the Hoxie case was whether a Federal statute

had altered the common law, as theretofore administered in the State courts of Connecticut. That the fellow servant rule was part of this common law in Connecticut was not questioned by any of the able counsel who participated in the argument. . . .

The Supreme Court of Errors had no power to repudiate this fellow-servant rule, as applicable to the case before it. It had become generally accepted as right and just in the middle of the last century by the American people. It had been recognized by the Supreme Court of Errors of Connecticut in many opinions. . . .

No change having been made since then by the Legislature of Connecticut, the rule was necessarily applied in the Hoxie case. Subsequently, and on account of the decision, the Federal law was altered so as to make it in terms applicable to actions in the State courts.[29]

The Springfield (Massachusetts) *Republican*, in commenting on the controversy between Baldwin and Roosevelt, made a significant point in a concluding paragraph:

It is not necessary . . . to call fresh attention to the fact that while the judge on the bench decided the Hoxie case as the law required, in the opinion of himself and his colleagues of the court, thus sustaining the decision of the court below, now that he is in a position to advocate a new law, Judge Baldwin does so, and supports the demand of his platform for a workman's compensation act in Connecticut.[30]

So completely did Roosevelt fail to face the charges which Baldwin leveled against him that the Governor finally threatened to sue the former president for libel.[31] When Baldwin appeared before his first law class after the election results were known, he said in response to the applause of his students:

I thank you, gentlemen. I stand before you as an instructor rather than as a politician. But I will say that in my campaign I was assisted by a controversy I had with a certain ex-president, and I have come to the conclusion that this ex-president knows less law than you and I do, and I am going to teach him some.[32]

A week later Baldwin informed the press that he had not changed his mind about suing former President Roosevelt.[33] Judge Alton B. Parker, the Democratic presidential candidate in 1904, admitted that he was drawing the papers for a fifty-thousand dollar libel suit against the former president.[34] Not until late in the following January did Baldwin announce that he had decided not to press the suit.[35] The New York *Times* said that the Connecticut Governor wanted the controversy submitted to a lawyer or judge in order to avoid publicity. Roosevelt, however, insisted upon an open suit.[36]

Meanwhile the lawyers of Connecticut were singing a new song entitled "The Ballad of Baldwin and Teddy," a copy of which they sent to the Governor-elect.

Oh, Teddy attacked Baldwin's legal repute—
He was not the poor man's best friend—
And Baldwin replied, "when I am elected
The sheriff to Teddy I'll send.

He don't know as much about law as my students,
But I'll teach him law some fine day."
And Baldwin's elected, just as he expected,
And now you can hear Baldwin say:

Chorus:

Yip I-addy-I-ay, yip I-addy-I-ay,
I don't care what he said of me,
I am glad that he said it because of the fact
It only made more votes for me.
Yes, indeed, I am glad that he said it, you bet.
For Teddy's our best campaign document yet.[37]

When a year later the United States Supreme Court unanimously reversed the Connecticut decision,[38] the pronouncement was seized upon as vindication of Theodore Roosevelt's stand in the 1910 controversy.

The United States Supreme Court decision overrules this view in every respect. The constitutionality of the act is unanimously affirmed. The decision as to the respective limits of state and national jurisdiction goes far beyond the exact issue. It holds that it is not competent for State courts or officials to plead that a Federal law is not in harmony with a State law and therefore no heed need be paid to it by the State. A Federal law, it says, is the expression through Congress of the will of all the people, and establishes a policy for all, with the following conclusion:

That policy is as much the policy of Connecticut (where the leading case originated) as if the act had emanated from its own Legislature, and should be respected accordingly in the courts of the State.

Recalling the logomachy between ex-President and ex-Chief Justice, now Governor of Connecticut, and the attendant condemnations of Roosevelt for "attacking the judiciary," it seems that the final chapter leaves Governor Baldwin's judicial infallibility in a very shaky condition.[39]

A different interpretation of the cases was that of the New York *Tribune:*

Governor Baldwin, while on the Connecticut bench, had held, among other things, that the federal employers' liability law was unenforceable through the Connecticut courts. Colonel Roosevelt declared that his decision was reactionary, and now the Supreme Court pronounces it wrong, and says that the state courts must enforce the law. The result will add new impetus to the debate on the question how much a judge's habit of thought unconsciously influences his decisions—an interesting question, to which the prompt success of remedial legislation in this country is closely related. But the lesson of the incident seems to be that even though there are judges on the bench whose cast of mind is an obstacle to much needed legislation, their influence is only temporary. Judge Baldwin's opinion made the federal employers' liability law unconstitutional in Connecticut for a few years, but it is so no longer.

The Supreme Court's unanimous decision sustaining the constitutionality of the law is fortunate and hopeful. The fellow servant and assumption of risk doctrines belonged to a simpler state of society, when men were freer in the choice of employment and employers and in determining whom they would work alongside of than they are today, and when machinery was less complex and its hazards slighter. They do not suit existing conditions, and it would be regrettable if the courts were to give them a sacrosanct character.[40]

It should be recalled that the quarrel between the two men originated on other grounds than these. Baldwin threatened to sue Roosevelt because the former president refused to retract certain statements which he alleged that Baldwin had made but which the latter denied having uttered. It should also be remembered that, although bound by all the rules and precedents of Connecticut law to uphold the fellow-servant rule as he did in the Hoxie decision, Baldwin unequivocably advocated and saw through the 1913 session of the Connecticut legislature a workmen's compensation act which reversed the ancient common law liability rule.

In the interim between the election and the inauguration Baldwin wrote to the National Democratic Club stating the three policies which he thought the party should emphasize. These were the tenets for which the Democracy had stood historically. The first was opposition to disturbing the equilibrium between the states and the federal government by undue extension of federal authority. The second was a lower tariff, permitting foreign competition but securing to American producers reimbursement for their higher labor costs. On at least one other occasion Baldwin had stressed that the United States must allow foreigners to sell in America, if it expected to market its products abroad. The extra cost of American over foreign labor he believed was greatly exaggerated by the high tariff advocates.[41] His third policy was simplicity and economy in the public establishment.[42]

On the fourth of January, 1911, the General Assembly of Connecticut convened for its biennial session and listened to the new Governor deliver his inaugural message.[43] Simeon E. Baldwin began by comparing the growth of Connecticut's population with the rise of the state's expenditures. While the population in the last seventy years had multiplied fourfold, state expenses had increased twelve times fourfold. Although many of the added outlays were necessary, due economy had not always been exercised, and Baldwin believed that such a policy should now be a paramount consideration of the legislature.

A first step in this direction would be the creation of a state purveyor, who would buy for all state institutions. This idea had also been proposed by Governor Woodruff in 1907. As another economy move Baldwin advocated eliminating the salaries of the board of directors of the county homes for tubercular patients. All other state charitable boards served without compensation, and the Governor believed that it should be possible to find public-spirited citizens to do likewise for the tubercular homes.

The Governor also called attention to the multiplication over the years of public agencies and positions. When he took office, there were nine commissioners or heads of departments and more than forty boards of commissioners or directors to manage other departments and institutions. In some instances the jurisdictions of these agencies overlapped. In others, a single commissioner could better perform the work of several. Baldwin suggested many simplifications in the state administrative structure which showed his detailed knowledge of the expenses, number of employees, and duties of the multifarious agencies.

Little knowing that the 1913 General Assembly would break all records for length, the Governor suggested that few new laws were needed and that a short legislative session should be possible. He urged that statutes be clearly written, that a lawyer be appointed clerk of bills to attend to the drafting of laws, and that the term of this officer be lengthened to good behavior, so that a more competent man could be secured. Questions of statutory construction or conflict should seldom arise if such steps were taken.

Turning to suffrage, Governor Baldwin recommended several measures. The election law of 1909 should be clarified so that its meaning would be unquestionable. The corrupt practices laws should be strengthened. The ballots should have the elector's oath on the back of them, a solemn and impressive statement of the responsibility of the voter to the state.

With respect to women's voting Baldwin believed that the time had not yet come to give the unrestricted exercise of the ballot to the female sex. Since many women were property holders, however, he recommended that the General Assembly make it possible for those who were taxed to vote on all questions of municipal management at town meetings or at the meeting of any municipal corporation. He pointed out that steps had already been taken in this direction by giving women the right to vote for school and library officers and upon any questions arising in a town relating to libraries, schools or education in general.

The Governor also urged the General Assembly to establish a public utilities commission which would merge the functions of the present Board of Railroad Commissioners with the new body. He suggested that the general plan recommended by the Special Commission to the General Assembly in 1909 be enacted with minor changes.

Baldwin further proposed that Connecticut join most of the western world in enacting a workmen's compensation act. As a basis for such legislation, he suggested that the unanimous report of a committee appointed by the General Assembly in 1907 be used.

In an allied field, the Governor suggested that the 1840 law limiting to five thousand dollars the recovery for accidental death due to negligence be changed. Because the purchasing power of money had declined considerably since 1840, the new limit should not be less than ten thousand dollars.

In addition, the Governor recommended that the County Commissioners be elected by the voters of each county rather than by the legislature. He also advocated transferring the power of appointment of local judges from the General Assembly to the governor, such appointments henceforth being merely confirmed by the legislature.

Since the supreme executive authority was vested by the constitution in the governor, it was his duty to see that the laws were faithfully executed. In order to enable him to discharge this duty, the state's chief executive ought to have the power to remove inferior administrative officers. The President of the United States, Baldwin pointed out, could take such action, and in the more recent city charters the mayors had been granted similar power.

Under the heading of miscellaneous recommendations Baldwin suggested a variety of actions: that a state civil service on a merit basis for minor employees be established; that a general law be enacted permitting the issuance of municipal bonds for certain specified purposes, an action which would save the General Assembly from considering each case separately; that opinions of the attorney general now made to state officers by courtesy should be made compulsory; that the state auditors be required to report to the governor any charges which seemed to them irregular or of doubtful propriety; and that no gratuities should be appropriated and no legislative souvenirs voted.

A proposal in which the Governor was especially interested pertained to the regulation of flying machines. He recommended their registry in the clerk's office of each town, the forbiddance of flights unless under control of a competent operator, the examination and licensing of such persons, and the assumption of responsibility for all damages by the owner. When subsequently enacted, this measure was the first passed by any government for the regulation of airplanes.[44]

Regarding federal constitutional revisions Baldwin urged the passage of a resolution requesting Congress to approve and send to the states an amendment providing for the direct election of United States senators. As for the income tax amendment he suggested some legal difficulties and recommended that the General Assembly seek an opinion from the attorney general before acting upon it. He pointed out advantages and disadvantages in the measure but made no appeal for its passage or rejection.

In his recommendations for the revision of the state constitution Baldwin once again trod the ground he had labored over for nearly a half century. As a final settlement to the long-standing difference between the representation of small and large towns in the General Assembly, he strongly advocated a return to the system existing in Connecticut from 1644 to 1828 of electing the Senate on a general ticket rather than by districts. He also suggested that special legislation be prohibited on any subject that was or could be as well covered by a statute of general application. He concurred in the recommendation of Governor Lilley, made in 1909, that an amendment be passed requiring a two-thirds vote of each house to override the governor's veto.

Baldwin was careful in his message to invoke the names of

his Republican predecessors whenever they had favored measures which he also advocated. Since both houses of the General Assembly were in Republican hands, this was of course an astute move. It was traditional in Connecticut, however, for the legislature to listen respectfully to the suggestions of the chief executive but disregard them in the session that followed. To a considerable extent Baldwin's administration was an exception to this rule, and in spite of his being of a different political party from that controlling the legislature, most of his major recommendations were accepted by that body.

One of the Governor's law students who later became Connecticut's Secretary of State remarked on how astonished the public was at the intimate knowledge of state affairs Governor Baldwin acquired between his election in November and his inaugural address on January 4.[45] Baldwin's message was indeed evidence that he was acutely aware of both the long-standing problems of Connecticut and the more recent ones. Such knowledge had not been acquired, however, in a few months but by nearly fifty years of close attention to state affairs and the study of its history.

One of the most interesting tributes to Baldwin's message came from former Governor Rollin S. Woodruff, a Republican, who said there was not one thing which Baldwin suggested that the state ought not to adopt.[46] Such complete endorsement of his program by a prominent Republican served to underline the basic similarity of the two parties and the essential conservatism of Simeon E. Baldwin. The New York *Times* with good reason rated the Governor of Connecticut as the most conservative Democrat in a conspicuous position at this time.[47]

During the early months of 1911 Governor Baldwin's schedule was a full one. Besides his official duties and his work with legislative leaders, he spoke frequently at banquets, dedications and similar affairs. A letter to his niece illustrates the variety of such activities:

> I am just back from New London, where I went to welcome the convention of the Atlantic Deeper Waterways Association. . . .
>
> Tomorrow I help dedicate a Russian synagogue here. Sunday I be-

gan the week with a commemorative address on General Booth of the Salvation Army, and Monday I helped dedicate the Harigari's new music hall in West Haven.[48]

So faithful was he in these duties that one newspaper said of him:

The fears expressed before Gov. Baldwin's election that on account of his advanced age he would be unable to mix at public functions as did past Governors, have not been borne out by Gov. Baldwin's public appearances since taking office, according to his friends today. Indeed, they say, that if the present chief executive keeps up his record of attendance at banquets, dedications, inspections and visits he will have eclipsed the reputations as mixer of all former governors.[49]

Baldwin's newspaper publicity while governor was generally favorable. The reaction to his early appointments, which he made on a nonpolitical basis,[50] is a case in point. After a little more than two months in office, the Springfield *Republican* said:

Although Gov. Baldwin had to retire from the Connecticut supreme court because he was 70, and although he was absolutely out of politics for some 20 years, he seems to be getting his appointments confirmed by the republican Senate and winning general recognition as a political antagonist well worth watching. Our correspondent at the Connecticut capital even reports that he "is coming to be recognized as a politician of no mean parts." A year or two from now the republican tribute to "Sim" Baldwin may be that he's the slickest politician seen in Connecticut in many years.[51]

Two weeks later the same paper predicted that much might be accomplished in Connecticut in spite of the legislature's being controlled by a different party than that of the Governor:

Gov. Baldwin fully appreciated, when he was elected, the obstacles a republican Legislature would throw up against his policies, and he is not being disillusioned any by the progress of events. The governor of Connecticut is steadily, persistently pursuing the right course. He is constantly urging upon the Legislature and especially upon the people the reasonableness of the measures he advocates, and thus he is doing what he can to make his views prevail. As between him and the Legislature, the final judgment may be deferred, but it is certain that the governor in the end will stand high on account of his unwearied and faithful labors. His appointments average unusually high in quality. And, after all, he may get out of a Legislature opposed to himself politically quite as much as Gov. Bass of New Hampshire will get out of a Legislature controled [*sic*] by his own party friends.[52]

This was actually the case, according to the Governor's Executive Secretary, who said that the high regard in which Baldwin was held by the legislators helped to smooth the way for his legislative program.[53] Undoubtedly the similarity of the two parties with respect to aims and means also facilitated the harmonious relationship between the lawmakers and the chief executive.

One of the first fruits of this amicable association was cooperative action in establishing a public utilities commission. Two bills were reported to the legislature in June, and Governor Baldwin expressed a preference for the minority bill, which the Republican Senate leader also favored. This version provided for appeals from the decisions of the Public Utilities Commission to the Superior Court, a stipulation which the Governor believed would satisfy the constitutional objections to the Commission that it would have power to take private property without due process of law.[54] This feature was included in the compromise measure which the legislature at length approved early in July.[55] The establishment of a Public Utilities Commission was the most significant accomplishment of the 1911 General Assembly and along with the Workmen's Compensation Act constituted the major measures of Baldwin's four years as governor.[56]

Regarding some minor legislation, on the other hand, there were instances of disagreement between the General Assembly and the Governor. In July Baldwin vetoed a resolution to appropriate four thousand dollars for a legislative souvenir. In his rejection message he suggested that such a memento might be paid for by the members of the legislature who desired it. By a very close vote his veto was overridden, the Lieutenant Governor having to cast the tie-breaking ballot in the Senate.[57] Next Baldwin vetoed a legislative divorce on the grounds that divorces came within the jurisdiction of the courts and were unconstitutional when granted by legislative bodies. This veto was sustained.[58] Another bill disapproved by the Governor involved setting the fares on the railroad service in and around New Britain. The Governor took the position that such a decision was the function of the Public Utilities Commission and not of the legislature.[59] One of his most notable vetoes was of a piece of special legislation which would have in effect taken from the governor the power of appointing the highway commissioner. Baldwin held that such a law would be unconstitutional, but on the question the General Assembly overrode the Governor.[60] Still another veto and one sustained by the Senate was that of a bill enlarging the franchises of a canal company at Windsor Locks on the Connecticut River. In this instance the Governor believed that the company's plans for expansion were not financially sound.[61]

On the last day of August Governor Baldwin sent a special message to the General Assembly urging action on redistricting the state for the election of members of the national House of Representatives. He also urged that the apportioning changes in the Connecticut Senate which he had previously recommended—the substitution of a general ticket for districts—be enacted.[62]

Late in September the legislative session finally adjourned. Probably the most concise account of its accomplishments and failures is the closing message of Governor Baldwin:

Mr. President, Mr. Speaker, and Gentlemen of the General Assembly:

This joint convention concludes by far the longest session ever held by the general assembly of Connecticut. You have given your assent to an amendment to the constitution proposed by the general assembly of 1909, which, if ratified by the people, will prevent any future legislative session from continuing beyond an early date in June. By letting your constituents know from your own legislative experience how necessary, in view of the growth of the state, the imposition of such a constitutional limit has become, you can remove all doubts as to its approval by the people at the October town meetings, soon to be held.

You have proposed for the consideration of the next general assembly another constitutional amendment, conceived in the same spirit. It is that forbidding, for the future, special legislation in cases where the same end can be as well accomplished by a general statute. . . .

Another amendment to our constitution which you have proposed for the consideration of the next assembly, requiring a two-thirds vote to override a veto of the governor, will, I believe, commend itself to the people and prove a useful preventive of unnecessary or ill-considered legislation.

Your creation of a public utilities commission will tend to relieve future general assemblies from the consideration of many matters affecting the administration of public service companies which can be more satisfactorily handled by a small body exercising quasi-judicial functions.

While you have not thought fit to proceed so far as I suggested in my inaugural message in the line of general public economy, and particularly in the direction of pruning off what have seemed to me unnecessary offices, I thank you for the careful consideration which you have given to all the various recommendations which that message contained.

I thank also the chairmen of the joint standing committees for the uniform attention and courtesy with which they have received such suggestions of amendments, as I have from time to time made to them personally, in respect to the form and contents of pending bills. In many instances causes of objection to a bill have thus been removed which might otherwise have made me deem it my duty to withhold my approval of it.

Most legislation on controversial matters is apt to take the shape eventually of a bundle of compromises. Many of the acts of this session came out at the end of the legislative process very different in appearance from what they were when they were introduced. It is probable, however, that they thus better represent the average judgment and common sense of our people.

It is to be regretted that it proved impossible for the two houses to agree on the terms of a proper workmen's compensation act, but it is not surprising that this was the result, in view of the inherent difficulties of bringing the positions of modern sociology and social economy into accord with all the guaranties of individual right to be found in our American constitutions.

It is better to have no change in the laws regulating the important subject of employers liability than to have them changed without due consideration of all the effects that might result from the new legislation. A law promising a workingman, injured in the course of his employment, a fixed compensation automatically ascertained, would be a delusion, unless he were sure of collecting it. It would seem that this assurance can be best afforded by some plan of insurance. This is particularly important where the employer has but a small capital.

You have provided for the appointment of a commission to study this subject and report to the next general assembly. Their recommendations will, no doubt, be an important guide in determining what legislation upon this subject ought to be adopted in this state.

You have adopted a fair and reasonable plan for dividing the state into five congressional districts. This duty had been left unperformed by previous legislatures, and I congratulate you in having dealt with this question in the manner contemplated by the laws of the United States. . . .

The failure to redistrict the state for senatorial districts, will make it incumbent upon me to consider with care whether it may be my duty at a later period to call you together again, in special session.

I congratulate you upon having adopted a corrupt practices act, well-guarded and self-executing. This and the amendments adopted in respect to the form of ballots can hardly fail to give us greater purity of elections.

You have made it your rule, when authorizing the issue of capital stock by corporations seeking charter privileges in that respect, to provide that the shares shall be paid for at not less than par, in cash or its equivalent.

In this your action has been in striking contrast to that of some previous general assemblies when dealing with similar questions, particularly in the case of street railways. The state has reason to thank you for your care in thus guarding the public interest.[63]

After the General Assembly had adjourned, the Governor and the first company of the Governor's Foot Guard journeyed to Georgia early in October for the unveiling in Atlanta of the Old Guard monument,[64] a memorial to both Confederate and Federal soldiers. Governor Baldwin made the main address at this celebration and emphasized the road to reunion that both the South and North had traveled since 1865. Among the milestones on this trail were the visits of Atlanta's Gate City Guards to the North in 1879 and the current journeys of military companies from the twelve other original states to Georgia.[65] From Atlanta the Connecticut visitors went to Charleston, South Carolina, where an informal smoker was tendered the guests.[66] On the return trip the group stopped at Richmond, and Governor Baldwin gave another well-received address.[67]

The successful visit to the South considerably strengthened the Governor's position at home. He arrived in Connecticut "trailing clouds of glory" which soon broke forth in a Baldwin-for-president boom. In a burst of local patriotism the papers of the state late in October, 1911, heaped acclaim upon the chief executive. The Hartford *Post* called Baldwin the equal of Champ Clark, Woodrow Wilson, or Governor Harmon.[68] The Governor's Executive Secretary, Edwin S. Thomas, declared that Baldwin's name would be presented to the Democratic National Convention as a candidate for president.[69] Some papers commented favorably on the idea but expressed grave doubts as to the possibility of a resident of such a small state as Connecticut receiving the nomination under the American electoral system.[70]

This was not the first time that Baldwin's name had been mentioned as a suitable candidate for the Democratic presidential or vice-presidential nomination.[71] During 1911 the press frequently alluded to this possibility, and in August of that year Baldwin took formal notice of these references:

> I have understood that for some months my name has been mentioned in connection with the vice-presidency, in several states of the east and middle west. . . . I am not a candidate for any office whatever and should not make any effort to obtain a nomination.
>
> If it is thought by my party friends that my nomination would tend in any way to strengthen the chances of Democratic success next year, had [*sic*] it come to me, I certainly should not decline it.[72]

Perhaps the most accurate appraisal of Baldwin's presidential expectations appeared in the New Britain *Herald* in January, 1912. Quoting a New Haven journal as saying that Democrats of that city have concluded that the Wilson boom had collapsed and as a result Baldwin's possibilities had been enhanced, the upstate paper said:

> . . . but not even the optimistic New Haveners think that it will secure him the nomination.
>
> Just at present no man has any license to predict the result of the Baltimore convention but at the same time there is no one who seri-

ously thinks that Governor Baldwin will be the choice. The Connecticut delegation, it is understood, will favor him but there is no sentiment for the governor outside of Connecticut except such as may have been created by an article in the New York *Sun* which made favorable comment on his candidacy and said that he was better equipped for the office than any other one mentioned. . . . No man could be expected to refuse a nomination for the presidency and Governor Baldwin evidently takes the view that if the nomination comes to him he will accept but that he hasn't the slightest notion that it will.[73]

On January 30, 1912, the Democratic leaders of Connecticut convened and in a gesture of loyalty and tribute to Governor Baldwin declared themselves for his candidacy. There was no doubt now but that his name would be presented at Baltimore.[74] With his endorsement by the Democratic state committee, the Baldwin boom in Connecticut was thoroughly launched.[75]

At a state convention of the Democratic party in May the delegates to the Democratic National Convention were chosen and instructed to vote for Baldwin on the first ballot. An effort to pledge the delegates to Champ Clark, should Baldwin not receive the nomination, was defeated.[76] The Governor was given a tremendous ovation by the assemblage, and the press declared that it was undoubtedly sincere. Commenting on Baldwin's endorsement a Bridgeport Democratic paper said:

There is, of course, no possible chance for the nomination of Governor Baldwin. He belongs to the past, to the distant past, and the Democratic party will not go so far back for their candidate in a campaign that is going to demand a stern consideration of the great issues of the day. Governor Baldwin might be useful in Connecticut, where the party lines are more closely drawn and delegates and voters still do the bidding of men who deal imperiously with them, as though they were so many strings to be pulled by master minds. But away from this section Governor Baldwin's name stands for very little. The rank and file of both parties know of him only through his controversy with Colonel Roosevelt. Nothing could suit the Republicans better than to have to fight the campaign on that Hoxie judgment.

But there is not the slightest chance of the Democrats making any such blunder, and no one knows it better than the shrewd leaders who so skillfully managed the late convention.[77]

Voicing the same point of view, the Republican Hartford *Courant* predicted that the Simeon E. Baldwin-for-governor movement would begin as soon as the Democratic national convention had rejected him for the presidential nomination.[78]

At the Baltimore convention in the early hours of June 28, the name of Simeon E. Baldwin was placed in nomination by his friend, Dean Henry Wade Rogers. He spoke twenty-two minutes, and a twelve-minute demonstration ensued.[79] Following upon the nomination of Champ Clark, who was cheered for over an hour, the ovation for Baldwin was rather meager. The occasion was somewhat enlivened, however, by a young man, whose story is told by a Hartford paper:

When Dean Rogers of the Yale Law school was addressing the convention in advocacy of the nomination for president of Governor Baldwin, between the hours of 1 and 2 Friday morning, a young man of Bohemian disposition named George O'Connor, who hails from Washington and who has relatives in Connecticut, went over to the press section to greet a friend. He was detained by James L. McGovern, the enthusiastic democratic representative of the Bridgeport *Farmer*, who had previously met O'Connor and had noted the possibilities of his cheering voice.

"George, we want you to lead a cheer for our governor, when the speaker gets through nominating him."

"What's his name?"

"Simeon E. Baldwin."

"What's his middle name?"

"Eli."

Just then the dean concluded the brilliant peroration, which ended one of the best speeches made to the convention and there went up a perfunctory cheer from the floor. O'Connor jumped upon a press table and with a shout that could be heard to the outer corners of the great hall cried, "Simoleon Eli Baldwin!" "Three cheers for Simoleon Eli Baldwin!" "Simoleon!" "Simoleon!" "Simoleon Eli Baldwin!" The working press dropped their pencils and took it up. The reporters jumped upon the tables and joined in the cry for "Simoleon" Baldwin. Yale men all over the hall, at first astonished at the variation in the name of their honored preceptor, appreciated the battle cry, and they added to the roar. O'Connor led like a college rooter at the annual football match and the name of "Simoleon" Baldwin was kept ringing over the hall for nearly fifteen minutes. It will be a long time before any who were present will forget the sound of the cheering for "Simoleon" Eli Baldwin.[80]

When the tumult induced by O'Connor was at its height, "Mr. Dooley" was heard to observe to Mr. Ade, "Let's go home, George. This is no place for us. There's a new king in American humor over there leading the cheering squad." [81]

During the forty-six ballots which were necessary to select a presidential nominee, there was occasionally a ray of hope that Baldwin might emerge as a dark horse candidate and break the deadlock between the major contenders, Governor Wilson of New Jersey and Speaker of the House of Representatives, Champ Clark of Missouri. Former Governor Henry St. George Tucker of Virginia told a member of the Connecticut delegation that he felt he was doing his country a disservice by not casting his vote for Governor Baldwin. Reporting the episode, the Hartford *Times* quoted Tucker as follows:

"He is the ideal man for the place" he said. And he added: "I hope it may yet break so that a lot of men who think as I do may cast their ballots for the great jurist whom you are fortunate to have as a governor of your state." And it can be added that there are a hundred other men in this convention who feel the same way and would like to do the same thing but they hesitate to vote for a man whom [*sic*] it was felt did not have any show.[82]

The nomination of Woodrow Wilson terminated whatever slight presidential possibilities Baldwin may have had, and the Governor was now free to devote himself to state affairs.

Ever desirous of correcting abuses in the public establishment and of furthering the Jeffersonian ideal of simplicity and economy in government, Governor Baldwin secured in December, 1911, a ruling from the attorney general regarding the mileage allowance for state legislators. The new interpretation cut the amount they could claim in the future for travel. Under the constitution legislators were allowed twenty-five cents a mile from their homes to Hartford at the beginning of the session and a like amount for their return. By using mileage tickets issued by the state comptroller, they had found a way to obtain several trips to and from the capital at the state's expense. According to the attorney general's interpretation of the constitution, the cost of transportation should be about seven thousand dollars for a legislative session, whereas in 1911 the actual amount paid for these services was over thirty-seven thousand dollars.[83] Undoubtedly Baldwin's action did not endear him to the hearts of the legislators.

During his first year in office Baldwin had two major critics, both of them fellow Democrats. One was Professor Willard C. Fisher of Wesleyan University, the Democratic mayor of Middletown. Among his many attacks on Baldwin's administration Fisher published in January, 1912, a lengthy article which was widely circulated, criticizing the conservativeness of the Governor and his failure to press vigorously for the progressive legislation desired by the people. What credit Fisher gave Baldwin for the accomplishments of his first year in office was bestowed grudgingly.[84] The other critic was the Democratic Bridgeport *Post*, which consistently flailed the Governor for the same reasons as did Mayor Fisher. The *Post*, however, was more apt to pay the Governor tribute when he accomplished something which accorded with its definition of progressiveness.[85]

At the close of his first year of office the most influential Republican paper in Connecticut summarized its impression of the Governor:

He is a serious-looking, spectacled gentleman, more likely to be picked up by the stranger for a college professor than for a politician, but under his sedate exterior there is a singularly keen mind and a choice sense of humor. He sees the fun of the passing show as readily as anybody else, and gets as much sport from the spectacle.[86]

This impression was borne out by two incidents which occurred during the year. A son was born to one of the members of the House of Representatives, a farmer from the country town of Tolland,[87] on Baldwin's inauguration day, and the father named the child Simeon Baldwin Luhrsen. Upon hearing of this, the Governor presented the legislator with a silver cup before the House of Representatives.[88] On another occasion a Hartford woman addressed the Governor in verse as follows:

Gov. Baldwin

For thee we rise and sing,
Homage to thee we bring,
We deem thee everything,
Pure, loyal, obliging.

Thy rule is without fear
That the money'd men will hear
Thy dealings through the year.
Justice is thy sphere.

Thy days are free from sin,
No bribery enters in,
Nor grafting, dire and grim,
We love thee, Gov. Baldwin.

Republicans are we,
But the Reps are few that be,
So honest, good and free.
Gov. Baldwin, we love thee.[89]

Recognizing the sincerity of the primitive verses, the Governor sharpened his poetic pencil and replied to Mrs. Murphy in kind:

Dear Madam:—
You are very kind
To say so many pleasant things
In grace of poetry entwined,—
Sweet poetry, which ever brings,
Child as it is of sentiment,
New charm to words of compliment.

To me, at least, your verses read
As if they spoke your honest thought,
And meant that you believe, indeed,
I try to do that which I ought,
However short I come of reaching
All that I may be fond of preaching.

Whoever holds a public place
Some praise, much blame, is sure to get.
The source of praise he oft' can trace—
'Tis a cheap way to pay a debt—
But yours—a stranger's tribute—must
Be honest, if it be not just.[90]

Many stories regarding the Spartan customs of Simeon Baldwin circulated during the years he was Governor. According to one he brought his lunch—a sandwich—with him to the capitol each day and ate it in his office. Another had him eating his sandwich on a train while the members of his official party dined sumptuously in a dining car. Baldwin enjoyed walking, and a cycle of stories centered around this avocation. On one occasion he was scheduled to participate in the dedication of a new bridge. When the last train to reach the town in which the ceremonies were to take place had come and gone without the Governor disembarking, the committee became concerned. Five minutes before the observances were to begin, however, Governor Baldwin appeared on foot. He explained that the weather had been so fine that he had gotten off the train a couple of stations back and walked the last few miles. Another episode occurred at the time Baldwin received an honorary degree from Wesleyan University in 1911. After the ceremonies were over, the seventy-one-year-old Governor departed on foot and began walking along the road from Middletown to his home in New Haven—a twenty-five-mile distance. Several motorists recognized the Governor and offered him a ride, but to all he politely declined. At Meriden or Wallingford, when he had walked enough for that day, he caught a train for New Haven.

All of these episodes and others were duly reported in the press and probably were not without political effect. In fact, Baldwin's grandson told the writer that he had never been able to decide whether or not there might have been a trace of political design in some of the Spartan practices of the old Governor.

During his second year in office the Governor maintained his record for making speeches and attending public functions.

Some examples will reveal the variety of these activities. In an address delivered to the businessmen's association of New Britain Baldwin referred to the high tariff as the germ of the disease of trusts.[91] At a similar conclave in Danbury he scored the growth of the Federal Government's power in controlling the business affairs of the states.[92] In February he spoke before the New Haven Teacher's League and tactfully suggested that American teachers raise the standards of education to those of Europe.[93] On Lincoln's birthday he addressed the Young Men's Republican Club of New Haven [94] and on February 22 the students of Smith College.[95] Referring to immigration later in the spring the Governor favored a liberal policy and opposed restricting the flow of Europeans to America.[96]

Speaking before the State Democratic Club, the Governor informed his hearers that there were no startling wrongs to redress in Connecticut. The Nutmeg State had invented the referendum over two centuries before. Nor was Connecticut a stranger to the recall. A two-thirds vote of the General Assembly could recall a judge at any time. Baldwin suggested, therefore, that the party not waste time the following fall on the questions of initiative, recall and referendum. Instead he advocated that its energy be concentrated on what he considered the great issue—the invasion of states' rights by the Federal Government.[97]

When this address was delivered late in April, the Governor probably realized that he would again be leading the state ticket in November. It was not, however, until the Baltimore convention had rejected his name in June that Baldwin declared his intention of seeking re-election. At once the Connecticut papers were full of confident reports that he would again be nominated and elected.[98] On September 12 the Democratic state convention did the expected, and the Governor was unanimously renominated by acclamation.[99]

The Democratic state platform called for self-government of the cities, towns and boroughs, repeal of the personal tax law, election of county commissioners by popular vote, and a fair workingmen's compensation act. Thorough revision of the state banking laws was also advocated, as was publication of the names of campaign contributors, appointment of local judges by the governor, adoption of the initiative and referendum, direct election of United States senators, direct primaries, and further extension of suffrage to women.[100]

As in 1910 the Republican state platform differed very little from the Democratic. The campaign was complicated by the defection of the Progressives from the Republican party. In state affairs the third party likewise offered few new proposals.[101]

The Republican state convention, although not as divided as in 1910 and apparently a far freer body,[102] witnessed a lively contest between the supporters of Lieutenant Governor Dennis A. Blakeslee, a prominent contractor, and Judge John P. Studley of the New Haven Probate Court. According to one who knew Mr. Blakeslee for many years, the latter refused to make any patronage commitments to the Republican State Chairman, and because of this many of his supporters were diverted to Judge Studley.[103] At any event Studley received the nomination, and a Republican newspaper observed that there was general satisfaction among the politicians upon this outcome.[104]

The election in Connecticut in 1912 was part of a much larger political drama. By that year the Progressive Movement in the United States was nearing its peak. This liberal urge had been gathering momentum for over a decade, and no party could hope for victory in 1912 which did not convince the voters that it would forge ahead to further progressive triumphs.

Upon the renomination of President William H. Taft by the conservative faction of the Republican party, Theodore Roosevelt and his liberal followers withdrew and formed the Progressive party in the summer of 1912. Familiarly referred to as the Bull Moose party, the new group promptly nominated Roosevelt as its presidential candidate. Its platform was similar to the Democratic, both standing for the reforms which the Progressive age believed would open the door to utopia—initiative, referendum, recall, and a variety of measures for curbing the overwhelming power of the industrial giants America had produced. There was a significant difference between the two parties, however, in the methods they advocated for achieving these ends. The Progressives' principles came to be called the New Nationalism. Under their plan the Federal Government and especially the president were to exercise all the power of which they were capable in order to curb the excesses of large accumulations of economic power. Paternalism was implicit in the New Nationalism.

The Democratic party's slogan in 1912 was the New Freedom —a policy emphasizing the return of control of the nation's affairs to the people. Not a paternalistic executive authority, but the laws passed by a Congress representing the people, would curb the great concentrations of economic power.

In comparison with the Progressives and the Democrats, the Republicans were the conservatives in 1912. William Howard Taft had tried to prove in the last part of his term as president that he was a moderate liberal, but his concessions and those of his party to the spirit of the times were belated and insufficient.

The differences among the parties on the national level were brought home to the people of Connecticut in the state campaign. Simeon E. Baldwin spoke widely and attacked Roosevelt's New Nationalism with all the artillery in his states-rights' arsenal.[105] He also condemned Herbert Knox Smith, the Progressive gubernatorial candidate, for advising former President Roosevelt against the prosecution of the harvester trust. One newspaper suggested that Baldwin made this assault to prevent Smith from attracting liberals from the Democratic party.[106] Baldwin also repeatedly denounced the "Lord High Commissioner" of Highways, James H. MacDonald, a Republican holdover, whom Baldwin had been unable to unseat because of a law passed over the Governor's veto by the Republican-controlled 1911 General Assembly specifically retaining MacDonald in this position.[107] A final major note in Baldwin's campaign was the tariff. On this topic he corrected the impression that the Democratic party was for free trade, emphasizing instead their support of a fair tariff.[108]

The national issues and campaigns of 1912 threw the state contests into comparative obscurity. When the votes were counted, Connecticut had returned a complete Democratic state administration, and the state's electoral votes had gone to Wilson. Baldwin ran ahead of his party, winning by a plurality of over ten thousand votes to one of sixty-four hundred for Wilson.[109] In addition, the Democrats secured twenty-one of the state Senate seats to fourteen for the Republicans. The House was still in Republican hands by the narrow margin of 132 to 120, and there were six Progressives.[110] The third party in Connecticut as in the nation was largely responsible for the results.

Early in January of 1913 the re-elected Governor appeared before the General Assembly and outlined with his customary clarity the legislative program he desired the lawmakers to enact.[111] As in 1911 Baldwin favored the direct election of United States senators and urged the General Assembly to approve the pending constitutional amendment on that subject. He also suggested that the time had come for the abolition of the electoral college and the substitution of direct election of the president and vice-president. He advocated retaining the system by which the candidates receiving a plurality in the states would be credited with all the electoral votes allotted to a state. He recommended that Connecticut take the initiative in urging a constitutional amendment to this effect on Congress.

With regard to Connecticut's constitution, of the seven amendments proposed by the last House of Representatives, and which had to pass a second time before their submission to the electorate, Baldwin endorsed three. The first was designed to place restraints upon special legislation and to forbid it in any case which was or could be covered by a general law. Another proposed a two-thirds vote in each house instead of a majority to override an executive veto. The third gave the Supreme Court of Errors unquestioned authority to review evidence in appealed cases and also to review orders and decisions of executive or administrative authorities.

The Governor disapproved of the proposed amendment providing for the direct election of local judges and suggested as an alternative that these officials be nominated by the governor and confirmed by the General Assembly. He also opposed the amendments providing for a four-year term for members of the General Assembly and an increase in their salaries from three hundred dollars to five hundred dollars. A final constitutional change which the Governor held in disfavor would have repealed the forfeiture of the voting privileges of a person convicted of several crimes and whose sentence was only a fine.

Baldwin renewed again his 1911 plea, on which the General Assembly had not acted, for a constitutional amendment electing state senators on a general ticket rather than by districts. Instead of the thirty-five members as at that time, he proposed a senate of twelve, the original number of the Connecticut upper house in colonial days. Revising the composition of the General Assembly was one of the Governor's favorite reforms for half a century, but he never succeeded in obtaining the support necessary for carrying it through.

The Governor repeated in 1913 several other recommendations he had made two years earlier. He requested again that the governor be granted power to remove inferior executive officers. He renewed his plea that the term of the clerk of bills be during good behavior. The Governor asked for the establishment of a State Civil Service Commission. He also advocated that county commissioners be elected by the voters of each county rather than by the General Assembly. Another proposal was the enfranchising of property-owning women in local elections. In contrast to his stand in 1911 Baldwin this time spoke of such a measure as preliminary to granting the suffrage to all women. The Governor recommended the passage with minor changes of the workmen's compensation bill agreed upon by the commission appointed by the last General Assembly.

Since the state was spending more than its income, Governor Baldwin again urged economy on the lawmakers. To reinforce his plea he appended to his message a table of state receipts and expenditures during the past decade, which showed an increase of almost 100% in both. For purposes of economy and efficiency Baldwin suggested several specific measures for the reorganization of the executive branch of the government. Chief among these was the request for the creation of a state purveyor to supervise all state purchases. As a means of more strictly controlling the expenditure of public funds, he recommended that state money should be disbursed only by the treasury rather than by the officers of institutions and departments.

The 1913 session of the General Assembly was considerably shorter than that of 1911. Relations between the Governor and legislature were generally harmonious, and the few tangles between them were usually over appointments. One such case involved William H. Caldwell, Baldwin's appointee as highway commissioner, whom the General Assembly refused to confirm for partisan reasons.[112] Again when the Governor nominated the incumbent Republican, William H. Corbin, for Tax Commissioner, the Democratic Senate rejected him in caucus. After a reminder from Baldwin that he was Governor of the whole state and not only of the Democrats,[113] the Senate finally confirmed the nomination.[114] Another controversy resulted when the members of the General Assembly tried to vote themselves free transportation from their homes to the capital and return daily. Baldwin vetoed the measure as a violation of the constitution and was sustained.[115]

Without a doubt the most significant measure enacted by the 1913 session was the Workmen's Compensation Act. Both parties had favored such legislation for several years, but the 1911 General Assembly had been unable to agree on details. As finally constituted the act declared accidents to be the liability of employers, regardless of where the blame for them lay. It then set forth the terms and rates of compensation to injured workmen. Finally, it made provisions for the establishment of mutual insurance associations by employers to finance compensation payments.[116] Thus remuneration for industrial accidents became one of the costs of doing business in Connecticut. With the passage of this measure Connecticut somewhat belatedly joined the many states and countries of the western world which were enacting progressive labor legislation early in the twentieth century.

At the close of the session Baldwin pocket-vetoed a large batch of bills of minor consequence.[117] The Republican Hartford

Courant in an editorial entitled "Nerve" said in this regard:

> Governor Baldwin may or may not have the senatorial bee buzzing in his chapeau. He certainly has nerve and the bee is not able to disturb it. He has signed some measures that it seemed impossible that he would give his signature to, and now he has killed off a bunch that nobody believed he would kill—some saying frankly that they did not believe he "had the nerve." They have found out. Others were sure the measures had so much merit that he could not turn them down. Down they are.[118]

In a survey of the reaction to Baldwin's vetoes in Connecticut newspapers, the Hartford *Times* said that the Governor was upheld in his policy even by those who were hurt by them.[119]

In his closing message to the General Assembly Baldwin reviewed the accomplishments of the session and congratulated the members on the general character of the laws they had enacted. He pointed out that if their time had not been so occupied with the distribution of local offices and the consideration of special legislation, they could have adjourned a month earlier.

He regretted that they had refused again to pass the constitutional amendment which would have placed the nomination of municipal judges in the governor's hands. He also was displeased by their rejection of the report of the House Committee on Constitutional Amendments to preclude the appointment by future General Assemblies of their own members to any state office.

The Governor, on the other hand, approved of their assent to the federal constitutional amendment permitting the direct election of United States senators and also of their resolution asking Congress to initiate another amendment providing for the direct election of the president and vice-president.

Baldwin called the session a historic one, because it had framed and passed a carefully considered Workmen's Compensation Act. He also approved the relaxation of the Sunday observance laws so as to accord with the general trend of public sentiment.

He heartily endorsed several general laws which would save the legislature in the future from consideration of many individual petitions. One of these increased the self-governing powers of cities, towns and boroughs. No longer would it be necessary for them to obtain special legislative acts for bond issues. With a local referendum, they could revise their charters in many particulars. Another was a general law allowing banks and trust companies to incorporate. This, in turn, would do away with the flood of individual petitions for charters. A third such measure granted charities complete exemption from the payment of legacy taxes.

Although Baldwin approved of the liberal provisions made for better roads, he reproved the lawmakers for spending more than the probable income of the state. He concluded by congratulating them on the rejection of many useless and harmful measures which had been pressed on them.[120]

While governor, Simeon E. Baldwin attended the annual conferences of the state chief executives. In 1912, at this assemblage, he summarized his thinking on crime and punishment in a lucid address entitled "Modern Penology" [121] and a year later exhibited the progressive side of his nature by advocating that states pay the expenses of candidates for nomination and election. Such a step would give poor men an opportunity to run for public office and not necessitate their accepting money from those whose help would be an encumbrance. The states, in Baldwin's opinion, should pay for the printing and distribution of ballots and other papers required by law, the copying of poll and registry lists, the remuneration of challengers, and the traveling expenses of the candidates and of their supporting speakers to and from meetings incident to the campaign. The state should regulate nominations as it did elections, either by instituting direct primaries or by regulating the nominating conventions of the parties.[122]

Although in favor of direct primaries on the state level, Baldwin was opposed to the plan of President Wilson for a national direct primary to nominate candidates for president. Such an innovation would, he affirmed, enhance the importance of large states and further diminish that of small ones.[123]

In the fall of 1913 Governor Baldwin displayed his economic

conservatism by opposing the Justice Department's investigation of the New York, New Haven and Hartford Railroad. The carrier had by this time secured a near monopoly of railroad, trolley, and ship transportation in New England. Attorney General McReynolds had made investigations and threatened to bring proceedings against the railroad under the Sherman Anti-Trust Act. Baldwin wrote to the Attorney General that there might be good grounds for such an action, but cautioned that if a suit were brought, it might have grave consequences to the banking system of the state. The company's bonds were legal investments for savings banks, and many had invested heavily in them. If litigation should be instituted, the price of the railroad bonds would decline, surpluses of banks would be drained, and possibly runs follow.

There is no general wish in this State [said the Governor] to have the New York, New Haven and Hartford Railroad system broken up. There is a general wish that nothing should be done which would essentially change its *status*, until the new management has had a fair opportunity to survey the field, and rectify what it may think needs rectifying.[124]

The Attorney General replied that the transportation system of New England had been under investigation for some months, and it seemed fairly clear that the law was being violated and that there must be an early and a radical change. Mr. McReynolds hoped these modifications could be brought about voluntarily by the owners. He observed, however, that a continuing disregard of the law could not be permitted.[125] The Governor re-emphasized his former objections and repeated his plea that the suit be postponed until the new management had had an opportunity to rectify conditions.[126]

One of the most active opponents of the monopoly of New England transportation by the New Haven Railroad was Louis Brandeis, a Boston lawyer. The disparate positions of Baldwin and Brandeis on this question was a measure of the conservatism of the former and the liberalism of the latter. This difference may have influenced Baldwin's reply when in 1916 he was asked to write to the chairman of the Senate Judiciary Committee in behalf of Brandeis' candidacy for the Supreme Court. The latter's character and reputation were not, in Baldwin's opinion, such as to justify his being placed upon the Supreme Court.[127]

As early as the spring of 1913 the newspapers of Connecticut were referring to the possibility of Baldwin's running for the United States Senate in 1914.[128] This would be the first direct election of a United States senator in the state, and there was a belief that Baldwin would like to parallel his father's political career by moving from the governor's chair to a seat in the Senate. On October 1, 1913, Baldwin announced that he would accept the Democratic senatorial nomination, if it were offered him, and would not be a candidate for governor again.[129]

The following September the Democratic state nominating convention was held at Hartford in Foot Guard Hall.[130] Baldwin's principal opponent was Congressman Bryan F. Mahan of the New London district. The odds definitely favored Baldwin, and when the delegates cast their ballots, he received 377 to Mahan's 225 votes. The convention then made the nomination unanimous.[131] The Governor was referred to as Connecticut's "peerless leader," about to step on to the national stage, and his choice was applauded by Democratic and Republican papers alike.[132] The Hartford *Times* said:

> That the governor's nomination will win general approval of the party cannot be gainsaid. He will bring to the campaign a dignity, a learning and a record second to that of no man who has ever held the office.[133]

The Democratic platform emphasized national issues, defending the vigorous actions of the national administration in enacting such important measures as the Federal Reserve Act, the Underwood-Simmons Tariff, the Clayton Anti-Trust Act, and the Federal Trade Commission Act. It also favored women's suffrage.

The Republicans had meanwhile met at the Hyperion Theater in New Haven. Only one action of the Republican convention seemed certain in advance: the nomination of Frank B. Brandegee for United States senator. Brandegee, who then held a senatorship by legislative appointment, gave the keynote address at the convention.[134] His nomination was unanimous.[135]

The Republican convention was a more harmonious affair than its predecessors in 1910 and 1912. Some observers professed to see a reunited Grand Old Party in Connecticut and a decided confidence that victory was in the air for the Republicans that year.[136] The convention was described as boss-ridden, however, by the political opponents of the party. The Progressives, for example, pointed to the fact that J. Henry Roraback had been elected state chairman again, even though C. E. Mellen, president of the New York, New Haven and Hartford Railroad, had testified that Roraback was a paid lobbyist of that corporation.[137]

The Republican state platform, like the Democratic, dealt largely with national affairs. It denounced the incompetent administration of the Democrats in Washington, scored the assumption of power by the Democratic chief executive, and endorsed the protective tariff. The brief section on state issues merely approved such innocuous programs as better roads and the drive to eliminate tuberculosis.[138]

The campaign in 1914 was overshadowed by the great war which had begun in August. News of Connecticut and even national politics was crowded off the front page by reports of the battles being waged in France.

Baldwin was on the defensive in the campaign of 1914. His opponent's position as an incumbent senator gave him a decided advantage in the ensuing race. In addition, Baldwin was compelled to defend the record of the national administration against a constant barrage of criticism by the Republicans. The latter blamed the Democrats in Washington for the business recession in 1914.[139] The confident Republicans also stressed that the policies of the national administration had been hostile to New England. They pointed to the tariff reduction, which allegedly was bringing suffering to manufacturing interests in that area, and to the anti-trust litigation which the government had instituted against the New York, New Haven and

Hartford Railroad.[140] These charges brought countercharges that the Republicans were waging a campaign of misrepresentation, that they were trying to throw dust in the eyes of the voters.[141] Although the Republicans generally dared not criticize Governor Baldwin, they tried to maintain that he was a free trader. They argued too that Baldwin's experience was all on the state level and that he would be an amateur in the national political game. Senator Brandegee, on the other hand, would be able to represent Connecticut more effectively because of his experience. He would not be at the bottom of the seniority list as would the newcomer Baldwin and hence would receive more important committee posts.

On the whole the campaign was a quiet one. As late as November 1, the Hartford *Courant* took notice of the dearth of political activity in the state.[142] Underlying the calm was a confidence that the Republicans would soon be in control of the state house at Hartford and would re-elect a United States senator.

The assurance of the Grand Old Party proved to be well-founded, for the Republicans swept Connecticut in 1914. The great surprise of the election was the sharp decline of the Progressive party which polled thirty-five thousand votes in 1912 but only five thousand in 1914.[143] The return of the Progressives to the Republican party accounted in large part for the Democratic defeat in Connecticut.

Along with the rest of the ticket Simeon E. Baldwin was among the losers. Senator Brandegee was elected by a plurality of thirteen thousand votes.[144] The Democratic defeat, Baldwin told friends, was a real case of "recall" by the people.[145] The attitude of the Democratic national administration towards the New Haven Railroad had materially affected the outcome. The indictment of many of Connecticut's most respected citizens with conspiracy in connection with the railroad case had cost the Democratic party thousands of votes, the Governor believed.[146] He of course also laid part of the blame to the return of the Progressives to the Republican fold.[147]

The brief period of Democratic power in Connecticut was

like an arctic summer between two long northern winters of Republican rule. From 1895 to 1911 and from 1915 to 1931 the Republicans controlled the Nutmeg State. In 1930 as in 1910 another Yale professor—Wilbur L. Cross—was to break a second sixteen years of Republican rule in Connecticut.

II

The varied tasks associated with the governorship necessarily limited Simeon E. Baldwin's other activities between 1911 and 1915. He continued to teach at the Yale Law School but on a restricted schedule, and his work with the scholarly associations was similarly reduced. His research and writings also suffered from the pressure of official duties, and the products of his pen were fewer than in any previous period of his adult life.

In December of 1910, a month after his first election to the governorship, Baldwin became the president of the American Political Science Association. In this office the Governor-elect of Connecticut succeeded the Governor-elect of New Jersey, Woodrow Wilson.[148] As his presidential address the following year the Governor read a paper entitled "The Progressive Unfolding of the Powers of the United States." [149] Tracing with a sure grasp of the facts the rise of the powers of the Federal Government since the adoption of the Constitution, Baldwin summarized this growth with the statement: "The powers of the United States were unfolded in arithmetical progression until 1861, and since then in geometrical progression." [150] The vast expansion of federal authority in the 1930s would not have surprised the Governor (although he would have disapproved of it), for in 1911 he stated that the Constitution was flexible enough to support legislation far in advance of anything yet attempted.

In 1912 Baldwin was chosen a fellow of the American Academy of Arts and Sciences.[151] Membership in the American Society for Jurisprudence [152] and the Sons of the American Revolution [153] was conferred upon him in 1913.

High academic honors also came to the Governor during these years. In June, 1911, Columbia University conferred an LL.D. upon him,[154] the first honorary degree he had received since 1891, when Harvard bestowed similar recognition. A year later Wesleyan University gave the Governor his third LL.D.,[155] and in 1916 Baldwin's Alma Mater honored her distinguished alumnus in like manner.

Baldwin's active interest in international affairs extended into these crowded years also. At the initial meeting of the newly organized American Society for Judicial Settlement of International Disputes in December, 1910, he was elected vice-president.[156] A year later he succeeded to the presidency.[157] In 1913 the Governor was received into membership of the Institute of International Law.[158]

While governor, Baldwin was unable to attend the annual meetings of the scholarly and professional associations with his customary regularity. Active participation as speaker or presiding officer, however, necessitated his presence at many. Thus each year he went to the American Bar Association meetings to deliver his annual report as Director of the Association's Bureau of Comparative Law.

While in the state capital the Governor did not forget the affairs of his native city. In 1911 as president of the board of trustees of Hopkins Grammar School he was for the second time involved in negotiations with the New Haven Board of Education over the question of uniting Hopkins with New Haven High School. Families whose boys formerly attended Hopkins, which was a day school, were by this time sending their sons to boarding schools. Faced with a diminishing clientele and always hard pressed to meet expenses, the board was once more considering the feasibility of entrusting the school to the care of the city. Although negotiations were carried on for some time, an agreement with the city was never reached, and the private school continued its precarious existence until more adequately financed during the 1920s, principally by Baldwin.[159]

During this period most of Simeon E. Baldwin's publications were adaptations of addresses. Research papers quite understandably were almost entirely absent. The subjects on which he wrote corresponded rather closely to those of the period of his judgeship.

His interest in international relations produced "The Proposed International Court of Arbitral Justice";[160] "The New Era of International Courts";[161] "The Constitutional Objection to the New Arbitration Treaties";[162] and "Justice Between Nations."[163]

In the field of legal studies Baldwin contributed several articles on varying aspects of law. These included *The Project of a Federal Incorporation Law for Corporations Engaged in Interstate or Foreign Commerce*,[164] an address before the New Haven Chamber of Commerce; "Legislative Divorces and the Fourteenth Amendment";[165] "Liability for Accidents in Aerial Navigation";[166] and "The Limits of the Legislative Power of an American State,"[167] an address before the New Hampshire Bar Association.

Baldwin's only papers on historical subjects were of a popular nature and were prepared as addresses for special occasions. Among these may be mentioned *Historical Discourse Pronounced at the Two Hundred and Fiftieth Anniversary of the Hopkins Grammar School of New Haven, June 18, 1910;*[168] "The Contributions of North Carolina to the Development of American Institutions,"[169] a commencement address at Wake Forest College in 1914; and "New England's Leadership in American History,"[170] an address at the annual dinner of the New England Society of New York in 1913.

In addition to these articles a series of lectures which Baldwin delivered at Yale was published in book form as *The Relations of Education to Citizenship*.[171] These were the Yale lectures on the Responsibilities of Citizenship for 1912. In them Baldwin emphasized the responsibility of the educated man for devoting himself to public service as well as to private gain.

The demands of the governorship forced Simeon Baldwin to restrict his other activities to a greater extent than he had ever done before. It may have been with something of a sense of relief, therefore, that in January, 1915, he retired from public office and was able to resume many of the pursuits which had formerly filled his life.

AUTUMN YEARS

I

When Simeon E. Baldwin's impending retirement from politics became known, he received scores of sincere letters from admirers in both parties and many walks of life. Among these was a greeting in verse which summarized Baldwin's significant achievements up to 1915 and made a facetious observation as to his future.

S. E. B.

The youngest Baldwin always was a very clever lad;
In school as well as college his record was not bad.

He raked in all the prizes and made full many a speech,
Took in the best societies and everything in reach.

After some practice at the Bar his record showed no flaw,
So they made him a professor to instruct the young in law.

"This surely is a fine career!" his friends and neighbors cried.
But not at all! Do not suppose that *he* was satisfied.

The judge's ermine took his eye; though something of a wrench,
He very shortly left the Bar and got upon the Bench.

But after eighteen years of this he found it rather slow,
So into active politics he thought that he would go.

And so they made him Governor and let him rule the state,
As his father did before him at a somewhat earlier date.

When through with this, the Nation tried to make him President
But this, he said, was something to which *he* could not consent.

He'd held that title far too oft to make it count for much
In leagues, associations, conventions, clubs and such.

So now he has no job at all. He's looking round to find
An office that is big enough to occupy his mind.

What is there, where his knowledge, force, experience can find scope?
The only thing *I* can suggest is that they make him POPE.

Envoi

Professor, Doctor, Governor, Judge, Chief Justice S. E. B.
The fruits of all your arduous toil you here may gathered see.[1]

The seventy-four-year-old Governor had worked hard and faithfully, and if he had drifted through the remainder of his life, most observers would have thought him justified in enjoying a few years of relaxation. But coasting was something Baldwin could not do, even in his mid-seventies, and almost at once he realigned his activities so as to absorb his leisure. He told a friend that he was enjoying his new freedom and pursuing all the activities in which he had been interested while on the bench except his judicial duties.[2] The year 1915 and the subsequent ones thus saw him once more delivering addresses, serving on boards and committees, both of local groups and of national scholarly associations, and writing prolifically.

Prominent among his speaking engagements during the years after his political retirement were bar association addresses. In January of 1916, for example, he spoke at the Ontario Bar Association's annual banquet [3] and in June was the principal speaker at the convention of the Wisconsin Bar Association.[4]

Besides law addresses Baldwin continued to serve the legal profession through his work with the American Bar Association. Early in 1915 he became chairman of its Committee on Publications and assisted in launching its new organ, the *American Bar Association Journal*.[5] He served as editor of the first three numbers.[6] Later in the year he resigned from this committee and the editorship,[7] but continued to serve as Director of the Bureau of Comparative Law until 1919.

The advent of war in Europe in 1914 brought other new duties to Baldwin. American sympathy for the devastation in Belgium produced relief drives for the stricken nation. Governor Baldwin loaned the prestige of his name to this movement in January, 1915, and was elected President of the Connecticut Committee of the Commission for Relief in Belgium. The group succeeded in raising many thousands of dollars during its two years of existence. In May, 1917, after American entry into the conflict, the United States government assumed the tasks of the volunteers and made loans directly to Belgium for relief purposes.[8]

Another activity which absorbed Baldwin's time during the post-gubernatorial years was his service on a state tax commission. The Connecticut General Assembly in 1915 authorized the governor to appoint a three-man commission to study the state's taxation system and to codify the laws relating thereto. Baldwin's Republican successor, Governor Holcomb, invited him to be chairman of this body.[9] His appointment indicated the esteem in which Baldwin was held by his Republican opponents. It also provided another example of his conservatism, for the Republicans would scarcely have permitted his being named to such an important commission, were they not confident that he would reflect their party's views on the subject. Charged with considering both changes in the tax laws and methods of better administering them, the commissioners conducted hearings in various parts of the state. In their report to the General Assembly in 1917 they recommended that the existing system of taxation be retained but suggested improved techniques for its execution.[10] That the membership was weighted on the conservative side became evident when the chairman and another member outvoted the proposal of the third to recommend a state income tax similar to that of Wisconsin.[11]

The aspects of Baldwin's career which were most neglected during his years as governor were his research and publications. After his retirement he wasted no time in resuming his writings, and a stream of articles appeared during the succeeding years. The subjects on which Baldwin wrote most frequently were international problems, American government, legal history, and colonial and early American history.

The following articles are representative of Baldwin's writings during this final period of his life. "The 'Continuous Voyage' Doctrine During the Civil War, and Now" [12] discussed the applicability of a nineteenth-century maritime rule during World War I. In "A Ride Across Connecticut Before the Revolution," [13]

Baldwin quoted from the journal of his grandaunt, Bethiah Baldwin, an account of the discomforts of a journey from Norwich to Danbury in 1770. "The United States Law Journal of 1822" [14] related the history of New England's first legal periodical. "The Founding of the American Bar Association" [15] referred in modest manner to the contributions of Simeon E. Baldwin in establishing the chief guild of the lawyers. "The Hartford Convention" [16] provided a reinterpretation of the 1814 meeting of New England sectionalists. "The time has long gone by," said Professor A. B. Hart, in commenting on Baldwin's paper, "when that meeting could be looked upon as a treasonable gathering; you are doubtless correct in saying that what they were after was a revision of the Constitution—only the proposed revision was incompatible with the national government." [17] In the field of government Baldwin produced "The Share of the President of the United States in a Declaration of War." [18] Professor Hart remarked that this was one of Baldwin's numerous contributions to the actuality of American government. "I have occasion every day to thank you for your book on the judiciary, on the same grounds—that it tells something about the real springs of action." [19]

Two of Baldwin's contributions to the debate over an international organization among the nations appeared in 1918 and 1919, respectively. These were "The Membership of a World Tribunal for Promoting Permanent Peace" [20] and "The Vesting of Sovereignty in a League of Nations." [21] Baldwin was sympathetic with the aims of the League of Nations and favored America's participation in it. He insisted, however, that it should be made clear that the United States would not be forced into war through membership in the League without the approval of Congress.[22]

Undoubtedly Baldwin's most ambitious literary undertaking of this period was the life of his grandfather, Simeon Baldwin, which appeared in 1919.[23] This book was largely a compilation from letters and journals of the elder Simeon Baldwin, whom the author permitted to tell his own story and reveal his own character. He was, in the words of one reviewer, "a fairly typical Connecticut Federalist, sharing every opinion and prejudice of his class." [24] Nothing new or startling pertaining to Federalism, but much illustrative material, was contained in the correspondence. The work was written, according to the preface, primarily for the author's family and descendants and was privately printed. This product of Baldwin's late seventies cannot be judged a great biography, but it decidedly was a competent one.

Another volume, which appeared early in 1920, was entitled *The Young Man and the Law*. In this Baldwin considered five main topics: the attractions of the legal profession, the principal objections to it, the personal qualities requisite to success in the law, the type of education necessary to prepare for the law, and the great ideals of the profession. The work was studded with references to and quotations from both ancient and modern writers on the law, fruits of Baldwin's long life of study. It was essentially a guide to the young man contemplating a career at the bar. The book was also a synthesis of the thinking of one of the great jurists of the times on the legal profession.

In 1919 Baldwin celebrated his seventy-ninth birthday and in that year began to shed some of his duties and offices. He resigned as Director of the Comparative Law Bureau of the American Bar Association and gave up all his responsibilities at the Law School.

He continued, however, to devote his energies to the recently established Connecticut College for Women at New London. Since 1911, the year in which its charter was granted, Baldwin had served on its board of trustees. He assisted in formulating plans for the college and in their fulfillment during its early years of operation. After its first president was asked to resign in 1917, Baldwin corresponded with several prospective successors and was instrumental in securing the appointment of Reverend Benjamin T. Marshall. Baldwin spoke at the commencement exercises in June, 1920, and in thanking him President Marshall paid him the following tribute:

How I wish that to all our students and our Faculty, and all our

Board there might come some share of the fidelity, devotion, zeal and generosity which you have ever shown toward the college.[25]

In 1920 Baldwin and the homestead in which he was raised celebrated their eightieth birthdays. Someone commemorated the event with the following verses, which were among the Baldwin papers:

The Baldwin House to its Oldest Friend

Drawing our life from the self-same source
On the self-same day we both were born.
My life began when over the hedge
You came to me one April morn.

Fair and square we both were built,
Simple and dignified, 'twas said.
But I was gray from my earliest day,
While the years have lightly touched your head.

Fast you grew to a good height,
I, too, have had an upward growth,
I've changed furniture, you ideas,
But the man who made us would know us both.

I was rather cold till my furnace came,
But you were always warm of heart,
With a hearty welcome for one and all,
In that I, too, have born my part.

Your head is full of original thought
My top is full of inherited junk,
Your own old cradle, spinning wheels,
Many a chest and horse-hair trunk.

Eighty years we've had together.
Some foul weather, but mostly fair,
From 1840 to 1920,
We are truly a wonderful pair.

I remember of old
You had a sweet tooth,
Accept these sweets
For the sake of our youth.

The 1920s coincided with Simeon E. Baldwin's ninth decade, and during these years illness came to him for almost the first time in his life.[26] Except for his chronic eye trouble, he had up to this time lived singularly free of serious maladies. When his health permitted, he took his accustomed walks and spent part of the day in his law office. But Baldwin's public engagements after 1920 were not numerous. Not often did he venture from his home city. He even resigned from several New Haven organizations in 1923: the Social Science Club, the Lawyers Club, the Board of Park Commissioners, and the board of directors of the Hospital Society of Connecticut.[27] Moreover, he was not well enough to attend the American Bar Association meetings in 1923;[28] nor was he present at the centennial exercises of the Yale Law School in June, 1924.

Baldwin did not stop his intellectual pursuits, however much infirmities forced him to reduce his physical activities. In September, 1923, he wrote that old age had dealt kindly with him. He could still read and was just finishing John Quincy Adams' *Journal*, which he had longed to peruse for forty years.[29] A month later he agreed to write the chapters on the colonial period for Norris G. Osborn's five-volume *History of Connecticut in Monographic Form*.[30] This was Baldwin's last large piece of writing and is a competent survey of Connecticut as a colony and one of the most substantial monographs in the volumes.

Baldwin's last years were made more pleasant by the presence of his daughter and her children in New Haven. Mrs. Gilman's husband had died in 1920, and soon thereafter she came to reside with her father during the remainder of his life. Baldwin's granddaughter, Charlotte Wentworth Gilman, graduated from Radcliffe College in 1920 and received her M.A. from Yale a year later. Soon thereafter she was married at her grandfather's home to Paul L. Penfield. The Penfields have lived in Michigan, where Mr. Penfield is an executive in a Detroit utility. Their two daughters are married, and their son is a college student.

Baldwin's grandson, Bradley Baldwin Gilman, graduated from Yale in 1925 and from Harvard Law School in 1928. For many years he was a practicing attorney in Worcester. He has recently withdrawn from the law to become an officer in a Worcester bank. Mr. Gilman is also a trustee and officer of the Bancroft School and of Memorial Hospital, both in Worcester. He is married and has two children, a son in college and a younger daughter.[31]

Baldwin's son, who had married in 1910, continued to live on his farm in Woodbury, Connecticut. He had been obliged because of poor health to abandon his promising legal career and to live an outdoor life. After spending some years as a forester in California, he prepared for his occupation as a gentleman-farmer at Connecticut Agricultural College, from which he graduated in 1916.[32]

During Simeon E. Baldwin's last years many tributes came to the aging man from his friends and associates. An anonymous poem thanked Baldwin for his services in developing the park system of New Haven:

To the Honorable Park Commissioner, Simeon E. Baldwin.

Whene'er I take my walks abroad
How many parks I view;
And all these beauty spots derive
Their origin from you.

First *East Rock Park*, the queen of all,
Work of your hand and brain.
With many a scramble through the woods
You planned each road and lane.

Fort Wooster Park, with glorious view,
Full of historic charms;
Fort Hale, where every sultry day
The small boy swims in swarms;

Bay View, well named; its graceful elms
Waving in soft sea breezes;
Quinnipiac, won inch by inch,
Where baseball never ceases.

In *Waterside* Young Italy
Does run and romp all day
While mothers sit and dream themselves
At home on Naples' Bay.

While *Edgewood* with its flowery lawns
And deep and shady drives,
And *Clinton* with its river view
Make happy many lives.

In *Beaver Ponds*, where long ago
The ancestral cow did graze,
Young hyphenates of every race
Play through the summer days.

And *West Rock Park*, whose rocky crest
Sheltered the Regicide,
Freed from the quarry's ravening tooth,
Our city's greatest pride.

But lest you waver in your task
And think your work is done,
This little tree is sent to you
To start another one.[33]

Baldwin's work as founder of the American Bar Association brought several acknowledgments. One of these was a resolution adopted at the 1923 meeting of the association:

The American Bar Association in convention assembled at Minneapolis, mindful of the debt which it owes the Honorable Simeon E. Baldwin for his great service in founding the Association and his unfailing devotion to its interests, sends him its hearty congratulation that he has in such abundant measure all that should accompany old age, and it is hoped that his years may be prolonged while life has for him more of pleasure than of pain.[34]

The 1926 meeting of the American Bar Association designated the three living survivors of the founding meeting at Saratoga on August 21, 1878, Simeon E. Baldwin, Francis Rawle, and Alfred Hemenway, as Honorary Life Members. The Association also invited them to attend the fiftieth annual meeting the following year as its honored guests.[35]

Before that date arrived, however, Simeon E. Baldwin's life had come to a close. He died at his home on January 30, 1927, a few days before his eighty-seventh birthday. Parkinson's disease followed by bronchial pneumonia were the immediate causes,[36] but a general physical breakdown had apparently been taking place for some time.[37]

The sense of stewardship which had characterized Simeon E. Baldwin's attitude towards the acquisition and possession of material goods was perhaps most tangibly reflected in his will. Of his million-and-a-half dollar estate he bequeathed fully two-thirds to the institutions he had served so well. Approximately one-half million dollars went to the Yale Law School; nearly a quarter million to United Church; and more than one hundred thousand dollars to Hopkins Grammar School and a similar amount to the City of New Haven for use in the parks. The remainder of his estate was divided among his children, other relatives and friends.[38]

II

Any estimate of Simeon E. Baldwin's significance should begin with his career as a lawyer, for Baldwin devoted the largest portion of his life to this profession. He was a practicing attorney for thirty years, during much of which time he specialized in corporation law with particular emphasis on railroads. He was acknowledged as one of the leading members of the bar in his state, and although his reputation did not extend much beyond Connecticut's borders, that was in substantial measure because Baldwin's roots were too deeply implanted in his home community. On one occasion, it will be recalled, he declined the general counselship of the New York and New England Railroad, apparently because the position would require his moving to Boston.

As a young man Baldwin served the legal profession of his state by preparing the elaborate *Digest* of cases which bears his name. Soon thereafter he was given the opportunity to assist in revising and simplifying the legal procedure of Connecticut and did the major share in formulating the practice act and the new forms and rules of procedure to accompany the introduction of code pleading. His work in this field left a permanent mark upon the state's legal system.

Another of Baldwin's major services to his profession was

his half century of teaching at the Yale Law School. His timely assistance and direction when it was about to expire in 1869 may have saved the very existence of one of present-day America's great institutions for legal study. As a professor of law Baldwin's reputation went far beyond the halls of Yale. Letters from students who attended his classes attest the high quality of his instruction. The many endorsements of his publications in numerous fields of law and legal education are tangible evidences of his excellence as a scholar and thinker. His presidency of the Association of American Law Schools was one mark of his eminence as a member of the guild of law teachers. So strongly was he devoted to the Yale Law School that he left a third of his fortune to it, even after the majority of its faculty adopted the case method of teaching, the exclusive use of which Baldwin had fought vigorously for years.

Another significant aspect of Baldwin's long association with Yale was his role in the transference of control of the university from clerical to secular hands. Baldwin's article, "The Ecclesiastical Constitution of Yale College," lent authority to the contention that Yale's charter did not require the university to have a ministerial president or board of fellows.

Baldwin's unique contribution to legal education was his introduction of graduate study in law for the first time in any American institution of learning. And for this innovation his place in the history of American legal education is secure.

Also in the field of law is the act for which Baldwin will probably be longest remembered, the founding of the American Bar Association. The deliberate manner in which he accomplished this singlehandedly is a story of careful planning and execution. The way in which he sensed the need for such an association and marshalled the great legal names of the country behind its organization was as amazing as it was admirable. It is a prize example of the imagination and the initiative to carry through an idea which Baldwin exhibited so often and so well.

Baldwin was first and last a man of principle, and though he was jeopardizing a political career of twenty years' building, he jettisoned the Republican party in 1884 and became the leader of Connecticut mugwumpery. His first major political office was his judgeship in 1893, which removed him from politics for nearly twenty years. In this capacity and as chief justice of the Supreme Court of Errors during his last few years on the bench, he attained a position of prominence and respect second to that of no man in the state. It was as Judge Baldwin that he was known in Connecticut, and his eminence as a jurist was attested by his most distinguished contemporaries.

And it was as a retired chief justice more than as a Yale professor that he was known to the voters when he ran successfully for governor in 1910. In this office his consistent independence constantly amazed the press and his opponents, as well as his own political associates. After one term no one could say a word against him, and with the assistance of the Progressive split of 1912 he carried a complete slate of state officials into office with him. When Baldwin ran at the age of seventy-four for a term of six years in the United States Senate, the voters, assisted by the return of the Progressives to their former berths in the Republican party, retired him from office.

All during the busy years as lawyer, judge, and governor, Baldwin won an enviable reputation for himself as a scholar and authority in several fields of the social sciences. Few, if any contemporaries, commanded enough respect in law, international law, government, history, and legal education to have been president of the national societies in each of these fields. Rare indeed is the man in more recent times who heads more than one of these.

With all of these accomplishments to his credit, it is somewhat perplexing to understand why, a generation after his death, Simeon E. Baldwin is so little remembered. One explanation may be that he dispersed his energies too widely, that he did not specialize in law or history or international relations to a sufficient extent to become a truly great figure. That he could have done so, had he chosen to, this writer does not doubt. Unfortunate "breaks" suggest another explanation. He almost became a Supreme Court Justice; and had he been ten or fifteen years younger when the opportunities arose, he might have become president of Yale or even President of the United States. A third reason for Baldwin's not reaching the very first rank may lie in his personality. Although he was warm and affectionate within his family, to the world he was austere and somewhat forbidding. He was the sort of man people could admire and respect but hardly the kind they could be genuinely fond of.

Perhaps a final reason for the rapid decline of Baldwin's fame is his lack of sympathy for many of the movements which were gaining success in his day. He opposed, for example, the case system which triumphed in the law schools during his active years; he did not appreciate what Louis Brandeis stood for, and he was hostile to the antitrust proceedings which the Federal Government was instituting against the New York, New Haven and Hartford Railroad. It is indeed difficult to recall very much of the program of the Progressive Era with which Baldwin was in sympathy. There were, however, two areas in which he displayed some liberalism. In religion his viewpoint was forward-looking, and in a period of triumphant nationalism Baldwin favored American entry into the League of Nations. Had he lived on into the 1930s, he almost certainly would have opposed the New Deal. If Baldwin can be called a liberal at all, it is only in the nineteenth-century sense.

In spite of his multitude of activities Baldwin appeared to be essentially a lonely man. Although in part true, this appearance was deceptive, for Baldwin was the center of a large family circle. After his daughter's marriage she and her children visited Baldwin's home several times a year. The relatives in large numbers customarily gathered at his house for Thanksgiving, and on one such occasion more than forty enjoyed dinner there.[39] As the most distinguished member of the family, Baldwin became increasingly the one to whom everyone turned for advice and assistance. Several nieces and nephews looked to him for counsel; and he helped numerous cousins and other relatives in a variety of ways. In short, he was the reliable, responsible pillar of the whole family.[40]

The accomplishments of Baldwin's lifetime were made possible by several factors. Primary, of course, was his first-rate intelligence. His excellent family background helped him in many ways. But most important was Baldwin's supreme passion for work. In this respect he was the source of constant wonder to his contemporaries. Very little came his way by chance; in fact, most "breaks" worked to his disadvantage. It was his superior native ability plus a strong desire to leave his mark upon the world which accounted in large measure for Simeon E. Baldwin's many achievements.

NOTES

NOTES

THE SETTING

1. Richard S. Fisher, *A New and Complete Statistical Gazetteer of the United States of America Founded on and Compiled from Official Federal and State Returns and the Seventh National Census*, pp. 540–41.

2. Richard J. Purcell in *Connecticut in Transition, 1775–1818*, deals competently with the course of events leading up to the disestablishment of Congregationalism. Fisher, *op. cit.*, p. 541, states that in 1853 New Haven had 22 churches: 8 Congregational, 4 Episcopal, 4 Methodist, 2 Baptist, 2 Catholic, 1 Universalist, and 1 Jewish Synagogue.

3. The chapter in Jarvis M. Morse's *A Neglected Period of Connecticut's History, 1818–1850*, on the rise of industry contains a survey of the developments in transportation.

4. Edward E. Atwater, ed., *History of the City of New Haven to the Present Time*, pp. 95–98. This work has been superseded by Rollin G. Osterweis', *Three Centuries of New Haven, 1638–1938*, published in 1953.

5. Thomas Jefferson to Abraham Bishop, November 13, 1808, as quoted by Atwater, *op. cit.*, p. 534.

6. Morse, *op. cit.*, p. 244.

7. Daniel P. Tyler, *Statistics of the Condition and Products of Certain Branches of Industry in Connecticut, for the Year Ending October 1, 1845*, pp. 38–41.

8. Morse, *op. cit.*, p. 23.

9. See letter from Jewish Congregation of New Haven to Governor Roger S. Baldwin, November, 1844, inviting him to their Thanksgiving services. Baldwin Collection, Yale University Library. All manuscript sources referred to are from the Baldwin Collection unless otherwise noted.

10. Thomas T. Sherman, *Sherman Genealogy*, pp. 293–94. This source gives Mrs. Baldwin's name as Emeline; the Vital Records of Hartford list her birth under the name of Emilia; Mrs. Baldwin always used and preferred the name of Emily.

11. William Pitkin and George Wyllys of Connecticut; William Bradford and Thomas Dudley of Massachusetts; and John Haynes of both colonies.

12. George W. Perkins, *Sermons by George W. Perkins with a Memoir* (by Rev. James T. Dickinson), p. 2. George W. Perkins was the brother of Mrs. Baldwin.

13. Simeon E. Baldwin, *Life and Letters of Simeon Baldwin*, pp. 1 ff.

14. Samuel W. S. Dutton, *An Address at the Funeral of Hon. Roger Sherman Baldwin*, p. 8.

15. *Ibid.*, p. 13. A concise account of this famous trial may be found in Simeon E. Baldwin, "Roger Sherman Baldwin," *Great American Lawyers* (ed. William Draper Lewis), III, 498–505.

16. Emily P. Baldwin to her son, Edward L. Baldwin, November 19, 1844.

17. Simeon E. Baldwin, "Roger Sherman Baldwin," *Great American Lawyers* (ed. William Draper Lewis), III, 525.

18. Philip Marett to an unknown correspondent, ca. February, 1863.

19. Emily P. Baldwin to her son, Roger S. Baldwin, Jr., undated (1853).

20. Philip Marett to his daughter, Mrs. Ellen Gifford, March 7, 1863.

21. Governor William A. Buckingham to Roger S. Baldwin, February 2, 1861.

22. Allan Nevins, *The Emergence of Lincoln*, II, 402, 412.

23. From an undated sketch of Edward L. Baldwin in the handwriting of his brother, Simeon E. Baldwin.

24. Emily P. Baldwin to her husband, Roger S. Baldwin, January 21, 1848.

25. Roger S. Baldwin, Jr., to his father, Roger S. Baldwin, October 24, 1848.

26. Roger S. Baldwin to his wife, Emily P. Baldwin, January 11, 1849.

27. Roger S. Baldwin, Jr., "Tarryings in Nicaragua," The *Century Illustrated Monthly Magazine*, XLII, 911–31.

28. Emily P. Baldwin to her husband, Roger S. Baldwin, January 3, 1848.

29. Emily P. Baldwin to her husband, Roger S. Baldwin, January 29, 1848.

30. Henrietta P. Baldwin to her brother, Roger S. Baldwin, Jr., July 19, 1848.

31. Emily P. Baldwin to her husband, Roger S. Baldwin, February 8, 1850.

32. C. A. Joy to Herman Camp, May 26, 1853.

33. Emily P. Baldwin to her son, Roger S. Baldwin, Jr., February 14, 1856.

34. Roger S. Baldwin to his son, Roger S. Baldwin, Jr., August 6, 1855.

35. Simeon E. Baldwin to his father, Roger S. Baldwin, August 27, 1858.

EARLIEST IMPRESSIONS

1. The Baldwin homestead no longer exists (the main building of the Southern New England Telephone Company now stands in its place), but it is pictured in Fanny Winchester Hotchkiss' *Winchester Notes*, opposite page 161.

2. Emily P. Baldwin to her son, Edward L. Baldwin, February 14, 1845.

3. Elizabeth W. Baldwin to her brother, Edward L. Baldwin, July 9, 1845.

4. Simeon E. Baldwin to his brother, Edward L. Baldwin, November, 1846.

5. Emily P. Baldwin to her son, Edward L. Baldwin, December 29, 1846.

6. Emily P. Baldwin to her son, Edward L. Baldwin, May 28, 1847.

7. Roger S. Baldwin, Jr., to his brother, Simeon E. Baldwin, undated (spring of 1848).

8. Emily P. Baldwin to her husband, Roger S. Baldwin, December 24, 1847.

9. Elizabeth W. Baldwin to her father, Roger S. Baldwin, February 28, 1848.

10. Emily P. Baldwin to her husband, Roger S. Baldwin, March 11, 1848.

11. Simeon E. Baldwin to his father, Roger S. Baldwin, March 3, 1848.

12. Emily P. Baldwin to her husband, Roger S. Baldwin, April 10, 1848.

13. Simeon E. Baldwin to his father, Roger S. Baldwin, July 14, 1848.

14. Simeon E. Baldwin to his father, Roger S. Baldwin, January 21, 1849.

15. Simeon E. Baldwin to his sister, Henrietta P. Baldwin, January 21, 1849.

16. Simeon E. Baldwin to his father, Roger S. Baldwin, February 4, 1849.

17. Henrietta P. Baldwin to her brother, Simeon E. Baldwin, April 3, 1849.
18. Memorandum, February 18, 1850.
19. Emily P. Baldwin to her husband, Roger S. Baldwin, August 4, 1850.
20. Roger S. Baldwin to his son, Simeon E. Baldwin, March 13, 1850.
21. Essay by Simeon E. Baldwin.
22. Emily P. Baldwin to her husband, Roger S. Baldwin, May 3, 1850.
23. Simeon E. Baldwin to his father, Roger S. Baldwin, June 7, 1850.
24. Emily P. Baldwin to her son, Roger S. Baldwin, Jr., January 9, 1851.
25. Emily P. Baldwin to her husband, Roger S. Baldwin, February 11, 1851.
26. Emily P. Baldwin to her husband, Roger S. Baldwin, January 18, 1851.
27. Mary E. Manchester, "Roger Sherman Baldwin," *Dictionary of American Biography*, I, 543.
28. Jarvis M. Morse, "Isaac Toucey," *Dictionary of American Biography*, XVIII, 600–601.
29. Simeon E. Baldwin to his sister, Elizabeth W. Baldwin, June 23, 1851.
30. Emily P. Baldwin to her husband, Roger S. Baldwin, October 9, 1851.
31. Emily P. Baldwin to her daughter, Henrietta P. B. Foster, December 12, 1851.
32. Roger S. Baldwin to his son, Roger S. Baldwin, Jr., March 19, 1852.
33. Roger S. Baldwin to his wife, Emily P. Baldwin, July 17, 1852.
34. Roger S. Baldwin to his son, Roger S. Baldwin, Jr., August 4, 1852.
35. Simeon E. Baldwin to his father, Roger S. Baldwin, May 22, 1853.
36. Emily P. Baldwin to her son, Simeon E. Baldwin, May 26, 1853.
37. Simeon E. Baldwin to his mother, Emily P. Baldwin, June 5, 1853.
38. Simeon E. Baldwin to his mother, Emily P. Baldwin, May 29, 1853.
39. Simeon E. Baldwin to his mother, Emily P. Baldwin, June 5, 1853.

40. Emily P. Baldwin to her son, Roger S. Baldwin, Jr., January 1, 1853.

41. Roger S. Baldwin to his son, Roger S. Baldwin, Jr., June 14, 1853.

42. *Ibid.*

43. C. O. Perkins to Emily P. Baldwin, August 29, 1853.

44. Miscellaneous undated manuscript.

45. Miscellaneous undated manuscript.

46. William H. Seward to Roger Sherman Day, January 29, 1854.

47. Edward F. Blake to Simeon E. Baldwin, August 2, 1854.

48. Miscellaneous manuscript dated March, 1854.

49. Diary of Simeon E. Baldwin, January through March, 1854.

50. Emily P. Baldwin to her husband, Roger S. Baldwin, February 13, 1854.

51. Simeon E. Baldwin to Edward F. Blake, May 11, 1854 (Blake Family Collection in Yale University Library).

52. Edward F. Blake to Simeon E. Baldwin, undated (ca. August, 1854).

53. Roger S. Baldwin to his son, Simeon E. Baldwin, August 28, 1854.

54. Emily P. Baldwin to her sisters, October 17, 1854.

55. Emily P. Baldwin to her son, Roger S. Baldwin, Jr., March 17, 1855.

56. Roger S. Baldwin to his son, Roger S. Baldwin, Jr., August 6, 1855.

57. *Ibid.*

58. Emily P. Baldwin to her daughter, Henrietta P. B. Foster, undated (ca. 1855–7).

59. *Ibid.*

60. Emily P. Baldwin to her son, Roger S. Baldwin, Jr., April 18, 1856.

61. Simeon E. Baldwin to his mother, Emily P. Baldwin, May 2, 1856.

62. Simeon E. Baldwin to his father, Roger S. Baldwin, May 10, 1856.

63. Simeon E. Baldwin to his mother, Emily P. Baldwin, June 12, 1856.

64. Emily P. Baldwin to her husband, Roger S. Baldwin, August 9, 1856.

65. James Blake to Simeon E. Baldwin, June 4, 1856.

66. See the oration on its history by Simeon E. Baldwin, dated January 23, 1857.

67. James Blake to Simeon E. Baldwin, June 4, 1856.

68. Simeon E. Baldwin to his sister, Elizabeth W. Baldwin, February 17 (1855).

69. Simeon E. Baldwin to his mother, Emily P. Baldwin, February 19, 1857.

70. Form letter dated July 27, 1857.

COLLEGE YEARS

1. Harris E. Starr, "Theodore Dwight Woolsey," *Dictionary of American Biography*, XX, 519–520.

2. Much of the information on Yale is from the college catalogues, 1857–58 to 1861–62.

3. The Department of Philosophy and the Arts consisted of (*a*) Yale Scientific School, and (*b*) a division offering instruction in philosophy, history, languages and literatures, mathematics and physics. Degrees of Civil Engineer, Bachelor of Philosophy, and Doctor of Philosophy were given in this department, the latter being first offered in 1860 and first awarded a year later.

4. See also the *Yale Banner*, September 30, 1857.

5. Franklin B. Dexter, *Sketch of the History of Yale University*, p. 87.

6. William C. Johnston, "The Literary Societies of Yale College," The *University Quarterly*, I, 115–126.

7. George W. Baldwin to his brother, Simeon E. Baldwin, October 21, 1857.

8. *Supplement to the Yale Banner*, October 6, 1857. See also undated balance sheet of Delta Kappa's financial affairs in Simeon E. Baldwin's handwriting.

9. Roger S. Baldwin to his son, George W. Baldwin, May 17, 1858.

10. The manuscript is in Simeon E. Baldwin's handwriting.

11. Draft of a speech by Simeon E. Baldwin, July 14, 1858.

12. Undated manuscript by Simeon E. Baldwin.

13. The *Yale Banner*, September 27, 1858.

14. Undated manuscript by Simeon E. Baldwin, ca. 1859.

15. *Secretary's Book of Alpha Sigma Phi Commenced by the Class of 1861* [,] *1858–62*, Memorabilia Room, Yale University Library.

16. Undated manuscript.

17. *Supplement to the Yale Banner*, September 29, 1860.

18. *Yale Banner*, September 24, 1859.

19. Simeon E. Baldwin to "Hebald," an unknown correspondent, January 18, 1859.

20. Simeon E. Baldwin to his father, Roger S. Baldwin, April 30, 1859.

21. Emily P. Baldwin to her son, George W. Baldwin, May 22, 1859.

22. Manuscript by Simeon E. Baldwin dated June 28, 1859.

23. Manuscript by Simeon E. Baldwin dated July 2, 1859.

24. The *Yale Banner*, September 24, 1859. For the latter prize Baldwin received a three-volume set of the *Essays of Montaigne*.

25. Simeon E. Baldwin's manuscript essay entitled "The Characteristics of Daniel Webster as a Statesman and Orator," February 26, 1859.

26. Simeon E. Baldwin to his mother, Emily P. Baldwin, July 26, 1859.

27. Emily P. Baldwin to her husband, Roger S. Baldwin, August 3, 1859.

28. Emily P. Baldwin to her husband, Roger S. Baldwin, August 4 and 6, 1859.

29. The *Yale Banner*, September 24, 1859.

30. W. E. Decrow, *Yale and "The City of Elms,"* p. 36.

31. The original essay is in the Baldwin Collection.

32. Emily P. Baldwin to her son, George W. Baldwin, March 23, 1860.

33. Peter Collier to Simeon E. Baldwin, June 24, 1884, indicated that Baldwin was its president. Frederick C. Hicks, *Yale Law School: 1895–1915, Twenty Years of Hendrie Hall*, p. 67, asserted that he was vice-president. Since no records of the organization can be found this discrepancy cannot be resolved. It is possible, of course, that he held both offices.

34. The first number (January, 1860) was called the *Undergraduate Quarterly Magazine*.

35. The *Yale Banner*, September 21, 1860. For an illuminating article on Yale secret societies see also the Boston *Globe*, July 2, 1874.

36. Decrow, *op. cit.*, pp. 32–33.

37. K. Stinnecke to Simeon E. Baldwin, December 8, 1860.

38. Emily P. Baldwin to her husband, Roger S. Baldwin, February 9, 1861.

39. Emily P. Baldwin to her husband, Roger S. Baldwin, February 14, 1861.

40. *Catalogue of the Officers and Students of Yale College, 1861–62.* The Townsend prize consisted of a nine-volume set of *The Works of Edmund*

Burke, the first volume of which is inscribed as follows: "Presented to Simeon E. Baldwin as one of the authors of the five best original compositions in the class of 1861—in accordance with the Townsend donation for the encouragement of the study of the English language in Yale College. Attest: William A. Larned."

41. Draft of letter from Simeon E. Baldwin to Alexander P. Root, undated (ca. June of 1861).

42. Emily P. Baldwin to her husband, Roger S. Baldwin, August 2, 1861.

43. Simeon E. Baldwin to his mother, Emily P. Baldwin, August 7, 1861.

44. *Triennial Record of Class of 1861, of Yale College*, p. 56.

45. The New York *Times*, November 14, 1861.

46. Anthony Higgins to Simeon E. Baldwin, April 20, 1862.

47. Francis E. Kernochan to Simeon E. Baldwin, January 16, 1862.

48. William E. Park to Simeon E. Baldwin, January 18, 1862.

49. Sextus Shearer to Simeon E. Baldwin, February 27, 1862.

50. Hubert S. Brown to Simeon E. Baldwin, June 8, 1862.

51. Edward F. Blake to Simeon E. Baldwin, March 18, 1862.

52. Dwight Foster to his father-in-law, Roger S. Baldwin, November 17, 1861.

53. George W. Baldwin to his father, Roger S. Baldwin, February 15, 1861; Simeon E. Baldwin to his father, Roger S. Baldwin, February 28, 1861.

54. Emily P. Baldwin to her son, George W. Baldwin, June 9, 1862.

55. Simeon E. Baldwin to Miss Evelyn MacCurdy, June 16, 1862.

56. Emily P. Baldwin to her daughter, Henrietta P. B. Foster, July 4, 1862.

57. *Ibid.* Two years later, while Simeon was away from New Haven, Mrs. Baldwin wrote, "Simeon . . . procured a substitute for the army before he left—that is deposited money for one—and that makes me feel better." (Emily P. Baldwin to her sisters, August 9, 1864.)

58. Simeon E. Baldwin to his mother, Emily P. Baldwin, July 23, 1862.

59. Simeon E. Baldwin to his mother, Emily P. Baldwin, August 4, 1862.

60. *Obituary Record of Graduates of Yale College Deceased from July, 1859, to July, 1870*, pp. 105 and 108.

61. Simeon E. Baldwin to his mother, Emily P. Baldwin, September 1, 1862.

62. Simeon E. Baldwin to his father, Roger S. Baldwin, September 7, 1862.

63. Simeon E. Baldwin to his sister, Elizabeth B. Whitney, October 20, 1862.

64. Simeon E. Baldwin to his mother, Emily P. Baldwin, October 2, 1862.

65. Simeon E. Baldwin to his father, Roger S. Baldwin, September 23, 1862.

66. Emily P. Baldwin to her son, Simeon E. Baldwin, September 9, 1862.

67. George W. Baldwin to his mother, Emily P. Baldwin, December 16, 1862.

68. Emily P. Baldwin to her daughter, Henrietta P. B. Foster, January 15, 1863.

69. Emily P. Baldwin to her daughter, Henrietta P. B. Foster, February 3, 1863.

70. Philip Marett to an unknown correspondent, ca. February, 1863.

71. Original is in the Baldwin Collection.

EXPANDING HORIZONS

1. His certificate of admission to the bar indicates that he had presented statements from his instructors and "been extensively and critically examined in the theory and practice of Law, by a committee of the Bar, appointed by and under the direction of the Court."

2. According to Probate Court records at New Haven his share of his father's estate was approximately $18,000. More than twice this amount came to him after his mother's death.

3. In the first will he left $5,000 to his mother, $2,000 to the Yale Law School for library purposes, the most prized volumes of his personal library to his best friends, and the residue to his brother and sisters. The will is dated March 31, 1863. The second document is dated April 13, 1863.

4. Anthony Higgins to Simeon E. Baldwin, December 1, 1863.

5. Efforts have been made through the Historical Society of Delaware and the Higgins family to unearth this letter, but no trace of it has been found.

6. Anthony Higgins to Simeon E. Baldwin, March 2, 1864.

7. Edward Rowland Sill to Simeon E. Baldwin, March 13, 1864.

8. New Haven *Daily Morning Journal and Courier*, June 17, 1864.

9. Anthony Higgins to Simeon E. Baldwin, June 28, 1864.

10. Anthony Higgins to Simeon E. Baldwin, July 23, 1864.
11. Anthony Higgins to Simeon E. Baldwin, May 19, 1866.
12. Henry Champion to Simeon E. Baldwin, August 9, 1866.
13. In library of the Law School of Yale University, entitled *Briefs, S. E. B., 1865–74.*
14. *Henry V. Freeman* v. *Selectmen of New Haven*, 1867.
15. *William C. Andrews, Administrator* v. *The Hartford & New Haven Railroad Company*, 1867.
16. *Harriet C. Jones* v. *City of New Haven*, 1867.
17. George A. Fay to Simeon E. Baldwin, May 29, 1871.
18. William Hamersley to Simeon E. Baldwin, May 27, 1873.
19. *Special Laws of the State of Connecticut*, VII (1871–75) May, 1873 session, 466–467.
20. George W. Baldwin to his brother, Simeon E. Baldwin, August 7, 1871.
21. New Haven *Daily Morning Journal and Courier*, April 1, 1863.
22. Anthony Higgins to Simeon E. Baldwin, May 10, 1863.
23. New Haven *Daily Morning Journal and Courier*, April 4, 1864 and April 6, 1864.
24. Simeon E. Baldwin to Anthony Higgins, July, 1864.
25. Simeon E. Baldwin to his mother, Emily P. Baldwin, September 9, 1864.
26. Simeon E. Baldwin to his mother, Emily P. Baldwin, October 17, 1864.
27. Simeon E. Baldwin to his mother, Emily P. Baldwin, March 28, 1866.
28. *Ibid.*
29. The upper house was the Board of Aldermen. In 1902 the lower house was abolished and the Board of Aldermen became the sole legislative body.
30. New Haven *Daily Morning Journal and Courier*, April 2, 1867.
31. John M. Morris to Simeon E. Baldwin, May 29, 1867.
32. John M. Morris to Simeon E. Baldwin, June 6, 1867.
33. William L. Kingsley, ed., *Yale College, a Sketch of its History*, II, 102.
34. Simeon E. Baldwin to his mother, Emily P. Baldwin, March 28, 1868.
35. Simeon E. Baldwin to his mother, Emily P. Baldwin, May 18, 1868.
36. Copy in Simeon E. Baldwin's handwriting of a letter from

Senator William A. Buckingham to Simeon E. Baldwin, March 19, 1869.

37. Hiram Willey to Simeon E. Baldwin, November 26, 1869.

38. S. W. Kellogg to Simeon E. Baldwin, December 1, 1869.

39. George W. Baldwin to his brother, Simeon E. Baldwin, December 6, 1869.

40. Calvin G. Child to Simeon E. Baldwin, March 3, 1870.

41. Calvin G. Child to Simeon E. Baldwin, March 10, 1870.

42. George A. Fay to Simeon E. Baldwin, May 23, 1871.

43. George A. Fay to Simeon E. Baldwin, June 6, 1871.

44. George W. Baldwin to his brother, Simeon E. Baldwin, March 29, 1873.

45. George W. Baldwin to his brother, Simeon E. Baldwin, April 2, 1873.

46. Governor Marshall Jewell to Simeon E. Baldwin, April 17, 1873.

47. Prefatory note to Baldwin's essay, *Constitutional Reform*, published by the Association.

48. N. Wheeler to Simeon E. Baldwin, November 17, 1873.

49. Calvin G. Child to Simeon E. Baldwin, November 7, 1873.

50. C. F. Cleveland to Simeon E. Baldwin, January 23, 1874.

51. Frederick C. Hicks, *Yale Law School: From the Founders to Dutton, 1845–1869*, pp. 36–37.

52. *Yale Shingle*, 1898, p. 68.

53. William C. Robinson, *An Address Commemorative of the Life and Character of Francis Wayland*, pp. 21–27.

54. These aims were listed in the section on the Law School in the annual volume entitled *Yale College. Needs of the University. Suggested by the Faculties. (July 10, 1871).*

55. Charles E. Clark, "Francis Wayland," *Dictionary of American Biography*, XIX, 560.

56. William C. Robinson, *op. cit.*, p. 23.

57. Robinson, in accepting his appointment as professor of law, said: "It is needless to say that I accept the appointment, and shall continue in the future, as in the past, to work for such compensation as the Providence, which watches over law teachers, may see fit to bestow." Quoted by Frederick C. Hicks, *Yale Law School: 1869–1894, Including the County Court House Period*, p. 11.

58. Frederick C. Hicks, *Yale Law School: 1869–1894 Including the County Court House Period*, p. 16. I am indebted principally to Mr. Hicks for information on the Yale Law School during this period.

59. Simeon E. Baldwin, "The Authority of the 'Provisional Court' of Louisiana," *American Law Register*, IV n.s., 385–390.

60. Simeon E. Baldwin, "The Constitutionality of the Concluding Exemption Clause in the Bankrupt Law," *The American Law Register*, VI n.s., 721–727.

61. *Connecticut Reports*, XXXIII (1865–1866). See also George W. Baldwin to his brother, Simeon E. Baldwin, July 14, 1866.

62. Little, Brown & Company to Simeon E. Baldwin, June 29, 1867.

63. Francis E. Kernochan to Simeon E. Baldwin, December 20, 1867.

64. Petition signed by nine persons dated May 1, 1868.

65. Little, Brown & Company to Simeon E. Baldwin, January 21, 1871.

66. Simeon E. Baldwin to his mother, Emily P. Baldwin, July 20, 1870.

67. Little, Brown & Company to Simeon E. Baldwin, March 6, 1871.

68. The volume was briefly reviewed by Oliver Wendell Holmes, Jr., in the *American Law Review*, V, 542–543, as follows: "A digest can to a great extent defy criticism, as about the same number of people will buy it whether it is well or ill done. It is the tool which every workman must have, and which none but workmen care to possess. The features which we most notice in this one are the excellence of the mechanical device by which the key word or words of each statement are doubleheaded so as to catch the eye at once; the usual want of sufficient cross references; and as it seems to us the satisfactory character of the digesting. In speaking of Mr. Brightly's new volume we have expressed our conviction that a digest like a head-note should state facts categorically, and give the judgment under a 'Held.' Mr. Baldwin leans to this form of statement, although he often allows himself an introductory 'Where,' which is superfluous."

69. William L. Kingsley, *op. cit.*, II, 102.

70. Certificate of Secretary of State to Comptroller that May session, 1874, of General Assembly authorized the payment to Baldwin.

71. *Special Acts and Resolutions Passed by the General Assembly of the State of Connecticut, at the May Session, 1876*, pp. 132–133.

72. Both pamphlets were published by the New Haven County Constitutional Reform Association, of which Baldwin was a prime mover.

73. Emily P. Baldwin to her sisters, August 9, 1864.

74. A brief account of the organization is contained in William L. Kingsley, ed., *Yale College, a Sketch of its History*, I, 329–337. On the one hundredth anniversary of its incorporation Simeon E. Baldwin

delivered a historical address on October 11, 1899, which appeared in the *Transactions of the Connecticut Academy of Arts and Sciences*, XI, xiii–xxxv.

75. Edward Y. Hincks to Simeon E. Baldwin, December 9, 1872.

76. Thomas B. Davis, Jr., *Chronicles of Hopkins Grammar School 1660–1935*, p. 439.

77. W. E. Decrow, *Yale and "The City of Elms,"* p. 35. See also ms. notebook of early minutes of the Trumbull Trust Association in Memorabilia Room, Yale University Library.

78. See Fanny W. Hotchkiss, *Winchester Notes*, pp. 138–39.

79. Henrietta P. B. Foster to her brother, Simeon E. Baldwin, June 18, 1865.

80. Emily P. Baldwin to her sisters, July 15, 1865.

81. Simeon E. Baldwin to his mother, Emily P. Baldwin, July 31, 1865.

82. Simeon Baldwin to his nephew, Simeon E. Baldwin, April 18, 1869.

83. Emily P. Baldwin to her daughter, Henrietta P. B. Foster, May 24, 1869.

84. Emily P. Baldwin to her son, Simeon E. Baldwin, August 11, 1869.

85. George W. Baldwin to his brother, Simeon E. Baldwin, March 15, 1871.

86. Simeon E. Baldwin to his sister, Henrietta P. B. Foster, August 3, 1874.

87. Frederick C. Hicks, *Yale Law School: 1895–1915, Twenty Years of Hendrie Hall*, p. 84, as quoted from Simeon E. Baldwin at William K. Townsend's memorial exercises.

88. Telegram from George W. Baldwin to his brother, Simeon E. Baldwin, July 29, 1874.

89. Anthony Higgins to Simeon E. Baldwin, March 1, 1875.

90. Simeon E. Baldwin to his sister, Henrietta P. B. Foster, August 3, 1874.

PROFESSIONAL SUCCESS

1. Statement of Honorable Frederick L. Perry, former Secretary of State of Connecticut, to the author, June, 1948.

2. General J. H. Wilson to Simeon E. Baldwin, August 12, 1881.

3. Draft of letter from Simeon E. Baldwin to General J. H. Wilson, August 18, 1881.

4. *Supplement to the Twenty-five Years' Record of the Class of 1861, Yale College*, p. 10. He resigned as general counsel and director May 16, 1893, but believed he could remain a trustee of the company's trust fund consistently with serving on the bench.

5. Charles P. Clark to Simeon E. Baldwin, October 3, 1876.

6. Charles P. Clark to Simeon E. Baldwin, November 16, 1876.

7. Published by State of Connecticut, General Assembly, January Session, 1883, pp. 1–13.

8. Letter and telegram from Frederick J. Kingsbury to Simeon E. Baldwin, May 3, 1883.

9. *James W. Townshend* v. *Alfred Todd and Philando Armstrong, U.S. Reports*, XCI (October term, 1875), Part I, 452–454.

10. *The Electric Railroad Signal Co.* v. *The Hall Railway Signal Co., U. S. Reports*, CXIV (October term, 1884), 87–103.

11. *George E. Coney and Peter R. Carll* v. *Alvred E. Winchell, U. S. Reports*, CXVI (October term, 1885), 227–231.

12. John W. Stedman to Simeon E. Baldwin, November 10, 1875.

13. Sherman W. Adams to Simeon E. Baldwin, January 14, 1875.

14. Copy of a letter from Simeon E. Baldwin to Sherman W. Adams, January 25, 1875.

15. "*F.*" *To the State Bar Association*, January 5, 1877.

16. Governor R. D. Hubbard to Simeon E. Baldwin, November 12, 1877.

17. Simeon E. Baldwin to Governor R. D. Hubbard, November 13, 1877.

18. W. D. Hubbard, Executive Secretary to the Governor, to Simeon E. Baldwin, May 30, 1878.

19. See *Rise and Progress of the Connecticut Practice Act, 1878–1880*, a collection of documents bound together by Simeon E. Baldwin and now in the Yale Law Library, for a complete account of this matter.

20. Lyman D. Brewster to Simeon E. Baldwin, November 22 and December 2, 1878.

21. Lyman D. Brewster to Simeon E. Baldwin, February 8, 1879.

22. Lyman D. Brewster to Simeon E. Baldwin, July 17, 1879.

23. Comptroller of Connecticut to Simeon E. Baldwin, February 10, 1880.

24. Anthony Higgins to Simeon E. Baldwin, October 16, 1877.

25. William Hamersley to Simeon E. Baldwin, February 20, 1878.

26. James Grafton Rogers, *American Bar Leaders*, pp. 64–65. Other sources for the founding and early years of the American Bar Associa-

tion include *Reports of the American Bar Association*, I, 4–11; Simeon E. Baldwin, "The Founding of the American Bar Association," *American Bar Association Journal*, III, 658–695; Max Radin, "The Achievements of the American Bar Association: a Sixty Year Record," *American Bar Association Journal*, XXV, 903–910; James Grafton Rogers, "Fifty Years of the American Bar Association," *American Bar Association Journal*, XIV, 521–526; and Francis Rawle, "How the Association Was Organized," *American Bar Association Journal*, XIV, 375–377. The recently published *History of the American Bar Association and Its Work* by Edson R. Sunderland (Chicago: The American Bar Association, 1953) also has a section on the founding and early years, which is based principally on sources included above.

27. James Grafton Rogers, "The American Bar Association in Retrospect," *Law, A Century of Progress, 1835–1935*, I, 188, note 1.

28. Thomas J. Semmes to Simeon E. Baldwin, April 18, 1887.

29. See annual reports of the American Bar Association.

30. Frederick C. Hicks, *Yale Law School: 1895–1915, Twenty Years of Hendrie Hall*, p. 59.

31. Charles C. Bonney to Simeon E. Baldwin, August 27, 1890.

32. Burton Mansfield to Simeon E. Baldwin, June 25, 1891.

33. P. R. Carll to Simeon E. Baldwin, September 30, 1875.

34. New Haven *Daily Palladium*, October 5, 1875.

35. Copy of a letter from Simeon E. Baldwin to Honorable George F. Edmunds, March 17, 1880.

36. George F. Edmunds to Simeon E. Baldwin, March 19, 1880.

37. Myron S. Dudley to Simeon E. Baldwin, February 21, 1881.

38. Henry P. Goddard to Simeon E. Baldwin, October 11, 1881.

39. Draft of a constitutional amendment in Baldwin Collection.

40. George M. Wallace to Simeon E. Baldwin, December 11, 1884.

41. Baldwin gave the credit for the organization of a Constitutional Reform Association in New Haven in 1882 to Dr. Leonard Bacon. Its officers were from every county of the state and from both political parties. Much of Baldwin's activity in the field of constitutional reform was carried on through this organization.

42. Simeon E. Baldwin to Governor-elect Morgan G. Bulkeley, December 18, 1888.

43. Morgan G. Bulkeley to Simeon E. Baldwin, December 20, 1888.

44. Simeon E. Baldwin to M. P. Yeomans, January 30, 1889.

45. Simeon E. Baldwin to M. P. Yeomans, February 5, 1889, and M. P. Yeomans to Simeon E. Baldwin, February 9, 1889.

46. Theodore D. Woolsey to Simeon E. Baldwin, August 30, 1884.

47. D. H. Chamberlain to Simeon E. Baldwin, October 13, 1884.

48. Edward J. Phelps to Simeon E. Baldwin, December 16, 1884.

49. New Haven *Evening Register*, September 24, 1885.

50. Official notice of appointment by Governor Harrison, February 8, 1886.

51. E. A. Joachinson to Simeon E. Baldwin, July 20, 1888.

52. Simeon E. Baldwin to E. A. Joachinson, August 1, 1888.

53. Draft of a letter from Simeon E. Baldwin to John S. Seymour, February 21, 1891.

54. Draft of a letter from Simeon E. Baldwin to William Hamersley, March 6, 1891. The nature of this plan is not known.

55. William Hamersley to Simeon E. Baldwin, April 7, 1891.

56. Lynde Harrison, "The Election Controversy in Connecticut," *New Englander and Yale Review*, XVIII n.s., 354–65.

57. Simeon E. Baldwin, "The Late Election in Connecticut," *New Englander and Yale Review*, XVIII n.s., 366–373.

58. "Is There Any Need of a Constitutional Convention?" *Tracts for the Times*, No. 2.

59. Simeon E. Baldwin to C. B. Davis, Chairman of the Democratic State Committee, September 5, 1891.

60. Albert H. Walker to Simeon E. Baldwin, September 14, 1892.

61. Simeon E. Baldwin to O. R. Wood, November 10, 1892.

62. A constitutional amendment permitting a plurality rather than a majority to elect state officers was later added to the constitution. All efforts to revise the apportionment of either representatives or senators have failed, and Connecticut remains a stronghold of the rotten borough.

63. Simeon E. Baldwin to Governor Luzon B. Morris, November 29, 1892.

64. Henrietta P. B. Foster to her brother, Simeon E. Baldwin, January 14, 1893.

65. Simeon E. Baldwin to his sister, Elizabeth B. Whitney, January 20, 1893. Baldwin was the first of two nominations to the five-man court so would rank the other appointee in seniority. New Haven *Evening Register*, January 11, 1893.

66. New Haven *Evening Register*, January 25, 1893.

67. William C. Robinson to Simeon E. Baldwin, January 25, 1893.

68. New Haven *Evening Register*, February 2, 1893.

69. Talcott H. Russell to Simeon E. Baldwin, February 3, 1893.

70. Frederick C. Hicks, *Yale Law School: 1869–1894, Including the County Court House Period*, pp. 50–53.

71. Theodore D. Woolsey, *Historical Discourse*, pp. 23–24.

72. Noah Porter, "Inaugural Address," *Addresses at the Inauguration of Professor Noah Porter . . . as President of Yale College*, pp. 58–59.

73. Frederick C. Hicks, *op. cit.*, p. 9.

74. Theodore D. Woolsey, *op. cit.*, p. 12.

75. The *Yale Shingle*, 1898, p. 69.

76. William C. Robinson, *An Address Commemorative of the Life and Character of Francis Wayland*, p. 28.

77. *Law Department of Yale College, 1876–77*, p. 6.

78. Simeon E. Baldwin, "Graduate Courses at Law Schools," *Journal of Social Science*, XI, p. 132.

79. *Ibid.*, pp. 123–137.

80. Frederick C. Hicks, *Yale Law School: 1895–1915, Twenty Years of Hendrie Hall*, p. 74.

81. Simeon E. Baldwin, "The Time Necessary to Get a Legal Education," *Columbia Jurist*, I, 67.

82. The three-year requirement had gone into effect at Harvard in 1877–78. See Charles Warren, *History of the Harvard Law School*, II, 523.

83. Frederick C. Hicks, *op. cit.*, pp. 36–38.

84. Catalogues of Yale College and Yale University, 1874–5 to 1892–3.

85. Sain Welty to Simeon E. Baldwin, July 3, 1883.

86. A. S. Vande Graaf to Simeon E. Baldwin, March 8, 1892.

87. Baldwin asserted that this was true as early as 1745. See "The Ecclesiastical Constitution of Yale College," *Papers of the New Haven Colony Historical Society*, III, 419.

88. *Papers of the New Haven Colony Historical Society*, III, 405–442.

89. *Ibid.*, p. 416.

90. *Ibid.*, p. 424.

91. *Ibid.*, p. 442.

92. New York *Evening Post*, May 7, 1881.

93. Honorable R. D. Hubbard to Simeon E. Baldwin, May 11, 1881.

94. Henry C. Robinson, July 16, 1885.

95. Reverend J. H. Twichell to Simeon E. Baldwin, July 27, 1885.

96. Reverend Joseph Anderson to Simeon E. Baldwin, August 31, 1885.

97. The *Nation*, number 1064, November 19, 1885, p. 419.

98. Morris Hadley, *Arthur Twining Hadley*, p. 104.

99. *Obituary Record of Graduates of Yale University Deceased during the Academical Year ending in June, 1901*, pp. 62–63.

100. Buchanan Winthrop to Simeon E. Baldwin, April [1], 1889.

101. Draft of a letter from Simeon E. Baldwin to Buchanan Winthrop, April 9, 1889.

102. *Obituary Record of Graduates of Yale University Deceased during the Academical Year ending in June, 1891*, pp. 466–67.

103. A search has not revealed this source.

104. Julius H. Ward to Simeon E. Baldwin, April 20, 1889.

105. Boston *Herald*, April 20, 1889.

106. *Ibid.* New York *Times*, April 14, 1889.

107. Daniel H. Chamberlain to Simeon E. Baldwin, October 30, 1898.

108. Roger Foster to Simeon E. Baldwin, November 21, 1898.

109. Hadley, *op. cit.*, p. 105.

110. *Historical Register of Yale University, 1701–1937*, p. 37.

111. In a review of J. Franklin Jameson, ed., "Essays in the Constitutional History of the United States in the Formative Period, 1775–1789," *New Englander and Yale Review*, XVI n.s., 171, Baldwin speaks highly of the modern historical seminars' emphasis on use of source materials.

112. Simeon E. Baldwin, "A Young Man's Journal of a Hundred Years Ago," *Papers of the New Haven Colony Historical Society*, IV, 195.

113. *Report of the Twelfth Annual Meeting of the American Bar Association, 1889*, pp. 235–264.

114. Simeon E. Baldwin, "*F.*" *To the State Bar Association.*

115. "Graduate Courses, at Law Schools," *Journal of Social Science*, XI, 123–137.

116. Charles A. Peabody to Simeon E. Baldwin, June 2, 1880, and A. P. Sprague to Simeon E. Baldwin, June 29, 1880.

117. "The Berne Conference of the Association for the Reform and Codification of the Law of Nations," *American Law Review*, XV, 209–213.

118. *Report of the Sixth Annual Meeting of the American Bar Association, 1883*, pp. 225–241.

119. Published by Albert B. Tavel, Nashville, 1884.

120. *Columbia Jurist*, I, 67.

121. *Ibid.*, I, 117.

122. *Ibid.*, II, 2–3.

123. *Report of the Eighth Annual Meeting of the American Bar Association, 1885*, pp. 25–32.

124. *Journal of Social Science*, XXII, 162–171.

125. *Report of the Fourteenth Annual Meeting of the American Bar Association, 1891*, pp. 163–195.

126. *Annual Report of the American Historical Association for the Year 1891*, pp. 225–241.

127. *Ohio State Bar Association Reports*, XIII, 137–148.

128. Printed as a pamphlet in New Haven, 1881.

129. *Report of the Special Investigating Committee to the Court of Common Council as to the Purchase of the New Haven Waterworks*, 1881.

130. *Address upon the Expediency of Consolidating the Town and City Governments in New Haven*, 1884.

131. See note 7 of this chapter.

132. Published as pamphlets. The first was entitled "Why You and I Ought to Vote for Morris and Alsop."

133. "The Late Election in Connecticut," pp. 366–373.

134. Printed privately, New Haven, 1884.

135. Printed privately, New Haven, 1886.

136. Published in the New Haven *Daily Palladium*, January 22, 1883.

137. *Ibid.*

138. *Ibid.*

139. George W. Baldwin to his brother, Simeon E. Baldwin, March 3, 1883.

140. Simeon E. Baldwin to Reverend Josiah Strong, March 17, 1889.

141. B. W. Maples to Simeon E. Baldwin, February 13, 1888.

142. Members of Sunday School Class to Simeon E. Baldwin, September 24, 1876.

143. *The Twenty-five Years' Record of the Class of 1861, Yale College*, p. 40.

144. *Ibid.*

145. *Ibid.*

146. George R. Chamberlin to Simeon E. Baldwin, September 25, 1886.

147. Dr. William H. Carmalt to Simeon E. Baldwin, October 24, 1881.

148. H. C. Kingsley to Simeon E. Baldwin, February 2, 1881.

149. Timothy Dwight to Simeon E. Baldwin, June 3, 1887.

150. See volumes III–IX of the Society's *Papers*.

151. See Simeon E. Baldwin, *Public Parks*, a lecture delivered March 17, 1881, and printed privately in New Haven. The development of New Haven's park system is told in a series of articles in the New Haven weekly, The *Saturday Chronicle*, for April 16, 23 and 30, 1904.

152. Statement of Baldwin's niece, Miss Emily Whitney, to the writer, April, 1948.

153. Miss Mary S. Packard of Brunswick, Maine, to the writer, May, 1949.

154. Simeon E. Baldwin to Mrs. Ellen M. Gifford, December 25, 1880.

155. These figures covering many years were recorded in a small notebook, which is in the Baldwin Collection.

156. The account book of the New Haven *Morning News* is in the Baldwin Collection.

157. Simeon E. Baldwin to Lynde Harrison, October 8, 1890.

158. R. B. Davenport to Simeon E. Baldwin, April 19, 1893.

159. Simeon E. Baldwin to his sister-in-law, Miss Charlotte Winchester, August 1, 1880.

160. A. P. Sprague to Simeon E. Baldwin, June 29, 1880.

161. Simeon E. Baldwin to his sister, Elizabeth B. Whitney, July 13, 1887.

162. James Bryce to Simeon E. Baldwin, July 19, 1887.

163. James Bryce to Simeon E. Baldwin, December 26, 1885.

164. Simeon E. Baldwin to James Bryce, December 16, 1887.

165. Roger S. Baldwin to his father, Simeon E. Baldwin, February 2, 1891.

166. Roger S. Baldwin to his father, May 10, 1891, and May 14, 1891.

MR. JUSTICE BALDWIN

1. Talcott H. Russell to Simeon E. Baldwin, July 25, 1893.

2. Francis Wayland to Simeon E. Baldwin, July 23, 1893.

3. Representative James P. Pigott to Simeon E. Baldwin, September 9, 1893.

4. Chief Justice C. B. Andrews to President Grover Cleveland, January 20, 1894.

5. John S. Seymour to Simeon E. Baldwin, January 19, 1894.

6. Actually, Edward D. White, the man who was finally appointed, after another, Wheeler H. Peckham, was rejected, did become Chief Justice.

7. Springfield *Republican*, September 7, 1906.

8. George W. Baldwin to his brother, Simeon E. Baldwin, January 31, 1907.

9. Simeon E. Baldwin to his sister, Mrs. Elizabeth B. Whitney, September 29, 1907.

10. Frank W. Hackett, "The Federal Employers' Liability Act of 1908—Is It Constitutional?" *Harvard Law Review*, XXII, 38–47.

11. *William H. Hoxie* v. *The New York, New Haven and Hartford Railroad, Connecticut Reports*, LXXXII, 352–373.

12. *Connecticut Reports*, LXXXII, 373–375.

13. *Second Employers' Liability Cases, United States Reports*, CCXXIII, 1–59.

14. Henry W. Osborn to Simeon E. Baldwin, September 10, 1894.

15. Simeon E. Baldwin to his sister, Mrs. Elizabeth B. Whitney, February, 1910.

16. The undated original is in the Baldwin Collection.

17. "Chief Justice Baldwin's Retirement," *Green Bag*, XXII, 207.

18. New Haven *Evening Register*, January 31, 1927.

19. "Obituary Sketch of Simeon E. Baldwin," *Connecticut Reports*, CVI, 735–738.

20. Catalogues of the Law School, 1893–4 to 1909–10.

21. Undated petition; also Law School catalogues for 1903–4 and 1904–5.

22. Anonymous letter to Simeon E. Baldwin, January 30, 1894.

23. Note from Miss Mary S. Packard of Brunswick, Maine, a friend of Baldwin's daughter, to the writer, May, 1949.

24. Charles P. Hine to Simeon E. Baldwin, December 30, 1906.

25. Charles P. Sherman, *Academic Adventures*, p. 100.

26. *Ibid.*, pp. 82–83.

27. Frederick C. Hicks, *Yale Law School: 1895–1915, Twenty Years of Hendrie Hall*, p. 79.

28. George W. Pierson, *Yale College, an Educational History, 1871–1921*, p. 220.

29. William C. Robinson to Simeon E. Baldwin, November 13, 1895.

30. Hicks, *op. cit.*, pp. 5–15.

31. See "Celebration of John Marshall Day in Connecticut," *Yale Law Journal*, X, 203–206.

32. See *Harvard Law Review*, XIV, 258–261; *Yale Law Journal*, XIII, 1–15; *American Political Science Review*, IX, 437–448.

33. Hicks, *op. cit.*, pp. 75–78.

34. *Ibid.*, pp. 79–80.

35. Simeon E. Baldwin to Chauncey M. Depew, August 2, 1897.

36. Chauncey M. Depew to Simeon E. Baldwin, August 11, 1897.

37. Hicks, *op. cit.*, pp. 40–41.

38. Pierson, *op. cit.*, pp. 219–21.

39. George M. Sharp to Simeon E. Baldwin, December 29, 1902.

40. Draft of a letter from Simeon E. Baldwin to George M. Sharp, January 16, 1903, on the back of a letter from Sharp to Baldwin, dated December 29, 1902.

41. Baldwin's will, New Haven Probate Court Records.

42. William W. Farnam to Simeon E. Baldwin, December 9, 1896.

43. Timothy Dwight to Simeon E. Baldwin, April 12, 1897.

44. H. J. Ostrander (of the Yale University treasurer's office) to Edwin A. Smith, Baldwin's secretary, December 17, 1926.

45. See the comment by Daniel H. Chamberlain quoted above on page 101.

46. Roger Foster to his uncle, Simeon E. Baldwin, November 21, 1898. He said that Judge Howland had told him that no clergyman would be chosen.

47. Simeon E. Baldwin to his sister, Mrs. Elizabeth B. Whitney, February 11, 1899.

48. President Arthur T. Hadley to Simeon E. Baldwin, June 5, 1908.

49. Walter B. Hill to Simeon E. Baldwin, June 4, 1897.

50. Albert B. Hart to Simeon E. Baldwin, November 10, 1897.

51. Simeon E. Baldwin to his sister-in-law, Miss Charlotte Winchester, August 15, 1897.

52. H. Holbrook Curtis to Simeon E. Baldwin, September 27, 1897.

53. Simeon E. Baldwin to his sister-in-law, Miss Charlotte Winchester, and to his daughter, Helen H. Baldwin, August 22, 1897.

54. Simeon E. Baldwin to his sister-in-law, Miss Charlotte Winchester, August 28, 1897.

55. G. G. Phillimore to Simeon E. Baldwin, September 2, and October 31, 1899.

56. *Journal of Social Science*, XXXVII, 1–17.

57. "The Constitutional Questions Incident to the Acquisition and Government by the United States of Island Territory," *Harvard Law Review*, XII, 393–416.

58. Draft of a letter from Simeon E. Baldwin to Senator O. H. Platt, January 12, 1899, on the back of a letter from Platt to Baldwin, dated January 10, 1899.

59. New York *Evening Sun*, December 30 and 31, 1898.

60. Senator O. H. Platt to Simeon E. Baldwin, January 10, 1899.

61. Card of invitation in Baldwin Collection.

62. Simeon E. Baldwin to his sister-in-law, Miss Charlotte Winchester, July 22, 1900.

63. Simeon E. Baldwin to A. de Malarce, March 20, 1900.

64. Simeon E. Baldwin to his sister-in-law, Miss Charlotte Winchester, July 28, 1900.

65. Simeon E. Baldwin to his sister-in-law, Miss Charlotte Winchester, August 25, 1900.

66. Simeon E. Baldwin to his sister, Mrs. Elizabeth B. Whitney, September 2, 1900.

67. Draft of a letter from Simeon E. Baldwin to Frank J. Goodnow on the back of a letter from Goodnow to Baldwin, dated March 22, 1904.

68. "Association of American Law Schools," *Report of the Twenty-fourth Annual Meeting of the American Bar Association, 1901*, p. 584 and "Proceedings of the Section of Legal Education," *Report of the Twenty-second Annual Meeting of the American Bar Association, 1899*, p. 565. The history of the first half century of the Association of American Law Schools has been recounted in Warren A. Seavey's "The Association of American Law Schools in Retrospect," *Journal of Legal Education*, III, 153–173.

69. "Association of American Law Schools," *Report of the Twenty-third Annual Meeting of the American Bar Association, 1900*, pp. 569–575, and "Association of American Law Schools," *Report of the Twenty-fifth Annual Meeting of the American Bar Association, 1902*, p. 732.

70. *Yale Law Journal*, XIII, 1–15.

71. Draft of a letter from Simeon E. Baldwin to Charles C. Soule, November 9, 1903, on a letter from Soule to Baldwin, dated November 7, 1903.

72. J. W. Jenks to Simeon E. Baldwin, January 20, 1903.

73. Draft of a letter from Simeon E. Baldwin to W. W. Willoughby, May 11, 1903, on a letter from Willoughby to Baldwin, dated May 6, 1903.

74. New York *Evening Post*, December 30, 1910.

75. New Haven *Leader*, January 27, 1904.

76. Simeon E. Baldwin to Simon Newcomb, January 6, 1904; Amos M. Thayer to Simeon E. Baldwin, February 27, 1904; and Jacob Klein, Chairman of the American Bar Association Committee on the Universal Congress of Lawyers and Jurists, to Simeon E. Baldwin, April 6, 1904.

77. Simeon E. Baldwin to his sister, Mrs. Elizabeth B. Whitney, October 4, 1904.

78. *American Historical Review*, XII, 219–243.

79. J. Franklin Jameson to Simeon E. Baldwin, July 3, 1897; *Writings on American History*, 1906, pp. iii–iv.

80. *Report of the Twenty-ninth Annual Meeting of the American Bar Association, 1906*, p. 81.

81. *Report of the Thirtieth Annual Meeting of the American Bar Association, 1907*, p. 1003.

82. *Report of the Forty-second Annual Meeting of the American Bar Association, 1919*, p. 397.

83. *Report of the Eighth Annual Meeting of the American Bar Association, 1885*, pp. 25–33.

84. Draft of a letter from Simeon E. Baldwin to Thomas D. Wells on a letter from Wells to Baldwin, dated February 20, 1897.

85. New York *Herald*, February 10, 1899. See also the Boston *Traveler*, March 6, 1899, for more extended remarks on the subject.

86. "Whipping and Castration as Punishments for Crime," *Yale Law Journal*, VIII, 371–386.

87. Simeon E. Baldwin to Judge Edgar M. Warner, February 6, 1900.

88. Samuel J. Barrows to Simeon E. Baldwin, June 17, 1905.

89. New York *Tribune*, September 5, 1905; New York *American*, September 5, 1905.

90. Simeon E. Baldwin to his sister, Mrs. Elizabeth B. Whitney, September 9, 1905.

91. Charles Matteson to Simeon E. Baldwin, January 27, 1896.

92. Simeon E. Baldwin to his sister-in-law, Miss Charlotte Winchester, February 22, 1896.

93. *Second Supplement to the Twenty-five Years' Record of the Class of 1861 Yale College*, p. 15.

94. The *Independent*, XLVIII, 613–614.

95. Draft of a letter from Simeon E. Baldwin to W. E. Dodge on the back of a letter from Dodge to Baldwin, December 4, 1899.

96. Draft of call of a National Arbitration Conference attached to a letter from Professor John Bassett Moore to Simeon E. Baldwin, December 1, 1903.

97. John W. Foster, President of National Arbitration Conference, to Simeon E. Baldwin, February 16, 1905.

98. Quoted from an unidentified newspaper clipping pasted to a letter from Mrs. Mary Ann Parker to her cousin, Simeon E. Baldwin, October 21, 1894.

99. Draft of a letter from Simeon E. Baldwin to President Alfred T.

Perry on the back of a letter from Perry to Baldwin, dated February 25, 1907.

100. *The Congregationalist and Christian World*, XCII, 418–420.

101. Draft of a letter from Simeon E. Baldwin to Reverend A. E. Dunning on the back of a letter from Dunning to Baldwin, dated June 27, 1898.

102. Report of a Committee Appointed in January, 1900, to Inquire into the Expediency of Altering the Articles of Faith of United Church, New Haven. (Typewritten with corrections in Simeon E. Baldwin's hand).

103. W. F. Warren to Simeon E. Baldwin, December 18, 1901.

104. *Zion's Herald*, LXXX, 744.

105. Simeon E. Baldwin to Representative James P. Pigott, January 12, 1894.

106. *Ibid.*

107. Simeon E. Baldwin to Albert Bolles, January 6, 1891. Hartford *Post*, March 5, 1912.

108. Oliver Wendell Holmes, Jr., to Baldwin, October 26, 1898.

109. *American Historical Review*, IV, 582–584.

110. *Ibid.*, p. 584.

111. Simeon E. Baldwin to his sister, Mrs. Elizabeth B. Whitney, August 18, 1901.

112. The London *Times*, December 25, 1901.

113. The *American Lawyer*, XII, 310–311.

114. Alfred Russell to Simeon E. Baldwin, November 16, 1904.

115. See *Law Notes*, IX, 155–156; The Baltimore *Sun*, June 28, 1905; and The New York *Evening Post*, December 11, 1905. The latter is the most critical.

116. The Baltimore *Sun*, June 28, 1905.

117. *Yale Law Journal*, X, 1–23 and *American Law Review*, XXXV, 214–237.

118. *Yale Review*, XII, 10–24.

119. Professor John Bassett Moore to Simeon E. Baldwin, June 9, 1903.

120. *Yale Law Journal*, XII, 487–494.

121. *Ibid.*, XIV, 1–8.

122. *Proceedings of the American Political Science Association*, II, 73–87.

123. *Yale Law Journal*, XVII, 21–25.

124. See pp. 140–141.

125. The *Independent*, XLVIII, 613–614.

126. *Advocate of Peace*, LXVII, 59–60.

127. The *Independent*, XLVIII, 1716–1717.

128. *Yale Law Journal*, XII, 1–7.

129. Professor John Bassett Moore agreed with Baldwin in this contention. John Bassett Moore to Simeon E. Baldwin, November 26, 1902.

130. *Yale Law Journal*, XV, 163–171.

131. *Columbia Law Review*, VII, 85–92.

132. *American Journal of International Law*, I, 565–578.

133. *The Lend a Hand Record*, XVI, 1–3.

134. *American Journal of International Law*, II, 307–312.

135. *Yale Law Journal*, V, 161–174.

136. *Revue du Droit Publique et de la Science Politique en France et à L'Étranger*, IV, 437–445.

137. *Harvard Law Review*, XII, 393–416.

138. The *Independent*, L, 962–964.

139. *Ibid.*, LI, 2101–2102.

140. *Yale Review*, X, 129–143.

141. *Report of the Fourteenth Annual Meeting of the Maryland State Bar Association, 1909*, pp. 266–285.

142. *Columbia Law Review*, IX, 567–586.

143. Senate Document No. 158, 55th Congress, 3d Session.

144. *Yale Law Journal*, VIII, 371–386.

145. *Medico-Legal Journal*, XVII, 61–73.

146. "Report on Prison Reform," *The Outlook Committee of the New Haven Congregational Club, April 16, 1900*. See also the New Haven *Union*, May 6, 1900.

147. *Leslie's Illustrated Weekly*, XCII, 50, 59.

148. *Green Bag*, XIII, 65–67.

149. Actes du Congrès Penitentiaire International de Budapest, III, 421–436.

150. *Charities and The Commons*, XVII, 137–140.

151. *Yale Review*, II, 133–158. Also published in *Annual Report of the American Historical Association for the Year 1893*, pp. 369–390.

152. Published in New Haven, 1896.

153. Vol. I, Series 5, pp. 1–19.

154. "Address of Mr. Chief Justice Baldwin," *Connecticut Reports*, LXXX, 719–721.

155. *Transactions of the Connecticut Academy of Arts and Sciences*, XI, xiii–xxxv.

156. *Proceedings of the American Antiquarian Society*, XIII n.s., 179–221.

157. *Papers of the New Haven Colony Historical Society*, VI, 263–281.

158. *Annual Report of the American Historical Association for the Year 1902*, I, 253–274.

159. See, for example, J. W. Jenks's review of Baldwin's *Modern Political Institutions* in the *American Historical Review*, IV, 582–584.

160. *Publications of the Colonial Society of Massachusetts*, XII, 55–82.

161. *Papers of the New Haven Colony Historical Society*, VIII, 1–19.

162. *Ibid.*, VII, 1–33.

163. *Proceedings of the Massachusetts Historical Society*, XVI, 2d Series, 478–521.

164. "Roger Sherman," *Two Centuries of New Milford, Connecticut*, pp. 232–255.

165. *Yale Law Journal*, VII, 1–19. Also published in *Journal of Social Science*, XXXV, 1–20.

166. See J. W. Jenks's review in the *American Historical Review*, IV, 582–584.

167. *Proceedings of the Twenty-fourth Annual Meeting of the West Virginia Bar Association*, 1908, XXIV, 72–85.

168. *Yale Law Journal*, IV, 133–136.

169. James Mark Baldwin, ed., *Dictionary of Philosophy and Psychology*, 3 vols. See also Simeon E. Baldwin to his sister-in-law, Miss Charlotte Winchester, August 15, 1897.

170. The *Independent*, LI, 3179–3180.

171. *Journal of Social Science*, XXXVII, 1–17.

172. The *International Monthly*, IV, 540–557.

173. *The Congregationalist*, LXXXVI, 177–178.

174. *Yale Law Journal*, XII, 226–233.

175. *Yale Review*, XII, 204–207.

176. *Michigan Law Review*, II, 597–600.

177. Printed as a pamphlet by the School and entitled *Legal Ethics. Lectures Delivered before the Students of Law Department of Union University*, pp. 27–43.

178. *Central Law Journal*, LVIII, 423–424.

179. *Congress of Arts and Sciences, Universal Exposition, St. Louis, 1904*, II, 331–349.

180. *Yale Review*, XV, 251–258.

181. *Harvard Law Review*, XXII, 27–37.

182. *Revue de l'Institut de Droit Comparé*, II, 353–364.

183. *American Journal of International Law*, IV, 95–108.

184. *Report of the Seventeenth Annual Meeting of the American Bar Association, 1894*, pp. 431–438.

185. *Yale Law Journal*, VIII, 1–23.

186. The *Independent*, LII, 1778–1780.

187. *Harvard Law Review*, XIV, 258–261.

188. The *International Monthly*, III, 634–647.

189. The *American Law School Review*, I, 101–113.

190. *Yale Law Journal*, XIII, 1–15.

191. Miss Charlotte Winchester to her brother-in-law, Simeon E. Baldwin, July 12, 1897.

192. Helen H. Baldwin to her father, Simeon E. Baldwin, August 16, 1897.

193. Simeon E. Baldwin to his sister-in-law, Miss Charlotte Winchester, February 12, 1899, and her undated reply.

194. Simeon E. Baldwin to his sister-in-law, Miss Charlotte Winchester, August 15, 1899.

195. William Noyes to Roger S. Baldwin, June 7, 1896.

196. Roger S. Baldwin to his aunt, Miss Charlotte Winchester, August 14, 1899.

197. Roger S. Baldwin to his father, Simeon E. Baldwin, November 3, 1902.

198. Simeon E. Baldwin to his sister, Mrs. Elizabeth B. Whitney, August 29, 1906.

199. Simeon E. Baldwin to his sister, Mrs. Elizabeth B. Whitney, September 9, 1906.

200. Simeon E. Baldwin to his sister, Mrs. Elizabeth B. Whitney, September 29, 1907.

201. Simeon E. Baldwin to his sister, Mrs. Elizabeth B. Whitney, September 12, 1908.

202. Simeon E. Baldwin to his sister-in-law, Miss Charlotte Winchester, August 3, 1898.

203. Simeon E. Baldwin to his sister-in-law, Miss Charlotte Winchester, August 10, 1902.

204. Simeon E. Baldwin to his sister, Mrs. Elizabeth B. Whitney, July 19, 1909.

205. *The Club*. New Haven, Connecticut, 1887—a pamphlet summarizing The Club's history and activities and listing its members and programs.

206. Simeon E. Baldwin to his sister-in-law, Miss Charlotte Winchester, May 12, 1897.

207. Simeon E. Baldwin to his sister-in-law, Miss Charlotte Winchester, March 27, 1898.

208. Simeon E. Baldwin to C. M. Mead, May 11, 1898.

209. Simeon E. Baldwin to his sister-in-law, Miss Charlotte Winchester, August 16, 1904; and Simeon E. Baldwin to his sister, Mrs. Elizabeth B. Whitney, August 18, 1904.

210. Mrs. Warren R. Gilman to the writer, May, 1949.

211. As quoted in a letter from Mrs. Warren R. Gilman to the writer, September, 1951.

GOVERNOR BALDWIN

1. George W. Baldwin to his brother, Simeon E. Baldwin, February 18, 1910.

2. James E. Beale to Simeon E. Baldwin, April 23, 1910.

3. Simeon E. Baldwin to James E. Beale, April 26, 1910.

4. Henry Wade Rogers to Simeon E. Baldwin, September 13, 1910.

5. John S. Seymour to Simeon E. Baldwin, August 1, 1910.

6. Draft of a letter from Simeon E. Baldwin to John S. Seymour, August 4, 1910, on the back of a letter from Seymour to Baldwin, dated August 1, 1910.

7. New Haven *Evening Register*, September 13, 1910.

8. *Ibid.*, September 8, 1910.

9. *Ibid.*, September 13, 1910.

10. New Haven *Union*, September 15, 1910.

11. New Haven *Evening Register*, October 29, 1910.

12. *Ibid.*, September 14, 1910.

13. *Ibid.*

14. *Ibid.*, September 15, 1910.

15. *Ibid.*

16. New Haven *Leader*, October 28, 1910.

17. The Honorable Kenneth Wynne, Judge of the Superior Court of Connecticut, to the writer, June, 1948.

18. *Ibid.*

19. New London *Telegram*, October 22, 1910.

20. New Haven *Evening Register*, October 24, 1910.

21. *Ibid.*, October 24, 1910.

22. Bridgeport *Post*, September 15, 1910.

23. New Haven *Evening Register*, October 21, 1910.

24. *Ibid.*, November 9, 1910.

25. Draft of a letter from Simeon E. Baldwin to H. T. Schaefer,

November 23, 1910, on a letter from Schaefer to Baldwin, dated November 21, 1910.

26. New York *Evening Post*, October 24, 1910.

27. New Haven *Union*, October 24, 1910.

28. Syracuse *Standard*, October 26, 1910.

29. Letter of Simeon E. Baldwin to Theodore Roosevelt as quoted by the New York *Times*, November 1, 1910.

30. Springfield *Republican*, October 30, 1910.

31. New Haven *Evening Register*, October 26, 1910.

32. *Ibid.*, November 9, 1910.

33. Boston *Globe*, November 15, 1910.

34. New York *American*, November 12, 1910.

35. New York *Globe*, January 26, 1911.

36. New York *Times*, January 27, 1911. The late Governor of Connecticut, Wilbur L. Cross, told the writer in April, 1947, that the altercation between Baldwin and Roosevelt was unlike Baldwin. Cross referred to such threats of libel suits as an old political trick.

37. New York *American*, December 11, 1910.

38. See pp. 121–122.

39. Pittsburgh *Dispatch*, January 19, 1912.

40. New York *Tribune*, January 16, 1912.

41. Undated ms. in Simeon E. Baldwin's hand, written during the Taft administration.

42. Simeon E. Baldwin to the National Democratic Club, December 7, 1910.

43. "Inaugural Message of His Excellency Simeon E. Baldwin, Governor of Connecticut, to the General Assembly, January Session, 1911," *Public Documents of the State of Connecticut*, Vol. I, Part I, 1910, pp. 3–41.

44. Baldwin had written a year before on this subject in "The Law of the Air-Ship," *American Journal of International Law*, IV, 95–108.

45. The Honorable Frederick L. Perry to the author, June, 1948.

46. Former Governor Rollin S. Woodruff to Simeon E. Baldwin, January 6, 1911.

47. New York *Times*, September 25, 1912.

48. Simeon E. Baldwin to his niece, Miss Emily Whitney, September 4, 1912.

49. New Haven *Union*, February 23, 1911.

50. Hartford *Courant*, February 25, 1911. Bristol *Press*, March 2, 1911.

51. Springfield *Republican*, March 9, 1911.

52. *Ibid.*, March 20, 1911.
53. The Honorable Kenneth Wynne to the writer, June, 1948.
54. New Britain *Herald*, June 3, 1911.
55. Bridgeport *Post*, July 12, 1911.
56. *Public Acts Passed by the General Assembly of the State of Connecticut in the Year 1911*, pp. 1387–1399.
57. New Haven *Leader*, August 3, 1911.
58. New York *Evening Post*, September 26, 1911.
59. New Haven *Journal-Courier*, August 11, 1911.
60. New Britain *Herald*, September 20, 1911.
61. Hartford *Times*, September 18, 1911.
62. Bridgeport *Post*, August 31, 1911.
63. Hartford *Times*, September 26, 1911.
64. Atlanta *Journal*, October 9, 1911.
65. Hartford *Times*, October 10, 1911.
66. Charleston *News and Courier*, October 11, 1911.
67. Hartford *Times*, October 10, 1911.
68. Hartford *Post*, October 31, 1911.
69. New York *Sun*, October 30, 1911.
70. New Haven *Evening Register*, November 2, 1911.
71. New York *Herald*, August 20, 1911; New Haven *Leader*, July 24, 1911.
72. New Haven *Leader*, August 21, 1911.
73. New Britain *Herald*, January 31, 1912.
74. New Haven *Leader*, January 30, 1912.
75. New Britain *Herald*, January 31, 1912.
76. New York *Times*, May 3, 1912.
77. Bridgeport *Post*, May 3, 1912.
78. Hartford *Courant*, June 21, 1912.
79. Hartford *Times*, June 28, 1912.
80. *Ibid.*, July 1, 1912.
81. *Ibid.*
82. *Ibid.*
83. *Ibid.*, December 13, 1911.
84. Hartford *Post*, January 17, 1912.
85. See, for example, an editorial in the Bridgeport *Post* for September 18, 1911.
86. Hartford *Courant*, November 7, 1911.
87. *State of Connecticut. Register and Manual*, 1911, p. 96.
88. Frank A. Luhrsen to Simeon E. Baldwin, January 24, 1911.

89. Original is in Baldwin Collection. See also Waterbury *Republican*, July 31, 1914.

90. Simeon E. Baldwin to Mrs. J. W. Murphy, undated.

91. Waterbury *Republican*, February 1, 1912.

92. Ansonia *Sentinel*, February 10, 1912.

93. New Haven *Evening Register*, February 9, 1912.

94. Hartford *Courant*, February 13, 1912.

95. Unidentified clipping under Northampton (Massachusetts) dateline, February 22, 1912.

96. Meriden *Record*, May 18, 1912.

97. New Haven *Evening Register*, April 26, 1912.

98. Hartford *Courant*, July 6, 1912.

99. New Haven *Evening Register*, September 12, 1912.

100. Hartford *Times*, September 12, 1912; New Haven *Evening Register*, September 12, 1912.

101. New Haven *Leader*, October 23, 1912.

102. New Haven *Evening Register*, September 12, 1912.

103. William Powell of Hamden, Connecticut, to the writer, July, 1948. See also New Haven *Evening Register*, September 11, 1912.

104. New Haven *Evening Register*, September 12, 1912.

105. *Ibid.*, October 29, 1912.

106. New Haven *Leader*, October 23, 1912.

107. Bridgeport *Post*, October 29, 1912; Bridgeport *Telegram*, October 29, 1912.

108. Hartford *Times*, October 25, 1912.

109. New Haven *Leader*, November 7, 1912.

110. *State of Connecticut. Register and Manual*, 1914, pp. 490–517.

111. "Inaugural Message of His Excellency Simeon E. Baldwin, Governor of Connecticut, to the General Assembly, January Session, 1913," *Public Documents of the State of Connecticut*, Volume I, Part I, 1912, pp. 3–35.

112. New Haven *Evening Register*, February 12, 1913.

113. Hartford *Courant*, March 24, 1913.

114. *Ibid.*, March 31, 1913.

115. *Ibid.*, March 19 and 24, 1913.

116. *Public Acts . . . of the State of Connecticut . . . 1913*, pp. 1735–1751.

117. Hartford *Times*, June 9, 1913; Hartford *Courant*, June 7, 1913.

118. Hartford *Courant*, June 9, 1913.

119. Hartford *Times*, June 10, 1913.

120. Hartford *Courant*, June 9, 1913.

121. *Proceedings of the Fifth Meeting of the Governors of the States of the Union Held at Richmond, Virginia, December 3–7, 1912*, pp. 34–43.

122. "State Assumption of Nomination and Election Expenses," *Yale Law Journal*, XXIII, 158–167. See also Providence *Journal*, August 28, 1913.

123. Hartford *Courant*, December 8, 1912.

124. Simeon E. Baldwin to Attorney General James C. McReynolds, November 24, 1913.

125. Attorney General James C. McReynolds to Simeon E. Baldwin, November 25, 1913.

126. Simeon E. Baldwin to Attorney General James C. McReynolds, November 26, 1913.

127. Draft of a letter from Simeon E. Baldwin to S. S. Gregory on the back of a telegram from Gregory to Baldwin, February 19, 1916.

128. Hartford *Courant*, June 9, 1913.

129. New York *Times*, October 1, 1913.

130. Hartford *Courant*, September 18, 1914.

131. Hartford *Times*, September 18, 1914.

132. Hartford *Courant*, September 19, 1914.

133. Hartford *Times*, September 18, 1914.

134. Hartford *Courant*, September 9, 1914.

135. New Haven *Evening Register*, September 10, 1914.

136. *Ibid.*, September 12, 1914.

137. *Ibid.*, September 14, 1914.

138. Hartford *Courant*, September 11, 1914.

139. *Ibid.*, October 29, 1914.

140. *Ibid.*, October 29 and 30, 1914.

141. *Ibid.*, October 29, 1914.

142. *Ibid.*, November 1, 1914.

143. *Ibid.*, November 4, 1914.

144. *Ibid.*

145. Draft of a letter from Simeon E. Baldwin to James Cray, November 6, 1914, on the back of a letter from Cray to Baldwin, dated November 4, 1914.

146. Draft of a letter from Simeon E. Baldwin to Moorfield Storey, November 6, 1914, on the back of a letter from Storey to Baldwin, dated November 4, 1914, and which expressed a similar belief.

147. Draft of a letter from Simeon E. Baldwin to Joseph E. Davies, November 18, 1914, on the back of a letter from Davies to Baldwin. dated November 12, 1914.

148. New York *Evening Post*, December 30, 1910.
149. *American Political Science Review*, VI, 1–16.
150. *Ibid.*, p. 11.
151. Notice of election, May 8, 1912.
152. W. J. O'Donnell to Simeon E. Baldwin, January 8, 1913.
153. Notice of election, May 10, 1913.
154. Nicholas Murray Butler to Simeon E. Baldwin, March 6, 1911.
155. William A. Shanklin to Simeon E. Baldwin, June 7, 1912.
156. *Proceedings*, I, 291.
157. *Ibid.*, II, 109–110.
158. James B. Scott to Simeon E. Baldwin, March 21, 1913.
159. Thomas B. Davis, Jr., *Chronicles of Hopkins Grammar School 1660–1935*, pp. 499–500, 529.
160. *Report of the Sixteenth Annual Meeting of the Lake Mohonk Conference on International Arbitration, 1910*, XVI, 78–85.
161. *Judicial Settlement of International Disputes*, I, 3–23.
162. The *Advocate of Peace*, LXXIII, 272–273.
163. *Judicial Settlement of International Disputes*, XVII, 3–21.
164. Published as a pamphlet in New Haven, 1910.
165. *Harvard Law Review*, XXVII, 699–704.
166. *Michigan Law Review*, IX, 20–28.
167. *Proceedings of the Bar Association of the State of New Hampshire*, III n.s., 221–240.
168. Published as a pamphlet in New Haven, 1910.
169. The *North Carolina Booklet*, XIV, 141–154.
170. *Address by Governor Simeon E. Baldwin at the 108th Annual Dinner of the New England Society in the City of New York, December 22, 1913.*
171. New Haven: Yale University Press, 1912.

AUTUMN YEARS

1. Anonymous undated manuscript.
2. Simeon E. Baldwin to Judge Charles B. Howry, March 18, 1915, on the back of a letter from Howry to Baldwin, dated March 16, 1915.
3. Program of the meeting on January 11, 1916.
4. George B. Hudnall to Simeon E. Baldwin, January 31, 1916.
5. Judge Charles B. Howry to Simeon E. Baldwin, March 16, 1915.
6. "Report of the Committee on Publications," *Report of the Thirty-eighth Annual Meeting of the American Bar Association, 1915*, p. 498.
7. Peter W. Meldrim to Simeon E. Baldwin, July 8, 1915.

8. Miscellaneous papers and correspondence on Belgian relief, Baldwin Collection.

9. Governor Marcus H. Holcomb to Simeon E. Baldwin, May 25, 1915.

10. *Report of the Special State Commission . . . on the Subject of Taxation . . .*, p. 22.

11. *Ibid.*, pp. 35-37.

12. *American Journal of International Law*, IX, 793–801.

13. *Papers of the New Haven Colony Historical Society*, IX, 161–169.

14. *American Bar Association Journal*, IV, 37–53.

15. *Ibid.*, III, 658–695.

16. *Papers of the New Haven Colony Historical Society*, IX, 1–28.

17. Albert Bushnell Hart to Simeon E. Baldwin, October 19, 1918.

18. *American Journal of International Law*, XII, 1–14.

19. Albert Bushnell Hart to Simeon E. Baldwin, May 14, 1918.

20. *American Journal of International Law*, XII, 453–461.

21. *Yale Law Journal*, XXVIII, 209–218.

22. New York *Times*, July 14, 1920.

23. *Life and Letters of Simeon Baldwin.*

24. Samuel E. Morison in *American Historical Review*, XXV, 142.

25. Benjamin T. Marshall to Simeon E. Baldwin, June 17, 1920.

26. In a letter to the Commissioner of Internal Revenue on April 21, 1923, he stated that he had been laid up for two years with a serious disorder.

27. Milton Winternitz to Simeon E. Baldwin, July 30, 1923.

28. Simeon E. Baldwin to H. St. George Tucker, July 12, 1923, on a letter from Tucker to Baldwin, dated July 6, 1923.

29. Simeon E. Baldwin to Moorfield Storey, September 26, 1923.

30. Agreement between Simeon E. Baldwin and The States History Company, October, 1923.

31. *Yale University. Obituary Record of Graduates Deceased During the Year Ending July 1, 1927, Number 86*, p. 11, and Mrs. Warren R. Gilman to the writer, September, 1951, and May, 1953.

32. Letter to the editor by Roger Sherman Baldwin, New York *Times*, April 21, 1917.

33. Anonymous undated manuscript.

34. W. Thomas Kemp to Simeon E. Baldwin, September 7, 1923.

35. Francis Rawle to Simeon E. Baldwin, July 28, 1926.

36. *Yale University. Obituary Record of Graduates Deceased During the Year Ending July 1, 1927, Number 86*, p. 11.

37. New Haven *Evening Register*, January 29 and 31, 1927.

38. Probate Court records, New Haven, Connecticut.

39. Bradley B. Gilman, Baldwin's grandson, to the writer, November 21, 1949.

40. *Ibid.*

BIBLIOGRAPHY

BIBLIOGRAPHY

MANUSCRIPT SOURCES

The Baldwin Collection

The primary source for this study is the more than one hundred boxes of manuscripts relating to Simeon E. Baldwin contained in the Baldwin Collection, Yale University Library.

Other Manuscripts

Blake Family Collection, Yale University Library.
A letter from Simeon E. Baldwin to Edward F. Blake, May 11, 1854.

Library of the New Haven Colony Historical Society, New Haven, Connecticut.
A letter from Simeon E. Baldwin to his children and executors, July 17, 1910.

Memorabilia Room, Yale University Library.
Manuscript notebook of early minutes of the Trumbull Trust Association.
Secretary's Book of Alpha Sigma Phi Commenced by the Class of 1861 [,] 1858–62.

A manuscript source of prime importance which will be unavailable for many years is the diary of Simeon E. Baldwin. Many of his innermost thoughts, he told his children, were confided to these volumes which he had kept since his childhood. In 1910 he left instructions as to their disposition and told his children that he preferred that they did not read them. "They have been my confidant, and I have written in them very freely of things I might have talked over with a wife, had I one (except in name), and for want of her sympathy and counsel have entered here.

"My wish and charge to you is that you will put them in a strong locked box, and give it to the New Haven Colony Historical Society, to be kept unopened for fifty years, and then delivered (i.e. 50 years after the society receives it) to my oldest then living descendant; and if no such descendant then survives, to my oldest then living relative, not more remote than fourth cousin computed by the rule of the civil law; and if no such relative then exists, the Society is to keep it for its own use." (This request was written in a letter from Simeon E. Baldwin to his children and executors, July 17, 1910, now in the possession of the New Haven Colony Historical Society.)

NEWSPAPERS

Newspaper accounts provided an important source especially for Baldwin's years as governor. The ones used in this study are cited in the appropriate footnotes.

WRITINGS OF SIMEON E. BALDWIN

The following is not a complete bibliography of Simeon E. Baldwin. Most of his book reviews have been omitted, and probably some items in his voluminous periodical literature have not been uncovered.

"Absolute Power, an American Institution." *Yale Law Journal*, VII, 1–19 (October, 1897). Also published in *Journal of Social Science*, XXXV, 1–20 (December, 1897).

"Address by Simeon E. Baldwin, LL.D." Laying of the Corner-Stone of the Connecticut State Library and Supreme Court Building at Hartford, May 25, 1909, 27–39. Hartford: Published by the State, 1909.

"Address of Mr. Chief Justice Baldwin." *Connecticut Reports*, LXXX, 719–721 (1907–1908).

"Address of the President." *Report of the Fourteenth Annual Meeting of the American Bar Association, 1891*, pp. 163–195.

Address upon the Expediency of Consolidating the Town and City Governments in New Haven. New Haven: Published by the New Haven Civil Service Reform Association, 1884.

"Advantages of a Permanent System of Arbitration." The *Independent*, XLVIII, 613–614 (May 7, 1896).

"American Business Corporations before 1789." *Annual Report of American Historical Association for the Year 1902*, I, 253–274.

The American Judiciary. New York: The Century Company, 1905. (The American State Series).

Reviews of this volume appeared in:

Law Notes, IX, 155–156 (November, 1905).

The New York *Evening Post*, December 11, 1905.

The Baltimore *Sun*, June 28, 1905.

"The American Jurisdiction of the Bishop of London in Colonial Times." *Proceedings of the American Antiquarian Society*, XIII n.s., 179–221 (1899–1900).

"American Jurisprudence." *Ohio State Bar Association Reports*, XIII, 137–148 (1892).

"American Opinions Regarding the Most Practicable Means of Promoting International Peace." The *National Economic League Quarterly*, I, 12–14 (August, 1915).

"The American Practice as to Jury Trials in Criminal Cases." *Schwurgerichte und Schöffenegerichte*, pp. 315–320 (1908).

American Railroad Law. Boston: Little, Brown and Company, 1904.
A review of this volume appeared in:
American Lawyer, XII, 310–311 (July, 1904).

"The American System of Supreme Courts, and What It Accomplishes." *International Monthly*, IV, 540–557 (October, 1901).

"An Anglo-American Prize Tribunal." *American Journal of International Law*, IX, 297–304 (April, 1915).

"An Anglo-American Tribunal within the Hague Court." *Advocate of Peace*, LXVI, 119–120 (July, 1904).

"Annual Address of Simeon E. Baldwin, Director of the Bureau of Comparative Law." *Report of the . . . Annual Meeting of the American Bar Association*. (1908–1919).

"The Authority of the 'Provisional Court' of Louisiana." *American Law Register*, IV n.s., 385–390 (May, 1865).

"The Authorship of the 'Quatre Lettres d'un Bourgeois de New-Heaven Sur l'Unité de la Législation' Published in Mazzei's 'Recherches Historiques et Politiques sur les États-Unis de l'Amerique Septentrionale.' " *Papers of the New Haven Colony Historical Society*, VI, 263–281 (1900).

"The Beginnings of an Official European Code of Private International Law." *Yale Review*, XII, 10–24 (May, 1903).

"The Berne Conference of the Association for the Reform and Codification of the Law of Nations." *American Law Review*, XV, 209–213 (March, 1881).

"The Boundary Line Between Connecticut and New York." *Papers of the New Haven Colony Historical Society*, III, 271–291 (1882).

Briefs S. E. B., 1865–74. (Bound printed briefs of Simeon E. Baldwin's law cases, Library of Yale Law School). Not published.

"Build on What Has Been Done." *World Court*, II, 58–59 (August, 1916).

"The Captives of the Amistad." *Papers of the New Haven Colony Historical Society*, IV, 331–370 (1886).

"Celebration of John Marshall Day in Connecticut. February 4, 1901, in Hendrie Hall, Yale Law School." *Yale Law Journal*, X, 203–206 (March, 1901).

"The Centenary of Modern Government." *Report of the Twelfth Annual Meeting of the American Bar Association, 1889*, pp. 235–254.

"Changes in International Law." *Report of the Thirty-Eighth Annual Meeting of the American Bar Association, 1915*, XL, 354–364.

"Charitable Institutions and Their Gifts: The Responsibilities of Managers." *Congregationalist*, XC, 607–608 (May 6, 1905).

"The Churches and the State." *Our City and Our State. Connecticut Bible Society Report*, pp. 10–12 (January, 1900).

"The Citizen of the United States." *Yale Law Journal*, II, 85–94 (February, 1893).

"Colonial Period." In: Osborn, Norris G., editor. History of Connecticut in Monographic Form, I, 1–463. New York: The States History Company, 1925.

"The Comparative Results, in the Advancement of Private International Law, of the Montevideo Congress of 1888–9 and the Hague Conferences of 1893, 1894, 1900 and 1904." *Proceedings of the American Political Science Association*, II, 73–87 (1905).

"Connecticut in Pennsylvania." *Papers of the New Haven Colony Historical Society*, VIII, 1–19 (1914).

Connecticut Reports, XXXIII (1865–1866). Edited by Simeon E. Baldwin.

"The Connecticut Statute for the Regulation of Air-Ship Voyages." *Zeitschrift für Völkerrecht und Bundesstaatsrecht*, V, 394–399.

Considerations on Constitutional Reform in Connecticut, Submitted to the Members of the Legislature of 1873, and to the People. New Haven: Published by the New Haven County Constitutional Reform Association, 1873.

The Constitution of the United States of America with the Several Amendments. New Haven: 1881. Edited by Simeon E. Baldwin.

The Constitution of the United States, with References to Judicial Decisions, etc., Prepared for the Use of the Yale Law School. New Haven: Hoggson and Robinson, 1875.

"The Constitutional Objection to the New Arbitration Treaties." *Advocate of Peace*, LXXIII, 272–273 (December, 1911).

"The Constitutional Questions Incident to the Acquisition and Government by the United States of Island Territory." *Harvard Law Review*, XII, 393–416 (January, 1899).

Constitutional Reform. A Discussion of the Present Inequalities of Representation in the General Assembly. New Haven: Published by the New Haven County Constitutional Reform Association, 1873.

"The Constitutionality of the Concluding Exemption Clause in the Bankrupt Law." *American Law Register*, VI n.s., 721–727 (October, 1867).

"Contemplated Changes in the General Incorporation Law of France." *Yale Review*, XII, 204–207 (August, 1903).

"The 'Continuous Voyage' Doctrine During the Civil War, and Now." *American Journal of International Law*, IX, 793–801 (October, 1915).

"The Contributions of North Carolina to the Development of American Institutions." *North Carolina Booklet*, XIV, 141–154 (January, 1915).

"Corporal Punishments for Crime." *Medico-Legal Journal*, XVII, 61–73 (June, 1899).

"The Courts, as Conservators of Social Justice." *Columbia Law Review*, IX, 567–586 (November, 1909).

"D'après Quels Principes Pourrait-on Autoriser et de Quelle Manière Pourrait-on Organiser l'Occupation des Condamnés aux Travaux des Champs ou à d'Autres Travaux d'Utilité Publique en Plein Air?" Actes du Congrès Penitentiaire International de Budapest, III, 421–436. Budapest et Berne: Bureau de la Commission Penitentiaire Internationale, 1906.

Definitions and explanations of terms of jurisprudence in James Mark Baldwin, editor. Dictionary of Philosophy and Psychology. New York: The Macmillan Company, 1901–5. 3 vols.

De la Responsibilité du Pouvoir Fédéral aux États-Unis au Cas où les États Particuliers s'Abstiennent de Réprimer les Délits Commis sur leur Territoire." *Revue du Droit Publique et de la Science Politique en France et à l'Étranger*, IV, 437–445 (November-December, 1895).

A Digest of all the Reported Cases Decided in the Supreme Court of Errors and the Superior Court of the State of Connecticut, and in the United States Courts for the District of Connecticut down to Those Contained in Volume XLVII "Connecticut Reports," and Volume XVII "Blatchford's Circuit Court Reports" Inclusive. Boston: Little, Brown and Company, 1871, 1882. 2 vols.

A review of this volume by Oliver Wendell Holmes, Jr., appeared in:

American Law Review, V, 542–543 (April, 1871).

"Divorces without Jurisdiction." *Independent*, XLIII, 181 (February 5, 1891).

"The Duty of the State in Suits Attacking Charitable Bequests." *Yale Law Journal*, IV, 133–136 (March, 1895).

"The Early History of the Ballot in Connecticut." *Papers of the American Historical Association*, IV, 407–422 (1886).

"The Ecclesiastical Constitution of Yale College." *Papers of the New Haven Colony Historical Society*, III, 405–442 (1882).

"Education for the Bar in the United States." *American Political Science Review*, IX, 437–448 (August, 1915).

"The Eleventh Convention Proposed by the Hague Conference of 1907." *American Journal of International Law*, II, 307–312 (April, 1908).

"The Encroachment of the American College upon the Field of the University." *International Monthly*, III, 634–647 (June, 1901).

"The Entry of the United States into World Politics as One of the Great Powers." *Yale Review*, IX, 399–418 (February, 1901).

"Equality Between Nations and International Conventions, as Determining Factors in Shaping Modern International Law." *Yale Law Journal*, XVII, 21–25 (November, 1907).

"The Evolution of a World Court." *Boston University Law Review*, I, 6–12 (January, 1921).

"The Exchange of Notes in 1908 Between Japan and the United States." *Zeitschrift für Völkerrecht und Bundesstaatsrecht*, III, 456–465.

"The Extent of the Judicial Power of the United States." *Yale Law Journal*, XVIII, 1–9 (November, 1908).

Ezra Stiles. (Address delivered in the old cemetery in New Haven before General David Humphreys Branch of the Sons of the American Revolution, June 14, 1908). Pamphlet.

"F." To the State Bar Association. New Haven: January 5, 1877. Pamphlet.

"Federal Taxation of Interstate Commerce." *Harvard Law Review*, XXII, 27–37 (November, 1908).

"The First Century of the Connecticut Academy of Arts and Sciences. An Historical Address Delivered before the Academy at its Centennial Anniversary, on October 11th, 1899." *Transactions of the Connecticut Academy of Arts and Sciences*, XI, xiii–xxxv.

"Flog the Kidnapers." *Leslie's Illustrated Weekly*, XCII, 50, 59 (January 19, 1901).

"The Founding of the American Bar Association." *American Bar Association Journal*, III, 658-695 (October, 1917).
"Franklin and the Rule of Free Ships, Free Goods." *Proceedings of the American Antiquarian Society*, XXV n.s., 345-357 (October, 1915).
"The French Jury System." *Michigan Law Review*, II, 597-600 (April, 1904).
"The Fundamental Principles of Criminal Justice." *Yale Law Journal*, XXII, 30-38 (November, 1912).
The Genius of Congregationalism: an Address Delivered before the New Haven Congregational Club, October 11, 1886. New Haven: Tuttle, Morehouse and Taylor, 1886.
"A German Law Suit." *Yale Law Journal*, XIX, 69-79 (December, 1909).
"The German Law-Suit without Lawyers." *Michigan Law Review*, VIII, 30-38 (November, 1909).
"The Government of Our New Territory." *Independent*, L, 962-964 (October 6, 1898).
"Graduate Courses, at Law Schools." *Journal of Social Science*, XI, 123-137 (May, 1880).
"The Hague Conference of 1904 for the Advancement of Private International Law." *Yale Law Journal*, XIV, 1-8 (November, 1904).
"The Hague Conference of 1907." *Lend a Hand Record*, XVI, 1-3 (November, 1907).
"The Hartford Convention." *Papers of the New Haven Colony Historical Society*, IX, 1-28 (1918).
"The Historic Policy of the United States as to Annexation." *Annual Report of the American Historical Association for the Year 1893*, 369-390. Also published in *Yale Review*, II, 133-158 (August, 1893).
An Historical Address at the Celebration of the One Hundredth Anniversary of the Organization of the Chamber of Commerce of New Haven on Monday Evening April 9th, 1894. New Haven: Tuttle, Morehouse and Taylor, 1896.
"Historical Address: The United Church, 1815-1915." Exercises Commemorating the One Hundredth Anniversary of the Dedication of the House of Worship of the United Church, New Haven, Connecticut, Sunday, January 16, 1916, pp. 3-15. New Haven: Tuttle, Morehouse and Taylor, no date.
Historical Discourse Pronounced at the Two Hundred and Fiftieth Anniversary of the Hopkins Grammar School of New Haven, June 18, 1910. New Haven: Privately printed, 1910.

"Historical Sketch of the Supreme Court of Errors of Connecticut." In: Bell, Clark, editor. The Supreme Court of the States and Provinces of North America, Vol. I, Series 5, pp. 1-19.

"The History of American Morals." *Journal of Social Science*, XXXVI, 1-55 (December, 1898).

"The History of the Common Law." Congress of Arts and Sciences, Universal Exposition, St. Louis, 1904, II, 331-349 (1906). Boston and New York: Houghton, Mifflin and Company, 1906.

"How Civil Procedure was Simplified in Connecticut." *Report of New York Bar Association*, XXXV, 829-833 (1912).

"How to Deal with Habitual Criminals." *Journal of Social Science*, XXII, 163-171 (1887).

"The Ideals of the American Advocate—a Symposium." The *Central Law Journal*, LVIII, 423-424 (May 27, 1904).

Illustrative Cases on Railroad Law. St. Paul: West Publishing Company, 1896.

"Inaugural Address." (As Chairman of the Subsection of Public Law of the Second Pan American Scientific Congress). Proceedings of the Second Pan American Scientific Congress, VII, 294-302. Washington: Government Printing Office, 1917.

"Inaugural Message of His Excellency Simeon E. Baldwin, Governor of Connecticut, to the General Assembly, January Session, 1911." Public Documents of the State of Connecticut, Vol. I, Part 1, pp. 3-41 (1910). Hartford: Printed by Order of the General Assembly, 1911.

"Inaugural Message of His Excellency Simeon E. Baldwin, Governor of Connecticut, to the General Assembly, January Session, 1913." Public Documents of the State of Connecticut, Vol. I, Part 1, pp. 3-35 (1912). Hartford: Printed by Order of the General Assembly, 1914.

Insanity as a Legal Fiction. An Address Delivered before the Bar Association of Tennessee, Thursday, July 3d, 1884. Nashville: Albert B. Tavel, 1884.

"The International Congresses and Conferences of the Last Century as Forces Working toward the Solidarity of the World." *American Journal of International Law*, I, 565-578 (July, 1907).

"International Outlawry as an Alternative for Force." The *World Court*, II, 290-293 (December, 1916).

"Introductory Address." Exercises at the Unveiling of the Monument to Adjutant William Campbell, Who Fell in the British Invasion of New Haven, July 5, 1779. New Haven: Monument Commission, 1891.

"Is There Any Need of a Constitutional Convention?" Tracts for the Times, No. 2. Published by the State Democratic Club, no date.

"The Italian Demand." *Independent*, LI, 2101–2102 (August 3, 1899).

"Japanese Courts." *Independent*, LI, 3179–3180 (November 23, 1899).

Judaic Christianity: A Paper Read before the New Haven Congregational Club, April 14, 1884. New Haven: Tuttle, Morehouse and Taylor, 1884.

"Justice between Nations." *Judicial Settlement of International Disputes*, XVII, 3–21 (August, 1914).

"The Late Election in Connecticut." *New Englander and Yale Review*, XVIII n.s., 366–373 (April, 1891).

"Law Latin and Roman Law." *Columbia Jurist*, I, 117 (May 19, 1885).

"The Law of Roads and Boundaries." Annual Report of the Secretary of Connecticut State Board of Agriculture, for 1875, pp. 99–134. Hartford: Case, Lockwood and Brainard Company, 1876.

"The Law of the Air-Ship." *American Journal of International Law*, IV, 95–108 (January, 1910).

"Law School Libraries, and How to Use Them." *Report of the Seventeenth Annual Meeting of the American Bar Association*, 1894, pp. 431–438.

"Legal Ethics." Legal Ethics. Lectures Delivered before the Students of Law Department of Union University, pp. 27–43 (1903).

"A Legal Fiction with Its Wings Clipped." *American Law Review*, XLI, 38–46 (January-February, 1907).

"Legislative Divorces and the Fourteenth Amendment." *Harvard Law Review*, XXVII, 699–704 (June, 1914).

"Liability for Accidents in Aerial Navigation." *Michigan Law Review*, IX, 20–28 (November, 1910).

Life and Letters of Simeon Baldwin. New Haven: Tuttle, Morehouse and Taylor Company, 1919.

A review of this volume by Samuel E. Morison appeared in: *American Historical Review*, XXV, 142 (October, 1919).

"The Limits of the Legislative Power of an American State." *Proceedings of the Bar Association of the State of New Hampshire*, III n.s., 221–240 (1913–14).

"The Membership of a World Tribunal for Promoting Permanent Peace." *American Journal of International Law*, XII, 453–461 (July, 1918).

"The Mission of Governor Taft to the Vatican." *Yale Law Journal*, XII, 1–7 (November, 1902).

"The Modern 'Droit d'Aubaine'." *Proceedings of the American Association for the Advancement of Science*, LIV, 533–552 (1905).

"Modern Penology." *Proceedings of the Fifth Meeting of the Governors of the States of the Union Held at Richmond, Virginia, December 3–7, 1912*, pp. 34–43.

Modern Political Institutions. Boston: Little, Brown, and Company, 1898.

A review of this volume by Jeremiah W. Jenks appeared in: *American Historical Review*, IV, 582–584 (1898–99).

"The Monroe Doctrine in 1896." *Independent*, XLVIII, 1716–1717 (December 17, 1896).

"The Narrowing Circle of Individual Rights." *Proceedings of the Twenty-fourth Annual Meeting of the West Virginia Bar Association Held at Huntington, West Virginia, December 29–30, 1908*, XXIV, 72–85.

"The Natural Right to a Natural Death." *Journal of Social Science*, XXXVII, 1–17 (December, 1899).

"The New American Code of Legal Ethics." *Columbia Law Review*, VIII, 541–547 (November, 1908).

"The New 'Association Internationale des Avocats.'" *Yale Law Journal*, XV, 163–171 (February, 1906).

"The New Code of International Family Law." *Yale Law Journal*, XII, 487–494 (June, 1903).

"New England Secessionists." *New Englander*, XXXVII, 145–159 (March, 1878).

New England's Leadership in American History, Address by Governor Simeon E. Baldwin at the 108th Annual Dinner of the New England Society in the City of New York, December 22, 1913. Pamphlet.

"The New Era of International Courts." *Judicial Settlement of International Disputes*, I, 3–23 (August, 1910).

"The New Haven Convention of 1778." *Papers of the New Haven Colony Historical Society*, III, 33–62 (1882).

"The New Reading of Due Process of Law." *Report of the Fourteenth Annual Meeting of the Maryland State Bar Association Held at Old Point Comfort, Virginia, July 7th, 8th, 9th, 1909*, pp. 266–285.

"Obituary Notice of Henry White." *Connecticut Reports*, XLVII, 615–617 (1879–80).

"The Objects of Criminal Procedure as They Appear to a French

Prosecuting Officer." *Yale Law Journal*, XII, 226–233 (February, 1903).

The Opening Argument for the Defence in the Andover Case. Boston: Rand, Avery Company, 1887.

"Outdoor Convict Labor." *Charities and The Commons*, XVII, 137–140 (October 20, 1906).

"The Part Taken by Courts of Justice in the Development of International Law." *American Law Review*, XXXV, 214–237 (March-April, 1901). Also published in *Yale Law Journal*, X, 1–23 (November, 1900).

"The Past and Future of This Society; Being the Annual Address of the President for the Year 1886." *Papers of the New Haven Colony Historical Society*, IV, 397–403 (1888).

"The People of the United States." *Yale Law Journal*, VIII, 159–167 (January, 1899).

"Philip Marett." *Papers of the New Haven Colony Historical Society*, V, 71–88 (1894).

"The Place of Law in the Studies of a University." The *American Law School Review*, I, 101–113 (Fall, 1903).

"Le Pouvoir Judiciare Américain Comparé au Pouvoir Judiciaire Européan." *Revue de l'Institut de Droit Comparé*, II, 353–364 (1909).

"Preliminary Examinations in Criminal Proceedings." *Report of the Sixth Annual Meeting of the American Bar Association, 1883*, pp. 225–241.

"The Progressive Unfolding of the Powers of the United States." *American Political Science Review*, VI, 1–16 (February, 1912).

The Project of a Federal Incorporation Law for Corporations Engaged in Interstate or Foreign Commerce. New Haven: Chamber of Commerce, 1910.

"The Proposed International Court of Arbitral Justice." *Report of the Sixteenth Annual Meeting of the Lake Mohonk Conference on International Arbitration, 1910*, XVI, 78–85.

"The Proposed Trial of the Former Kaiser." *Yale Law Journal*, XXIX, 75–82 (November, 1919).

Public Parks: a Lecture Delivered in the Mechanics' Course at the Sheffield Scientific School, March 17, 1881. New Haven: Punderson and Crisand, 1881.

Railroad Taxation, Facts Submitted to the Joint Standing Committee on Finance, in Support of the Bill for an Act to Reduce the Rate of Railroad Taxation. (State of Connecticut. General Assembly. January Session, 1883). Pamphlet.

"The Re-adjustment of the Collegiate to the Professional Course." *Yale Law Journal*, VIII, 1–23 (October, 1898).

"Recent Changes in Our State Constitutions." *Journal of Social Science*, X, 136–151 (December, 1879).

"Recent Progress Towards Agreement on Rules to Prevent a Conflict of Laws." *Harvard Law Review*, XVII, 400–405 (April, 1904).

"The Recitation System." *Columbia Jurist*, II, 2–3 (September 30, 1885).

The Relations of Education to Citizenship. New Haven: Yale University Press, 1912.

"Religion Still the Key to History." *American Historical Review*, XII, 219–243 (January, 1907).

Reparation for Crime. (Senate Document No. 158, 55th Congress, 3d Session. Penological Questions. Reports Prepared for the International Prison Commission). Washington: Government Printing Office, 1899.

"Report of the Committee on Award of Medal." *Report of the Thirteenth Annual Meeting of the American Bar Association, 1890*, pp. 339–343.

"Report of the Committee on Jurisprudence and Law Reform on Forms of Verdicts in Criminal Proceedings." *Report of the Thirteenth Annual Meeting of the American Bar Association, 1890*, pp. 313–316.

"Report of the Committee on Jurisprudence and Law Reform on Methods of Improving the Form of American Legislation." *Report of the Twelfth Annual Meeting of the American Bar Association, 1889*, pp. 343–346.

"Report of the Committee on Publications." *Report of the Thirty-Eighth Annual Meeting of the American Bar Association, 1915*, p. 498.

"Respect for International Law, and the Hague Tribunal." *Report of the Thirteenth Annual Meeting of the Lake Mohonk Conference on International Arbitration, 1907*, pp. 40–46.

"The Responsibilities of the United States, Internationally, for Acts of the States." *Yale Law Journal*, V, 161–174 (March, 1896).

"The Restoration of Whipping as a Punishment for Crime." The *Green Bag*, XIII, 65–67 (February, 1901).

"Résumé du Rapport Présenté par M. Siméon-E. Baldwin." Actes du Congrès Pénitentiaire International de Washington, Octobre, 1910, II, 2–8. Groningen: Bureau de la Commission Pénitentiaire Internationale, 1912.

"Rev. John Higginson, of Salem." *Proceedings of the Massachusetts Historical Society*, XVI, second series, 478–521 (1902).

Review of James Bryce, The American Commonwealth. In: *New Englander and Yale Review*, XIV n.s., 229–243 (April, 1889).
Review of Woodrow Wilson, Division and Reunion, 1829–1889. In: *Yale Review*, II, 211–213 (August, 1893).
"A Ride Across Connecticut before the Revolution." *Papers of the New Haven Colony Historical Society*, IX, 161–169 (1918).
Rise and Progress of the Connecticut Practice Act, 1878–1880. (Edited and written in part by Simeon E. Baldwin). Not published.
"Roger Sherman." In: Two Centuries of New Milford, Connecticut, pp. 232–255. New York: The Grafton Press, 1907.
"Roger Sherman Baldwin." In: Great American Lawyers (ed. William Draper Lewis), III, 498–505. Philadelphia: The John C. Winston Company, 1908.
"The Salient Points in the German Constitution of 1919." *Michigan Law Review*, XVIII, 736–748 (June, 1920).
"Schooling Rights under Our Treaty with Japan." *Columbia Law Review*, VII, 85–92 (February, 1907).
"The Seal of Connecticut." *Papers of the New Haven Colony Historical Society*, VIII, 82–108 (1914).
"The Secession of Springfield from Connecticut." *Publications of the Colonial Society of Massachusetts*, XII, 55–82 (1908).
"The Share of the President of the United States in a Declaration of War." *American Journal of International Law*, XII, 1–14 (January, 1918).
"Should International Law Be Codified? And If So, Should It Be Done Through Governmental Agencies or by Private Scientific Societies?" Proceedings of the Second Pan American Scientific Congress, VII, 279–282. Washington: Government Printing Office, 1917.
"The Significance of 'John Marshall Day.'" *Congregationalist*, LXXXVI, 177–178 (February 2, 1901).
"State Assumption of Nomination and Election Expenses." *Yale Law Journal*, XXIII, 158–167 (December, 1913).
"The Study of Elementary Law, the Proper Beginning of a Legal Education." *Yale Law Journal*, XIII, 1–15 (October, 1903).
Summary of the Ellen M. Gifford Charities New Haven, 1891. Pamphlet. Written with E. E. Beardsley.
"The Supreme Court and the Insular Cases. *Yale Review*, X, 129–143 (August, 1901).
"Suspension from the Society of Nations, a Sufficient Sanction for a

World-Court Judgment." *American Law Review*, LII, 695–700 (September-October, 1918).

"Taxation by One State of Goods in Another." *Yale Review*, XV, 251–258 (November, 1906).

"Teaching Law by Cases." *Harvard Law Review*, XIV, 258–261 (December, 1900).

"The Tendency to Push the Lex Fori Beyond its True Limits." *Blätter für Vergleichende Rechtswissenschaft und Volkswirtschaftslehre*, I, 91–98 (1905).

"Theophilus Eaton, First Governor of the Colony of New Haven." *Papers of the New Haven Colony Historical Society*, VII, 1–33 (1908).

"The Three Constitutions of Connecticut." *Papers of the New Haven Colony Historical Society*, V, 179–245 (1894).

"Three Years Enough for a College Course." *Independent*, LII, 1778–1780 (July 26, 1900).

"The Time Necessary to Get a Legal Education." *Columbia Jurist*, I, 67 (March 31, 1885).

"To the Editor of *Yale Alumni Weekly*." *Yale Alumni Weekly*, XII, 209 (March 18, 1903).

"The United States Law Journal of 1822." *American Bar Association Journal*, IV, 37–53 (January, 1918).

"The Vesting of Sovereignty in a League of Nations." *Yale Law Journal*, XXVIII, 209–218 (January, 1919).

"The Visitorial Statutes of Andover Seminary." *Annual Report of the American Historical Association for the Year 1891*, pp. 225–241.

"Voting-Trusts." *Yale Law Journal*, I, 1–15 (October, 1891).

"War and Militarism in Relation to Government and Politics." *Publications of the American Sociological Society*, X, 75–81 (1915).

"Whipping and Castration as Punishments for Crime." *Yale Law Journal*, VIII, 371–386 (June, 1899).

"Why the Decisions of the Hague Tribunal Are and Will Be Obeyed." *Advocate of Peace*, LXVII, 59–60 (March, 1905).

"Why You and I Ought to Vote for Morris and Alsop." Tracts for the Times, No. 1. (Published by State Democratic Club of Connecticut, 1890).

"William Kneeland Townsend." Commemorative Addresses at the Yale Law School, June 18, 1907, pp. 5–10. New Haven: Tuttle, Morehouse and Taylor Press, 1907.

"Yale Men as Writers on Law and Government." *Yale Law Journal*, XI, 1–8 (November, 1901).

"Yale University." *New Englander and Yale Review*, IX n.s., 882–887 (November, 1885).

The Young Man and the Law. New York: The Macmillan Company, 1920.

"A Young Man's Journal of a Hundred Years Ago." *Papers of the New Haven Colony Historical Society*, IV, 193–208 (1886).

SECONDARY SOURCES

Addresses and Proceedings, Including the Oration Pronounced by Reverend Dr. Bushnell, at the Commemorative Celebration, Held July 26, 1865, in Honor of the Alumni of Yale College Who Were in the Military or Naval Service of the United States during the Recent War; together with the Names Comprised in the Roll of Honor. New Haven: Tuttle, Morehouse and Taylor, 1866.

American Bar Association.

The American Bar Association. Call for a Conference; Proceedings of Conference; First Meeting of the Association; Officers, Members, etc. Philadelphia: Jackson Brothers, 1878.

Report of the . . . Annual Meeting of the American Bar Association, 1879 and following.

"Report of Committee of Jurisprudence and Law Reform." In: *Report of the . . . Annual Meeting of the American Bar Association*, 1879–1890.

American Society for Judicial Settlement of International Disputes.

Proceedings of International Conference Under the Auspices of American Society for Judicial Settlement of International Disputes. December 15–17, 1910, Washington, D. C. Baltimore: The Waverly Press, no date.

Proceedings of Third National Conference of American Society for Judicial Settlement of International Disputes. December 20–21, 1912, Washington, D. C. Baltimore: Williams and Wilkins Company, 1913.

"Association of American Law Schools." *Report of the . . . Annual Meeting of the American Bar Association*, 1900–1902.

Atwater, Edward E., editor. History of the City of New Haven to the Present Time. New York: W. W. Munsell and Company, 1887.

Ausubel, Herman. Historians and Their Craft; a Study of the Presidential Addresses of the American Historical Association, 1884–1945. New York: Columbia University Press, 1950.

Baldwin, Charles Candee. The Baldwin Genealogy. Cleveland, Ohio: The Leader Printing Company, 1881. 2 vols.

Baldwin, Roger S., Jr. "Tarryings in Nicaragua." *Century Illustrated Monthly Magazine*, XLII, 911–931 (May to October, 1891).

Beach, John Kimberly. "Obituary Sketch of Simeon E. Baldwin." *Connecticut Reports*, XVI, 735–738 (1927).

"Boston University Commencement." *Zion's Herald*, LXXX, 744 (June 11, 1902).

"Chief Justice Baldwin's Retirement." *Green Bag*, XXII, 207–208 (April, 1910).

Clark, Charles E. "Francis Wayland." Dictionary of American Biography, XIX, 560–561.

Clark, George L. A History of Connecticut, Its People and Institutions. New York and London: G. P. Putnam's Sons, 1914.

Congregationalist and Christian World, XCII, 418–420 (March 30, 1907).

Connecticut, State of. General and Miscellaneous Public Documents.

The Practice Act of the State of Connecticut, with the Orders, Rules, and Forms under the Same, Prepared by the Judges of the Superior Court; and the General Rules of Practice of the Supreme Court of Errors, and the Superior Court, as Revised in June, 1879. Hartford: The Case, Lockwood and Brainard Company, 1879.

Public Acts Passed by the General Assembly of the State of Connecticut in the Year 1911. Hartford, Connecticut: Published by the State, 1911.

Public Acts Passed by the General Assembly of the State of Connecticut in the Year 1913. Hartford, Connecticut: Published by the State, 1913.

Report of Commission for Simplifying Legal Procedure. Printed by Order of the Legislature. Hartford: Case, Lockwood and Brainard Company, 1880.

Report of the Special Commission, Appointed under the Resolution of the General Assembly, Approved April 4, 1884, on the Subject of Taxation, with Bills Recommended for Adoption and Statistical Tables. New Haven: Hoggson and Robinson, 1887.

Report of the Special State Commission Appointed in 1915 on the Subject of Taxation Submitted to the General Assembly in 1917. New Haven: Tuttle, Morehouse and Taylor Company, 1917.

Report of the Tax Commission to the General Assembly of 1886. Printed by Order of the House of Representatives. Hartford: Case, Lockwood and Brainard Company, 1886.

Revision of 1875. The General Statutes of the State of Connecticut. Hartford: The Case, Lockwood and Brainard Company, 1875.

Rules and Forms for Making up Records of Judgments, under the Practice Act. Prepared by the Judges of the Superior Court Especially for the Use of Clerks of Court. New Haven: Hoggson and Robinson, 1880.

Special Acts and Resolutions Passed by the General Assembly of the State of Connecticut, at the May Session, 1876. Hartford, Connecticut: Wiley, Waterman and Eaton, 1876.

Special Laws of the State of Connecticut, Vol. VII (1871–75). Hartford, Connecticut: Press of the Case, Lockwood and Brainard Company, 1880.

State of Connecticut. Register and Manual, 1911. Hartford: Published by the State, 1911.

State of Connecticut. Register and Manual, 1914. Hartford: Published by the State, 1914.

Daggett, Leonard M. "The Yale Law School." *Green Bag*, I, 239–253 (1889).

Davis, Thomas B., Jr. Chronicles of Hopkins Grammar School 1660–1935. New Haven, Connecticut: Quinnipiak Press, 1938.

Decrow, W. E. Yale and "The City of Elms." Boston: W. E. Decrow, 1882.

Dexter, Franklin B. Sketch of the History of Yale University. New York: Henry Holt and Company, 1887.

Dutton, Samuel W. S. An Address at the Funeral of Honorable Roger Sherman Baldwin. New Haven: Thomas J. Stafford, 1863.

Edgar G. Mondou v. The New York, New Haven and Hartford Railroad Company. *Connecticut Reports*, LXXXII, 373–375.

Edgar G. Mondou v. The New York, New Haven and Hartford Railroad Company. *United States Reports*, CCXXIII, 1–59.

Fisher, Irving, editor. Bibliographies of the Present Officers of Yale University, together with the Bibliography of the Late President Porter. New Haven: Tuttle, Morehouse and Taylor, 1893.

Fisher, Richard S. A New and Complete Statistical Gazetteer of the

United States of America Founded on and Compiled from Official Federal and State Returns and the Seventh National Census. New York: J. H. Colton, 1853.

Fitzgerald, David E. The Democratic Party of Connecticut to the Independent Voters of Connecticut. (Printed leaflet, 1914).

Four Years at Yale. (By a Graduate of '69). New Haven, Connecticut. Charles C. Chatfield and Company, 1871.

Hackett, Frank W. "The Federal Employers' Liability Act of 1908—Is It Constitutional?" *Harvard Law Review*, XXII, 38–47 (November, 1908).

Hadley, Morris. Arthur Twining Hadley. New Haven: Yale University Press, 1948.

Hall, John L. "The Federal Employers' Liability Act." *Yale Law Journal*, XX, 122–130 (December, 1910).

Harno, Albert J. Legal Education in the United States. San Francisco: Bancroft-Whitney Company, 1953.

Harrison, Lynde. "The Election Controversy in Connecticut." *New Englander and Yale Review*, XVIII n.s., 354–365 (April, 1891).

Hicks, Frederick C. Yale Law School: From the Founders to Dutton 1845–1869. New Haven: Yale University Press, 1936. (Yale Law Library Publications, No. 3).

—— Yale Law School: 1869–1894 Including the County Court House Period. New Haven: Yale University Press, 1937. (Yale Law Library Publications, No. 4).

—— Yale Law School: 1895–1915 Twenty Years of Hendrie Hall. New Haven: Yale University Press, 1938. (Yale Law Library Publications, No. 7).

Hotchkiss, Mrs. Fanny Winchester. Winchester Notes. New Haven, Connecticut: Tuttle, Morehouse and Taylor Company, 1912.

Jacobs, Albert P. The Psi Upsilon Epitome. Boston: Rand, Avery and Company, 1884.

Johnston, William C. "The Literary Societies of Yale College." *University Quarterly*, I, 115–126 (1860).

Kingsley, William L., editor. Yale College, a Sketch of its History. New York: Henry Holt and Company, 1879. 2 vols.

Law: A Century of Progress, 1835–1935. New York: New York University Press, 1937. 3 vols.

Lewis, William Draper, editor. Great American Lawyers. Philadelphia: The John C. Winston Company, 1908. 8 vols.

Manchester, Mary E. "Roger Sherman Baldwin." Dictionary of American Biography, I, 542–543.

Morgan, Forrest, editor. Connecticut as a Colony and as a State. Hartford: The Publishing Society of Connecticut, 1904. 4 vols.

Morse, Jarvis M. "Isaac Toucy." Dictionary of American Biography, XVIII, 600–601.

Morse, Jarvis M. A Neglected Period of Connecticut's History 1818–1850. New Haven: Yale University Press, 1933.

Nevins, Allan. The Emergence of Lincoln. New York: Charles Scribner's Sons, 1950. 2 vols.

Nichols, Roy F. The Disruption of American Democracy. New York: The Macmillan Company, 1948.

Norton, Frederick Calvin. The Governors of Connecticut. Hartford, Connecticut: The Connecticut Magazine Company, 1905.

Osborn, Norris Galpin, editor. History of Connecticut in Monographic Form. New York: The States History Company, 1925. 5 vols.

Osterweis, Rollin G. Three Centuries of New Haven, 1638–1938. New Haven: Yale University Press, 1953.

Perkins, George W. Sermons by George W. Perkins with a Memoir. New York: Anson D. F. Randolph, 1859.

Perry, Frederick L. The Life and Services of Simeon E. Baldwin with Some Reference to his Speeches. New Haven: The New Haven Colony Historical Society, 1941. (mimeographed).

Phillips Academy. The Andover Case, 1886–1892. (Documents relating to the case of the Visitors of the Theological Institution in Phillips Academy in Andover v. Egbert C. Smyth, including Simeon E. Baldwin's brief on final hearing of the appeal of Smyth).

Pierson, George W. Yale College, an Educational History, 1871–1921. New Haven: Yale University Press, 1952.

Porter, Noah. "Inaugural Address." Addresses at the Inauguration of Professor Noah Porter, D.D. LL.D., as President of Yale College, Wednesday, October 11, 1871, pp. 27–65. New York: Charles Scribner and Company, 1871.

Purcell, Richard J. Connecticut in Transition, 1775–1818. Washington: American Historical Association, 1918.

Records and Addresses in Memory of Simeon E. Baldwin 1840–1927. New Haven: Privately Printed, 1928.

Report of the Special Investigating Committee to the Court of Common Council as to the Purchase of the New Haven Waterworks. New Haven: Stafford Printing Company, 1881.

"Report on Prison Reform." The Outlook Committee of the New Haven Congregational Club, April 16, 1900. New Haven: The Price, Lee and Adkins Company, no date.

Robinson, William C. An Address Commemorative of the Life and Character of Francis Wayland Delivered before the Law School of Yale University at Hendrie Hall, April 22, 1904. New Haven: Tuttle, Morehouse and Taylor Press, 1904.

Rogers, James Grafton. "The American Bar Association in Retrospect." Law, a Century of Progress, 1835–1935, I, 166–190. New York: New York University Press, 1937.

Rogers, James Grafton. American Bar Leaders, Biographies of the Presidents of the American Bar Association, 1878–1928. Chicago: American Bar Association, 1932.

Seavey, Warren A. "The Association of American Law Schools in Retrospect." *Journal of Legal Education*, III, 153–173 (Winter, 1950).

Second Employers' Liability Cases, *United States Reports*, CCXXIII, 1–59 (October Term, 1911).

Shepard, Odell. Connecticut Past and Present. New York and London: Alfred A. Knopf, 1939.

Sherman, Charles P. Academic Adventures: A Law School Professor's Recollections and Observations. Cincinnati: The W. H. Anderson Company, 1947.

Sherman, Thomas T. Sherman Genealogy. New York: Tobias A. Wright, 1920.

"Simeon E. Baldwin." *Yale Law Journal*, XXXVI, 680–682 (March, 1927).

Starr, Harris E. "Theodore Dwight Woolsey." Dictionary of American Biography, XX, 519–520.

Sunderland, Edson R. History of the American Bar Association and Its Work. Privately printed, 1953.

Two Centuries Growth of American Law, 1701–1901. New York: Charles Scribner's Sons, 1901.

Tyler, Daniel P. Statistics of the Condition and Products of Certain Branches of Industry in Connecticut, for the Year Ending October 1, 1845. Hartford: John L. Boswell, 1846.

University Quarterly, Vols. I–IV (1860–1861).

Warren, Charles. History of the Harvard Law School and of Early Legal Conditions in America. New York: Lewis Publishing Company, 1908. 3 vols.

Weir, Forrest C. The Social Opinions of Simeon E. Baldwin. (A typewritten doctoral dissertation accepted by Yale University in 1941.)

William H. Hoxie v. The New York, New Haven and Hartford Railroad Company. *Connecticut Reports*, LXXXII, 352–373 (1909–1910).

Woolsey, Theodore Dwight. Historical Discourse, by Theodore D. Woolsey, and Oration on the Influence of Lawyers upon Free Governments, and the influence of Moral Forces upon the Prosperity of Governments, by Honorable Edwards Pierrepont, LL.D., Pronounced before the Alumni of the Law Department of Yale College at the Fiftieth Anniversary of the Foundation of the Department, in the Centre Church at New Haven, June 24th, 1874. New Haven: The Law Department of Yale College, 1874.

Yale College and Yale University.

Catalogue of the Officers and Students in Yale College. 1857–58 through 1861–62 and 1874–5 through 1885–6.

Catalogues of Yale University. 1886–7 through 1892–3. Law Department of Yale College. Fifty-third Year. 1876–77.

Catalogues of the Law Department of Yale University. 1894–95 through 1899–1900.

Yale University. Department of Law (Yale Law School). 1900–01 through 1902–03.

Yale Law School. Law Department of Yale University, 1903–04. Bulletin of Yale University. Law School Catalogue, 1904–05 through 1909–10.

Obituary Record of Graduates of Yale College Deceased from July, 1859, to July, 1870. Presented at the Annual Meetings of the Alumni 1860–1870. New Haven, Connecticut: Tuttle, Morehouse and Taylor, 1870.

Obituary Record of Graduates Deceased during the Year Ending July 1, 1927. New Haven: Published by the University, 1927.

Historical Register of Yale University, 1701–1937. New Haven: Yale University Press, 1939.

Yale College. Records of the Class of 1861 edited by Winthrop D. Sheldon, Secretary.

Triennial Record of the Class of 1861, of Yale College. New Haven: Tuttle, Morehouse and Taylor, 1864.

The Second or Sexennial Meeting, of the Class of Sixty-one, Yale College, with a Biographical Record. New Haven: Hoggson and Robinson, 1867.

Decennial Record of the Class of 1861, Yale College, Containing Reports of Class Meetings, and a Biographical Sketch of Each Member. Cleveland: Leader Printing Company, 1872.

Supplement to the Decennial Record of the Class of 1861 Yale College, 1871–1876. New Haven: Tuttle, Morehouse and Taylor, 1877.

Fifth Report of the Class of 1861, Yale College 1876–1881. Springfield, Massachusetts: Springfield Printing Company, 1882.

The Twenty-five Years' Record of the Class of 1861, Yale College. Springfield, Massachusetts: Springfield Printing and Binding Company, 1888.

Supplement to the Twenty-five Years' Record of the Class of 1861 Yale College. Springfield, Massachusetts: Springfield Printing and Binding Company, 1892.

Second Supplement to the Twenty-five Years' Record of the Class of 1861 Yale College. Philadelphia: J. B. Lippincott Company, 1897.

Yale Banner
September 30, 1857
September 27, 1858
September 24, 1859
September 21, 1860
September 21, 1861

Supplement to the Yale Banner
October 6, 1857
September 29, 1860

"Yale College in 1871." Yale College. Annual Statements 1868–1886. Not Published.

Yale College. Needs of the University. Suggested by the Faculties. (July 10, 1871). Pamphlet.

Yale Shingle, 1898. New Haven: "Mac" Printing Company, 1898.

INDEX

Bei Fragen zur Produktsicherheit wenden Sie sich bitte an:
If you have any questions regarding product safety,
please contact:

Walter de Gruyter GmbH
Genthiner Straße 13
10785 Berlin
productsafety@degruyterbrill.com